THE DAIRY BOOK OF

BRITISH FOOD

THE DAIRY BOOK OF

BRITISH FOOD

OVER 400 RECIPES FOR EVERY OCCASION

Published by Ebury Press
Division of The National Magazine Company Ltd
Colquhoun House, 27–37 Broadwick Street,
London W1V 1FR
On behalf of the Milk Marketing Board
And distributed by The Dairy Industry

First impression 1988

EDITORIAL DIRECTION:	Yvonne McFarlane
ART DIRECTION:	Frank Phillips
EDITORS:	Helen Dore
	Ann Wilson
	Beverly Le Blanc
EDITORIAL ASSISTANT:	Rachel Gosling
TEXT:	Elizabeth Martyn
	Cassandra Kent
SENIOR HOME ECONOMIST:	Susanna Tee
DESIGNER:	Grahame Dudley
FOOD PHOTOGRAPHY BY	James Murphy
	Laurie Evans
	Grant Symon
STYLISTS:	Cathy Sinker
	Lesley Richardson
	Gina Carminati
FOOD PREPARED FOR	
PHOTOGRAPHY BY	Jacki Baxter
	Allyson Birch
	Maxine Clark
	Sue Philpot
	Janet Smith
ILLUSTRATIONS BY	Susan Robertson
	Gill Tomblin
	Kate Charlesworth

THE PUBLISHERS WOULD ALSO LIKE TO THANK
THE DAIRY PRODUCE ADVISORY SERVICE,
MILK MARKETING BOARD, FOR THEIR HELP
IN COMPILING THE RECIPES

Computerset by MFK Typesetting Ltd, Hitchin, Herts.
Printed and bound in Singapore

CONTENTS

A Taste of the Regions

Come with us on a fascinating journey from north to south through the British countryside. The lavishly illustrated pages that follow are a celebration of Britain's culinary heritage and focus on the fresh ingredients and high quality produce available throughout Britain today. We have divided the country into eight regions, each of which opens with a beautiful map of the area showing its wealth of fresh local produce. Each region features a 'calendar' of traditional food-related festivals and events of special interest.

A Taste of the Regions

The West Country

Avon, Cornwall, Devon, Dorset, Gloucestershire, Somerset, Wiltshire.

The mild climate and long coastline make this region not just a holiday-makers' paradise but the source of many delectable foods. Tender young vegetables and fruits, fine fish and shellfish, refreshing ciders and, above all, superb cream and cheeses are typical West Country temptations.

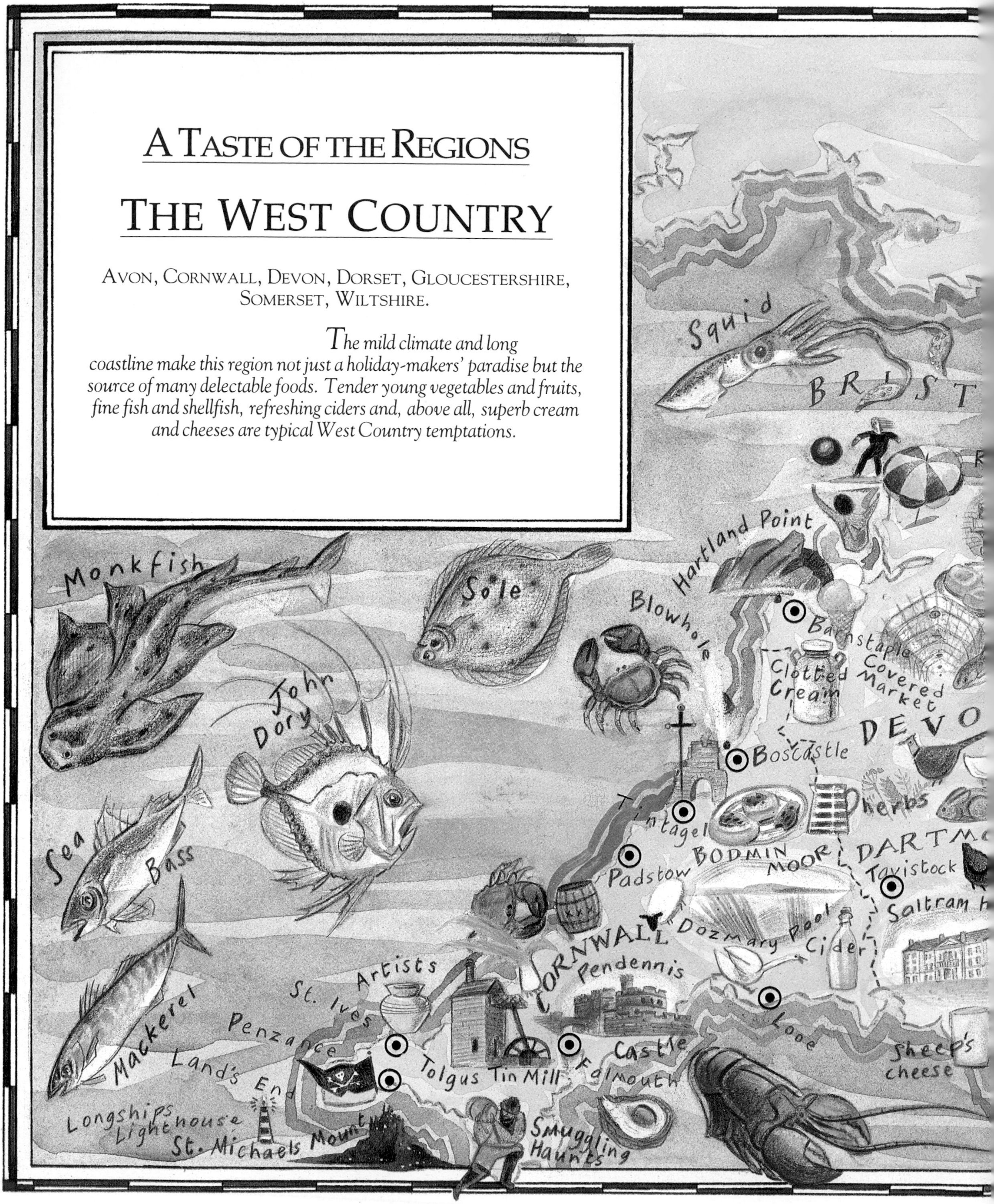

Squid

BRIST

Monkfish

Sole

Hartland Point

Blowhole

Barnstaple Covered Market

Clotted Cream

John Dory

Boscastle

DEVO

herbs

Sea

Bass

Tintagel

BODMIN MOOR

DARTM

Tavistock

Padstow

Saltram h

Artists

Dozmary Pool

Cider

St. Ives

CORNWALL

Pendennis

Penzance

Mackerel

Looe

Land's End

Tolgus Tin Mill

Falmouth

Castle

sheep's cheese

Longships Lighthouse

St. Michaels Mount

Smuggling Haunts

ABOVE

The early morning sun casts long shadows over dew-laden blossom in a Devon orchard by the River Exe. Spring and summer come early to these lush green valleys, and it's from this region that the first early berries and cherries speed their way to market long before similar produce from the rest of the country.

OPPOSITE

Cream tea in the garden is a perfect afternoon treat for visitors to the area, who find it well worth while interrupting their countryside explorations to linger over a tempting home-made spread.

The land of the West Country is so fertile that it spills over with a wealth of good produce. Add to this the fact that the area enjoys the mildest climate in England and it's not hard to see why there's so much agricultural activity. To sum up the food story of this generous region, think of cream teas, cooling ciders, ripe strawberries and mellow cheeses. Many people have sampled these West Country delights on family holidays, and will have travelled through the lush pastures past gently grazing cattle on their way to the glorious beaches of Devon and Cornwall.

The seas are warmed by the Gulf Stream, another plus for holiday-makers, and the occupation of fishing goes back for centuries. There are many bustling ports, busy handling the vast quantity of fish and shellfish that are landed here.

Spring arrives early in the West, ripening fruit and vegetables well before they are ready elsewhere. Apple orchards abound, filled with fruit to make the famous cider, and everywhere there are grassy fields supporting the dairy herds, which have made the production of cream and cheese such a popular part of the farmer's livelihood. Pig farming is also traditional, especially in Wiltshire. Crops tend to come second to livestock, although wheat, barley and oats are grown in Gloucestershire.

Moving away from the countryside, the elegant towns of Bath and Bristol have each made a contribution to West Country eating. Bath has given its name to several local goodies, mentioned later in this chapter, and Bristol, which as a port was once second only to London, used to trade in food and drink from all over the world.

FAMOUS DAIRYING

All the breeds of cattle raised on the rich green grazing of the West Country give milk with a high butterfat content, perfect for making the cream, cheese and butter for which the region is justly renowned. No visit here would be complete without a traditional cream tea – a plate heaped high with fresh scones or splits, lavishly spread with strawberry jam and, of course, clotted cream. This type of cream is one of the best-known regional products and, as it both keeps and travels well, is often brought or posted home as a souvenir by the tourists who throng to this part of the country every summer.

Clotted cream is widely made in Cornwall and Devon, and some also comes out of Dorset. A handful of farms make it by the traditional method, but most producers use automatic separators and more up-to-date equipment. The basic idea is simple: double cream is heated, held at a high temperature for up to 40 minutes, and then cooled. The clotted cream that forms has a yellowish colour, wrinkled appearance, distinctive flavour and a very thick, grainy texture. Cream, clotted or otherwise, features in many West Country recipes (try Pork Fillet in Mustard Cream Sauce, see recipe, page 141). Luscious ice creams are another dairy product that is being more widely made.

It is, however, cheese for which the West Country is truly celebrated. The best-known variety of all must be Cheddar, which originated in Somerset and is now the most widely made cheese in the world. Its history dates back over the centuries – it was already highly thought of in the time of Henry II and has been prized ever since. English Farmhouse Cheddar is made by traditional methods. The milk will have been produced on the maker's farm, although by agreement milk from other local farms can also be used. The cheese is allowed to mature for at least six months and is carefully graded, with only the best being selected for its rich, mellow flavour. Cheddar comes with many different flavouring variations; you can also choose between mild and mature, depending on strength of flavour preferred.

Gloucestershire cheeses have an equally long history. They were originally made from the milk of the now rare Gloucester cattle, and came in two sizes. Double Gloucester is disc-shaped and, at 5 inches thick, was twice the depth of Single Gloucester, which is very hard to find these days. The two cheeses also differed in colour and flavour. Gloucester cheese was originally made with a tough rind, which enabled it to withstand the annual cheese-rolling ceremonies. These still take place, although today the cheese is wrapped in hessian to help it stand up to its downhill journey (see Food Fairs and Festivals, page 17).

A cheese with a somewhat shorter history is Lymeswold, which has quickly become popular since its launch in 1982 as the first new, natural English cheese for centuries.

Blue Vinney, a hard, white, blue-veined cheese, is an interesting variety that is well worth seeking out, although it is hard to track down. It was made only in

WEST COUNTRY CHEESES

Whether you are putting together an English cheeseboard or looking for a well-flavoured cheese for cooking, the West Country has something to offer. The most popular and famous of these cheeses are widely available at supermarkets, while others, made on a smaller scale, are stocked by delicatessens or specialist cheese shops.

CHEDDAR

A hard, golden yellow, firm cheese. Sweet and mild when young, stronger when mature. An excellent cheeseboard choice, and also good for cooking. Comes with added flavourings such as smoky paprika (Applewood and Charnwood); beer and garlic (Ilchester); chives (Cheviot) and several others.

DOUBLE GLOUCESTER

Golden straw colour with a good mellow flavour. Melts beautifully, so ideal for cooking and toasting.

CURWORTHY

A semi-hard cheese made in Devon. A creamy buttery taste, develops a fuller flavour when matured. Good for cheeseboards.

CORNISH YARG

Full-flavoured and creamy, with a coating of nettle leaves.

DEVON GARLAND

A Jersey milk, semi-soft cheese that has a band of herbs running through it.

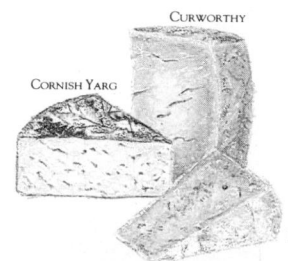

DOUBLE GLOUCESTER

CORNISH YARG

CURWORTHY

CHEDDAR

DEVON GARLAND

RIGHT
Cutting wedges from a Cornish Yarg cheese. The recipe for this cheese came from an old book, found in a farmer's attic, and the cheese was first marketed in 1981. It is made from cows' milk and has a pleasing texture and clean flavour with no sharpness. The wrapping of nettle leaves gives it an unusual and attractive appearance.

BELOW
The ideal accompaniment to a slice of English cheese, Bath Olivers are made from flour, butter, yeast and milk. In the background are the city's Roman Baths, where therapeutic waters can still be taken.

Dorset, from partly skimmed cows' milk, and local rumour claimed that the blue veining came from the mould of horses' leather tack. One farm in the area is now making Blue Vinney again, by more acceptable methods, so snap some up if you should come across it. However, you may have more luck in the search for Dorset Blue, which is similar but made from full-fat milk.

Many other cheeses originate from this part of the country. Look out for Cornish Yarg, Curworthy, Devon Garland, all delicious in their own ways (see fact panel for more details). And there are tasty goat and sheep cheeses emerging from the West too.

MORE-ISH BAKES AND CAKES

Probably the best-known bake of the West Country is the Cornish pasty, a portable meal originally made for farmers and miners to take to work. A good one has chunks of meat, not mince, plus potatoes and onions, inside a crisp pastry overcoat. But sometimes pasties don't live up to these high ideals – there is even a legend that the Devil refused to cross the Tamar into Cornwall because he had heard that the Cornish would put anything into their pasties!

Lots of lovely cakes come from these parts, including fruit cakes and honey cakes. The flowers of the countryside provide the perfect feeding ground for bees, and one of the monks at Buckfast Abbey maintains over 300 colonies in Devon and Cornwall, and sells the

honey in the Abbey shop. The colour and texture differ according to where the bees have gathered the nectar.

Ginger and spice feature strongly among the flavourings – they used to arrive at the ports from strange foreign places, and were pounced on by local cooks to add interest to their recipes. Saffron, although now quite hard to come by, was a popular if expensive flavouring and colouring ingredient. Apples, of course, crop up in cakes and puddings (try Somerset Apple Cake and Cider Cake, recipes, pages 265 and 266), and another favourite, Lardy Cake (recipe, page 292), also comes from the region. Devon Flats are a very more-ish biscuit, made with clotted cream (recipe, page 278). There are plenty of different flours for home-bakers to choose from, as several mills in the south-west produce organic and stone-ground varieties.

The spa town of Bath is known for three baked delicacies. Bath buns are made from a rich, yeasty mixture; they are beautifully yellow inside and are topped with crushed lump sugar. The Pump Room still serves them for tea. Dr W. Oliver, who founded the Bath Mineral Water Hospital, performed another great service when he invented the Bath Oliver biscuit as part of the simple diet required by those taking the waters for their health. These crisp crackers are still made today,

and are the ideal accompaniment to a chunk of Cheddar cheese. Look for the portrait of their originator, imprinted on one side of each biscuit. Thirdly, from Bath, comes Sally Lunn, a round, light, yeast cake. There are various legends attached to the name, but whether Sally Lunn was really an 18th-century street seller will never be known. Again, you can buy the cakes in the town, and apparently the best way to eat them is split and filled with whipped, sweetened cream.

FISH AND SHELLFISH GALORE

Cornish coasts face two seas, and consequently the fleets bring home a wide variety of fine-quality fish. Pilchards were formerly the biggest catch, but mysteriously disappeared earlier this century and have now been replaced by huge hauls of mackerel. Pilchards still turn up occasionally but in unpredictable quantities. They were traditionally used to make the delightfully named Stargazey Pie, in which the heads of the fish are left poking out through the pastry crust, to gaze at the stars.

Newlyn and Falmouth are the big ports in Cornwall, where monkfish, sole, hake, skate and many other varieties are landed. Fishing is big business in Devon

BELOW
Lobster pots line the harbour at Boscastle, Cornwall. This baited pot or 'creel' is the most common way of catching them. Lobsters are ideal for special occasions – allow two servings per average-sized lobster.

OILY FISH

A lot of oily fish are caught and brought into western ports. These varieties tend to be excellent value for money and, as well as being full of flavour, they are exceptionally nutritious. You'll find some tempting fish recipes on pages 184 to 204.

PILCHARDS

Rarely available fresh and usually only found locally to fishing port. Most are exported or canned. A strong, oily flavour, best enjoyed grilled or fried whole. Best between November and February.

HERRING

A streamlined fish, with a steely-blue back and silvery belly. At their best from July to February. Braise, bake, fry or grill. Also available smoked or kippered, and as rollmops in vinegar.

MACKEREL

Larger than herring, with a pattern of dark zigzags on the back and a silver belly. Firm, well-flavoured flesh. Cook as for herring, or can be soused in vinegar. In season all year round. Also available smoked.

SPRATS

A smaller member of the herring family (but not a young herring). Has a bluish-green back and silvery sides and belly. In season October to March. Bake, fry or grill. Also available smoked.

MACKEREL

HERRING

PILCHARDS

SPRATS

RIGHT
A fisherman lands a basketful of crabs. Fishmongers sell them live, boiled or dressed. Crabs provide two types of meat: white (legs and claws) and brown (the body meat), which is stronger in flavour with a creamier texture. Both are delicious.

OPPOSITE TOP
Small, hardy breeds of sheep, such as the Welsh Mountain, can survive the harsh winter conditions on Dartmoor in Devon. The animals are good foragers, and can live through the coldest weather without needing extra fodder.

OPPOSITE BELOW
Feeding time for these Gloucester Old Spot piglets, which are allowed to roam freely in orchards as they fatten. Each sow produces two litters per year.

too, and trawlers out of Brixham and Plymouth catch about 10 per cent of the total English haul. Dover sole are common, despite their name, and turbot, brill, dabs, conger eel and red and grey mullet also feature among the catch. You'll find interesting recipe ideas for fish between pages 184 and 204.

A great deal of this fish is exported or sent up to London. But some is sold fresh locally, and more finds its way into West Country smokeries, which produce smoked mackerel, kippers and bloaters. Fish for smoking has to be in tip-top condition, with a high oil content to make sure that the finished product is still deliciously moist. Most mackerel is hot-smoked, which means that no further cooking is needed and it can be eaten cold, just as it is. Alternatively, you can use it in recipes such as Smoked Mackerel Soufflé (page 196). Cold-smoked mackerel has a mavellous succulent flavour but needs to be cooked, or served cut in wafer-thin slices, like smoked salmon.

The waters of the West are well stocked with shellfish, and spider crabs, crayfish, scallops and lobsters are all considered local delicacies (you'll find recipes for crab and lobster on page 202). The crabs in Cornwall are larger than those caught in East Anglia, but the two areas both claim that *their* crabs have the finest flavour! Besides these luxurious treats, the everyday favourites – cockles, winkles, prawns and mussels – also thrive in these seas. There are oyster beds too, in Devon and Cornwall, producing both Native and Pacific oysters.

Freshwater fish, especially salmon and trout, from rivers such as the Dart, Exe and Tamar, feature on the menus of local restaurants and are frequently served cooked with cider or cream. Fish farms have sprung up here as they have elsewhere in the country. As well as trout and salmon, some enterprising fish farmers are producing more unusual fish, including pike, grayling and carp. Shellfish are also farmed on a small scale and oysters, crayfish and mussels are all commercially grown. Again, many of these fish end up in the smokeries or are made into fish products such as pâté and mousses.

Gloucestershire is well known for Severn salmon, and perhaps less famed for its elvers. The salmon are thought to have a fine flavour and are caught in May, by skilled fishermen using either traditional 'lave nets' or basket traps. Elvers, or baby eels, swim thousands of miles from the Sargasso Sea to come swarming up the Severn, and have been much relished for centuries. You're not likely to find them on the fishmonger's slab, however, and probably the only way to taste them is to join in the annual elver eating contests (see Food Fairs and Festivals, page 17).

PRIME MEAT

Pork is the prime meat of the West and is produced mainly in Wiltshire, which has been famous for pig farming for centuries. This is the county to visit for traditional sausages and faggots, and the hams and bacon are also well worth trying. The 'Wiltshire cure' produces sweet-flavoured, mild bacon, smoked or unsmoked. And Bradenham hams are a great treat, and are still prepared to a special, secret recipe. Soaked in juniper-flavoured molasses before smoking, they have a black, shiny outer coating which is unmistakable. Another West Country pork speciality is Bath chaps, which are the cured cheeks of the pig. Originally they came from a breed called the Gloucestershire Old Spot, an attractive dappled creature which has fortunately been saved from dying out completely. The pigs were fed on windfalls from the many apple orchards, which was said to give the flesh a particularly sweet flavour.

Plump, tender chickens and turkeys are bred all over the region, with ducks found particularly in Wiltshire, and the more unusual guinea fowl being reared in Somerset. If cooked carefully (see page 172 for roasting details) these birds compare well with the more costly pheasant. There is, of course, a wide variety of wild game to be found on the moors of Wiltshire, Devon and Cornwall, including rabbit and duck.

There is no shortage of cattle or sheep in these parts, and both Devon and Dorset produce good beef and excellent lamb. Cornwall, with its harsher landscape, has less of a tradition of livestock rearing and used, in the past, to rely mainly on the hardy goat for meat. However, the county does produce early lambs which have a superb flavour.

WEST COUNTRY CIDER

Traditionally, cider from this part of the country is made from cider apples, rather than the culinary and dessert varieties used in other regions. This gives farmhouse ciders their distinctive dryness.

FARMHOUSE CIDERS

From bone dry to reasonably sweet, many types of cider are brewed by small producers and sold locally 'over the gate'. These farmers tend to use the cider apples known as bittersharps and bittersweets to get the flavour they want.

Production is simple: the apples are pulped and allowed to ferment naturally in barrels. Different fruits might be blended or the cider may be made from one variety only.

These ciders vary widely in quality and can be excellent. They are only available locally, and it is wisest to try before you buy.

COMMERCIALLY PRODUCED CIDERS

Two of the country's largest cider producers are in the West Country and make a range of ciders of a consistent standard and flavour. Again, special cider apples are widely used. The drink is aged in oak vats and then carefully blended.

Types available include still, dry ciders, which are fairly strong; sweet, sparkling bottled ciders; and still, mellow, dryish ciders, which are almost like wine.

Blossom time in a cider apple orchard. The trees are planted close together and kept well pruned. Fertile valleys are ideal for apples, as they provide shelter from the frosts and winds that can damage the flowers and threaten the fruit crop.

YOUNG AND TENDER FRUIT AND VEG

The fertile land and well-warmed climate, with its regular rainfall, make the West Country ideal for growing vegetables. In fact the unusual warmth of these southerly parts means that crops are ripe well before those grown further north. In Cornwall, farmers can start planting potatoes in February, a month earlier than in less sheltered places. The very first crop is ready by May and these young early potatoes and other vegetables, such as peas and broad beans, have a tenderness and delicacy of flavour that is unbeatable. Other staple main-crop vegetables, such as carrots, Brussels sprouts and onions, also grow well. A scattering of herb farms, some salads and asparagus, and sizeable crops of sweet peppers, cauliflower and turnips complete the vegetable picture in the West.

Early strawberries from the Tamar valley are another great delicacy, and Cornwall also grows gooseberries, no doubt in order to cook one of the county's best traditional dishes, Baked Mackerel with Gooseberry Sauce (recipe, page 195). However, this is not really a great area for soft fruit, as the climate in Dorset and Devon is too wet to guarantee a good harvest, although strawberries are produced under intensive market gardening methods in Somerset, and in Gloucestershire they grow apricots, cherries and plums.

But it is apples, apples and more apples in the West Country, reflected deliciously in regional recipes like Somerset Apple Cake or Pork Fillet in Mustard Cream Sauce (recipes, pages 265 and 141). Apple orchards

FOOD FAIRS AND FESTIVALS

JANUARY

Wassailing the Apple Trees, Carhampton, Somerset: annual festival of toasting the orchard to bring a good crop.

EASTERTIDE

Easter Tuesday. Distribution of Twopenny Starvers, St Michael on the Mount Without, Bristol: buns are distributed to the young and old of the parish in a ceremony dating from 1739.

APRIL

Wimborne Horticultural Society Spring Show, Allendale Community Centre, Hanham Road, Wimborne, Dorset: spring flowers and produce, cookery, handicrafts.

MAY

Cheese Rolling Ceremony, Randwick, Gloucestershire, and Cooper's Hill, Brockworth, Gloucestershire (held on Whit Monday): large Double Gloucester cheeses are rolled downhill; originally carried out to protect grazing rights.
Devon County Show, County Showground, Exhibition Way, Whipton, Exeter, Devon: agricultural show.

JUNE

Royal Cornwall Agricultural Show, Wadebridge: livestock, crops and flowers.
Royal Bath and West Show, Showground, Shepton Mallet, Somerset: includes British Farm Food Fair, crafts, conservation, forestry.

JULY

Stithians Show, Playing Fields, Stithians, Truro, Cornwall: horses, cattle, goats, dogs, chickens, horticulture.

AUGUST

Harvest Home. Procession at East Brent, Somerset: church service, followed by procession of women carrying plum puddings; a huge loaf and 100 lb cheese are carried through the streets.

OCTOBER

Taunton Annual Illuminated Carnival and Cider-Barrel Rolling Race, Taunton, Somerset: carnival procession and race between teams pushing wooden cider barrels.

NOVEMBER

Great Western Beer Festival, Bristol Exhibition Centre, Canon's Road, Bristol, Avon: over 200 real ales and ciders, plus food and entertainments.

---

flourish all over the region. In the main, the apples are grown for cider-making (see Cider Fact Panel, opposite).

DRINKS FOR SIPPING AND SLURPING

Cider, in all styles and strengths, is the hallmark of West Country drinking. From farmhouse, scrumpy-type brews, to dry, smooth ciders, there is something to suit every taste. Some beer is also brewed in the region.

Wine-making is a growing venture in the West Country, even though the climate is not quite as suitable as it is in drier parts of the country. But there are commercial vineyards in Avon, Somerset, Wiltshire, Devon and Cornwall, producing a range of white wines. Many vineyards are experimenting with different grape varieties, but it is too soon yet to say how successful these will be.

Devon is home to the manufacturers of a rich cream liqueur, which combines local cream with brandy and whisky to make a sumptuous after-dinner drink. Another company in the area produces a range of fruit liqueurs, including raspberry, strawberry and blackcurrant. And in Somerset, they are distilling their cider to make an apple wine and have plans to launch an apple brandy in the near future. Plymouth has its very own gin distillery, where Plymouth gin has been made since 1793, and mead, an alcoholic drink made from fermented honey, is produced on a small scale.

Part-time pickers gather the harvest into baskets, to be taken for pressing. Cider apples are left on the trees until they start to fall, as the autumn sunshine helps the fruit to build up a high sugar content, vital for the strength and flavour of the cider.

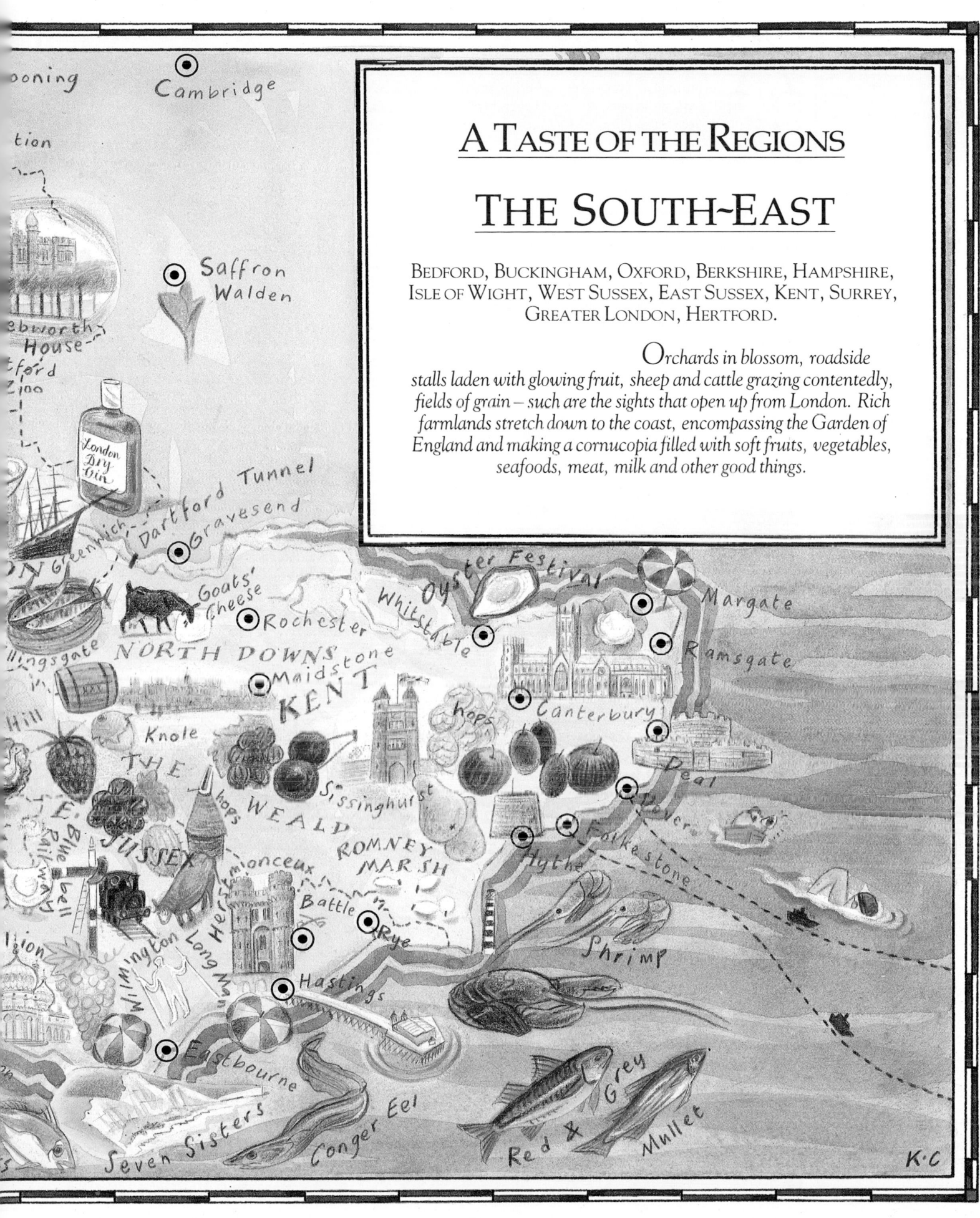

A Taste of the Regions

The South-East

Bedford, Buckingham, Oxford, Berkshire, Hampshire, Isle of Wight, West Sussex, East Sussex, Kent, Surrey, Greater London, Hertford.

Orchards in blossom, roadside stalls laden with glowing fruit, sheep and cattle grazing contentedly, fields of grain – such are the sights that open up from London. Rich farmlands stretch down to the coast, encompassing the Garden of England and making a cornucopia filled with soft fruits, vegetables, seafoods, meat, milk and other good things.

Cambridge

Saffron Walden

London Dry Gin

Dartford Tunnel

Gravesend

Greenwich

Goats' Cheese

Rochester

Whitstable

Oyster Festival

Margate

Ramsgate

NORTH DOWNS

Maidstone

KENT

Canterbury

Deal

hops

Knole

Dover

THE WEALD

Sissinghurst

hops

ROMNEY MARSH

Folkestone

Hythe

E. SUSSEX

Herstmonceux

Long Man

Battle

Rye

Shrimp

Wilmington

Hastings

Eastbourne

Seven Sisters

Conger Eel

Red & Grey Mullet

K·C

English wines

Most are white, and range from dry to medium sweet. They are similar to German Hock or Moselles in style and the best have a good crisp acidity, a fresh taste and a deeper flavour than their continental counterparts. Delicious with fish, light meats, or as an aperitif.

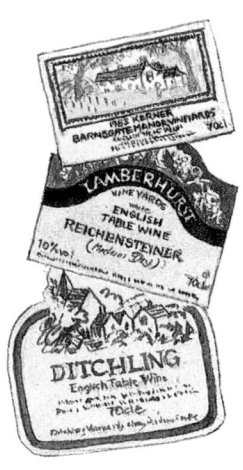

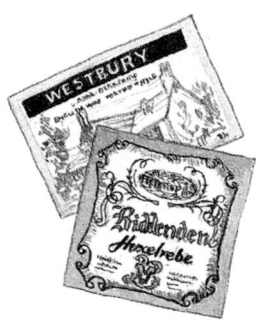

A kind climate, enough rain to keep the crops watered and a fertile soil – all these bonuses are enjoyed by farmers in the South-East. Farming of all types goes on here. Cereals, such as wheat, barley and oats, and root vegetables are grown, but the area is most famous for market gardening, with the Kent and Sussex Weald especially producing large amounts of fruit and vegetables. Relative newcomers to the scene are grape vines, rapidly becoming more widespread as the fine ancient tradition of English wine-making is revived.

As well as producing top-quality crops, the land is ideal for raising cattle and sheep, while the fishing industry is still important around parts of the south-east coast.

In the heart of the region is London. The days are long gone when London produced some of its own food. Everything has to be brought in. Billingsgate, Smithfield and Covent Garden, major centres of food distribution, are still here. But no crops are grown near London, no animals reared. Even the Home Counties have lost some of their farming tradition, as they have been gradually swallowed up by the capital. You can buy food of every possible type and nationality in London's markets and specialist shops, and you can sample the cuisines of the world in the city's numerous restaurants. It's the place to visit for traditional dishes like jellied eels or boiled beef and carrots, or for exotic ethnic food from far-flung countries like India, Africa, Mexico, China and Thailand, to name just a few.

But travel just that bit further towards the south coast and you reach the fertile acres and overflowing market gardens from which the rest of Britain gains tender lamb, fine fruit, superb shellfish and much more.

SUCCULENT PASTURES

Herds of dairy cattle are a common sight in the fields of the South-East. By far the most are found in Hampshire, where the lush pastures make ideal fodder.

These labels illustrate just a few of the many English wines available. Look out for them in your supermarket or off-licence, or pay a visit to your local vineyard – most welcome visitors.

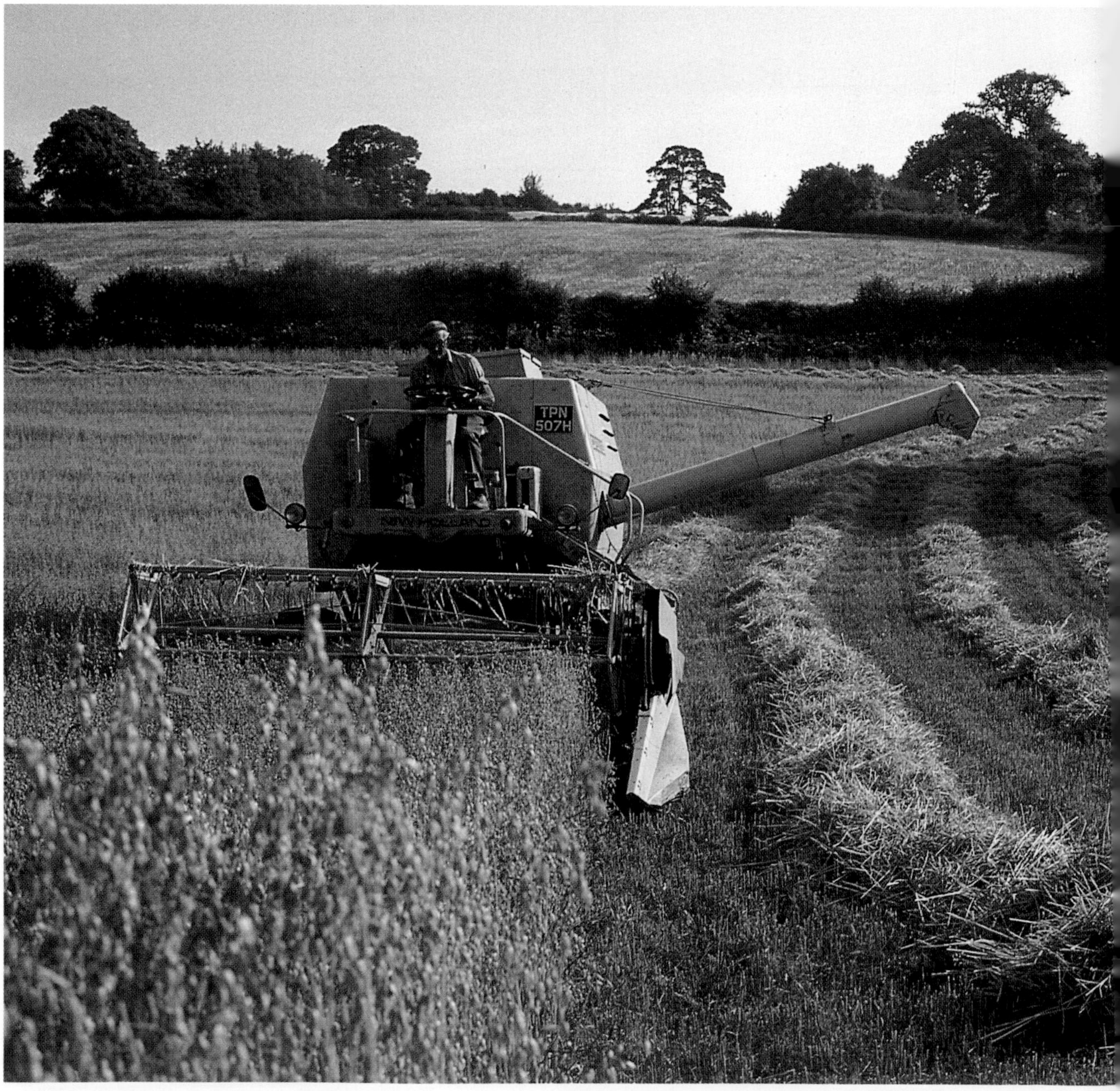

Cutting the barley by combine harvester. The relatively dry late summer and autumn in these parts means there's less chance of the crops being ruined by rain.

There are sizeable dairy herds, too, on the Isle of Wight and in Berkshire, Sussex and Kent. The number of cows kept for milk in Greater London, where until the mid-19th century large herds grazed on Clapham Common and Hampstead Heath, has diminished to almost nothing. Nowadays, London gets all its milk from the surrounding counties and 169 million gallons are brought into the capital every year.

The South-East has no tradition of cheese-making. Some new cheeses are being created as part of the national revival of interest in the farmhouse cheeses, but none of these is widely obtainable. Oxford cheese is a Cheddar type, available plain or smoked, which has recently been re-introduced. There is only one producer, but you should be able to find Oxford cheese in specialist delicatessens countrywide.

Other small-scale enterprises in the South-East include many dairy sheep and goat farms, producing milk, yogurt and cheeses. Look out for these delicacies if you are in the area. Loseley Park Farm near Guildford in Surrey use the milk of their pedigree Jerseys to make a range of natural, additive-free dairy products and these are widely found in wholefood shops in the south of England.

FLOURISHING FRUIT

Its warm, moist climate and rich soil make the Kent Weald exceptionally fertile. Fruit and vegetables thrive here in the Garden of England, as they have since the 16th century. But fruit was flourishing in this area long before then. Cherries first came to England with the Romans and still turn the orchards of the South-East into a mass of blossom every spring, even though far fewer cherry orchards exist than 30 or 40 years ago. The numbers have dwindled because the trees are tall and the crops had to be harvested from ladders – a costly and time-consuming business. However, small trees are gradually being introduced which make mechanised gathering possible.

Several varieties of sweet cherry are grown in Kent. You'll see many different types in the shops and it's worth buying them as they arrive. The picking period in any orchard is only about a week, so the supplies to the markets are constantly changing. If you want to cook cherries in a savoury dish, like Lamb with Cherries (see recipe, page 116), look out for red-skinned, sour types. Morellos are also a good choice – they have dark skin and flesh, and are also used for canning, bottling and making cherry brandy.

Apples are the other major fruit crop of Kent, the trees laden with more of that breathtaking spring blossom. Cox's Orange Pippins, one of Britain's favourite apples, were first grown in the South-East, and many other eaters, cookers, especially Bramley's, and cider apples are cultivated here.

Conference pears are frequently planted alongside dessert apple orchards. Also widely grown are Doyenne du Comice, which has a melting, fragrant flesh, and Williams' Bon Chrétien, a juicy sweet pear, often used

DESSERT APPLES

Numerous varieties of apple are grown and those listed here and overleaf are just a few of the types most widely available. Choose unblemished fruit without bruises, buy little and often, and store in a cool place, not in a bowl in a warm room. Many dessert apples can also be used successfully for cooking.

Cox's Orange Pippin
Crisp, juicy and very aromatic. (October to May.)

Ida Red
Succulent and crisp with white, juicy flesh. (November to March.)

Discovery
Firm, white and juicy. Fairly sweet. (August to September.)

Egremont Russet
Small and crisp with a distinctive nutty flavour. (October to December.)

Cox's Orange Pippins, fresh from the tree in a Sussex orchard, waiting to be graded according to size and skin quality before going to market. The picker, who has just emptied her fruit into the central collecting point, would belong to the team of extra casual labour taken on every year for the harvest.

Worcester Pearmain
Sweet, with crisp white flesh.
Eat when really ripe.
(September to October.)

Spartan
Firm, crisp and juicy. Refreshing
flavour. (November to March.)

Laxton Superb
Very sweet and juicy with firm
flesh. (November to April.)

ABOVE
The Georgian shop-front of
one of the most celebrated
cheesemongers in the country
– Paxton & Whitfield, in
central London's exclusive
Jermyn Street. The store
stocks over 50 varieties of
English cheeses, as well as
English hams.

RIGHT
English's Oyster Bar in
Brighton has been serving
delicious fresh shellfish to
satisfied customers for 150
years from premises in the
charming olde worlde area of
the town, known as The
Lanes.

for canning. South Buckinghamshire is known for its plums and damsons, while Victoria plums from Kent also make excellent eating.

As well as acres of fruit trees, the South-East boasts bushels of soft fruit – much of it on offer at pick-your-own farms. Black- and redcurrants, gooseberries, raspberries and strawberries make a brightly coloured display throughout the summer.

A WEALTH OF FRESH VEGETABLES

No market gardening area would be complete without plentiful vegetables, and salads galore are grown in the South-East, as well as broccoli, beans, cauliflower and almost every other vegetable you care to name. Some counties have specialities: Brussels sprouts are big news in Bedfordshire, Sussex has a large number of mushroom farms and Hampshire grows most of Britain's native watercress. Its deliciously tangy flavour is good for enlivening a dish like Warm Watercress, Potato and Bacon Salad (see recipe, page 89).

That deliciously aromatic member of the lily family, garlic, is produced on a small scale in the UK, mostly on the Isle of Wight. As well as adding flavour to recipes, garlic is said to have many medicinal properties, not to mention being useful for warding off evil spirits.

Kentish cob nuts, sometimes called Lambert's Filberts, were first grown by Mr Lambert in about 1830. They are a variety of hazelnut which has pleasant, sweet flesh. The crop is smaller now than in the past but you should still be able to find Kentish cobs in the shops during October.

GOOD GRAZING

Most farms in the South-East are mixed, and sheep are kept on more than half of them, as they are happy to graze on pasture which is unsuitable for cattle. The ewes are mainly cross breeds, bought from upland farms. They are crossed again with good meat breeds to produce hardy lambs with the best characteristics of both types. The Suffolk sheep, a hornless creature, with a black, bare face and legs and a long body, is probably most commonly used as a sire in the South-East.

Pure breeds are used only when their special characteristics make them ideal for a particular area. One famous pure breed is the Romney Marsh, which feeds on the salty pastures that border Sussex and Kent, and is robust enough to withstand the winds that sweep across the grazing grounds from the Channel.

Sheep normally produce lambs once a year, usually in the early spring, always a busy time for sheep farmers. The young start nibbling grass at about three to four weeks old and are fully weaned by mid-summer. Lambs sold for meat are under a year old, and English lamb is reckoned to be at its best from August to November.

Cattle also do well in the South-East and although many belong to dairy herds, beef production is also important. The two types of farming are closely interlinked. Some of the calves born to the dairy herd are kept to supplement the milk-producers, others are used for breeding and the remainder are reared for meat.

Sussex cattle – which are large and reddish-brown – are a breed commonly found in the area. But once again, they are cross bred in order to combine the good qualities of beef bulls and dairy cows.

Poultry and turkeys are important in the South-East, where almost half the 13 million chickens kept are for egg production, the rest being reared for the table. Surrey has been famous for capons and chickens for centuries, since they were bred for the royal table at Hampton Court. The Aylesbury duck, a large, plump, white species, originated in Buckinghamshire, but the pure breed has now almost disappeared.

Pig farms are scattered throughout the South-East, mainly in Kent and Hampshire, and there's good game to be had, with venison from the New Forest as well as excellent pheasant, partridge, quail and hare.

RICH IN SHELLFISH

The long coastline of Sussex and Kent has made fishing an important part of life in those counties for centuries. However, the inshore fishing industry has gradually decreased over the years, especially in Kent. Dover, the port once renowned for the superb sole that was landed there and sent to London, now has no fishing boats. The fishing tradition does continue in Sussex, with sea bass, conger eel, and red and grey mullet all found among the catch. A growing number of small manufacturers are setting up business near the coast, producing a variety of smoked seafoods.

Shellfish are plentiful all round the south coast. Fine lobsters are caught in pots from May to October, and shrimps, scallops, clams, whelks and superb crabs are also found in these waters.

Good-quality, well-fattened oysters are farmed in quantity in the Solent and in smaller numbers at Whitstable. Two main varieties are produced – the Flat oyster and the Pacific oyster – both of which are at their most delicious eaten raw with a squeeze of lemon and some bread and butter, although they can also be cooked (Oyster Loaves, page 201). The old 'R in the month' method of telling when oysters are in season still holds good, so look for them from September to April.

Oysters have had a rather chequered history. From being cheap and plentiful up until the start of the 19th century, they then became far scarcer and more of a luxury, because overfishing had severely depleted the oyster beds. The industry has been revived but the stocks are always at risk from disease, bad weather and predatory sea creatures.

From a food that used to be cheap and is now a luxury, to one that used to be pricy and is now much more affordable. Rainbow trout are farmed extensively all over the South-East and because the methods are so efficient, trout is more widely available – and therefore cheaper – than ever before. Farms spring up wherever there is a good supply of clean cool water and many of them welcome visitors. The trout are fed on a high-protein diet and grow rapidly, producing a good weight of sweet, succulent flesh for their size.

If you're lucky, you may find 'wild' trout from Sussex, or from the River Test in Hampshire, although these tend to be consumed close to where they are caught. Other freshwater fish, such as pike and zander, a relative of perch, are farmed to a small extent in the South-East, but may be hard to come by outside the local area.

London is home to Billingsgate, the famous fish market, where much of the British catch ends up. Although now moved from its former site in the City of London to the Docklands, the market continues to ply its trade as it has done for centuries. Most fish is sent directly by road from the ports and arrives in the early hours of the morning, to be rushed to fishmongers all over the country while it is still fresh.

WARM FROM THE OVEN

The streets of London no longer resound to the cries of traders ringing their bells as they walk along with a tray of fresh crumpets or muffins for sale on their heads. Such picturesque scenes disappeared in the 1930s, but we can still buy those wonderfully comforting foods, or even make them at home (see recipe, page 297).

Chelsea buns are another London delicacy, which fortunately has survived (see recipe, page 295). They were originally sold from the Old Chelsea Bun House in Pimlico, destroyed in 1839. King George III was a regular customer.

Kentish Maids were keen on baking and many traditional recipes exist, although few are made commercially. Huffkins (see recipe, page 287) have a long history, and although you won't see them in the shops, they are easy to make yourself. For an authentic Kentish touch, fill the hole in the centre of each huffkin with hot cherries and serve as a dessert. Not surprisingly,

Fly-fishing on the River Test, Hampshire. The most likely catch is brown trout, which can weigh as much as 5 kg (11 lb). However, smaller fish, although less impressive, make better eating, as they are more tender.

RIGHT
The cakes for which Banbury is renowned are made by The Original Cake Shop. They are rather like Eccles cakes to look at, but the mincemeat-style filling is flavoured with rum.

BELOW
Oast houses in the Darent Valley, Shoreham. In the foreground, the hop shoots can be seen growing up strings, supported by poles. After lying dormant all winter, hops start to grow fast in April and are about 18 feet high by the end of June. They then ripen during the summer, ready to be harvested in September. Hop shoots are a delicacy and are sometimes available for eating as a green vegetable.

recipes featuring cherries and apples are common in Kent. Ripe Tart (see recipe, page 241) is a more-ish cherry flan, and Apple and Hazelnut Layer (see recipe, page 258) uses two of the country's best-known products.

Banbury cakes, shown opposite, can still be bought in the town of Banbury, Oxfordshire, which is also famous for the Cross mentioned in the nursery rhyme 'Ride a Cock Horse'. A Victorian replacement of the original Cross still stands. Another sweet speciality from Oxford is Frank Cooper's Oxford Marmalade. This essential part of the British gentleman's breakfast was first made in 1874 by Sarah Cooper. Her husband was so delighted with the result that he packaged the marmalade in earthenware jars and sold it in his grocery shop. Its success soon led to the full-scale production of this mouthwatering, coarse-cut confection.

DRINKS NEW AND OLD

The English wine industry has seen an amazing upsurge in the last 20 years. Although wine-making has gone on here since the time of the Romans, it was an activity mainly confined to the monasteries and more or less disappeared when they were dissolved by Henry VIII. Interest in wine-making revived in the late 1940s and now there are over 1000 growers, many of them in the South-East.

Vines need a south-facing slope with well-drained soil to thrive, and are at the mercy of the climate. Frost kills the buds, high winds break down the vines, and if there's not enough sun, the grapes won't ripen properly.

FOOD FAIRS AND FESTIVALS

JANUARY

Wassailing the Apple Trees, Gill Orchard, Henfield, West Sussex: annual ritual of toasting the orchard to bring a good crop.

EASTERTIDE

Shrove Tuesday: Pancake Race, Olney, Buckinghamshire: race, run since 1445, of local women who dash from the market place to the church tossing pancakes as they go.
Good Friday: Easter Bun Ceremony, The Widow's Son Inn, 75 Devons Road, Bromley-by-Bow, London E3: a sailor adds a bun to those already hanging from the inn's ceiling, to commemorate the poor widow who baked a bun for her only son, who was expected home from sea and never returned.
Good Friday: Butterworth Charity, St Bartholomew-the-Great, London EC1: hot cross buns and coins are presented to the 'poor widows of the parish' after the 11.00 service.
Rogation Day: Blessing of the Nets and Mackerel, on the beach opposite the Old Ship Hotel, Brighton, East Sussex; also at Hastings.

MAY

Festival of English Wines, Leeds Castle, Maidstone, Kent.
Greenwich Real Ale Festival, Greenwich Town Hall, London.
Hertfordshire Show, Showground, Friars Wash, Redbourn, Hertfordshire: agricultural show with show jumping.
Surrey County Show, Stoke Park, Guildford, Surrey: agricultural show with sheepdog display, vintage farm machinery, heavy horses and other attractions.

JUNE

Annual South of England Show, Ardingly, West Sussex: livestock.

JULY

Blessing the Sea Ceremony, Whitstable: ceremony dating back to Saxon times, held as near to St James's Day as high tide permits.
Kent County Show, Detling, Maidstone, Kent: livestock and produce.
Rare Breeds Show, Weald and Downland Open Air Museum, Singleton, Chichester, West Sussex.
Whitstable Oyster Festival: celebration of oyster harvest, held towards end of month.

SEPTEMBER

English Wine Festival and Regional Food Fair, The English Wine Centre, East Sussex.

DECEMBER

Royal Smithfield Show, Earl's Court Exhibition Centre, Warwick Road, London SW5: major event in farming calendar, with livestock and exhibition of machinery.

Despite these problems, English wine growers have experimented with different grapes and found that there are several types, mainly German, which can cope with our uncertain climate. If you happen to be visiting the South-East, remember that many vineyards are happy to show you around and let you sample their products.

Although most English wine is sold 'over the farm gate', many brands are starting to appear in shops further afield. EEC regulations mean that all English wines have to bear the words 'Table Wine' on the label. However, the English Vineyards Association have introduced a Seal of Quality, so look out for that when buying. Don't confuse *English* wines, made in England from grapes grown here, with *British* wines, made from grapes and concentrates imported from Europe.

When you're shopping for wines, keep an eye out for the growing range of English country wines, made not from grapes but from apples, redcurrants, gooseberries, elderflowers and berries and other old-fashioned ingredients – delicious, and well worth trying.

Hops have been an important crop in Kent for centuries and although less widespread now, fields of hop cones and oast houses are still a familiar part of the Kent countryside. Families from London's East End used to make an annual holiday of hop-picking, but the operation is now mechanised. Hops were originally grown as a vegetable and weren't used in brewing until the 16th century. After harvesting, they are placed in the oast houses to dry out over slow-burning fires, before being sent to breweries around the country. Beers brewed in Kent tend to have a strong hoppy flavour, which can be something of an acquired taste.

The vast crops of fruit produced every year in Kent have other delicious alcoholic spin-offs. Cider is made from local apples, and Morello cherries are used to make delectable cherry brandy. The slight hint of almonds in the flavour comes from the crushed cherry stones which are added to the pulped fruit.

Some beer is brewed around London, which has independent breweries at Wandsworth and Chiswick. London Dry Gin is another tipple associated with the capital and the recipe, based on juniper berries and various herbs, has been the same for 200 years.

And if you're starting to feel the effects of all this booze, try a glass of refreshing mineral water from the Hertfordshire Chilterns. The water is exceptionally pure, having permeated slowly through the chalk hills.

Penshurst vineyards in Kent were first planted in 1972, and now cover 12 acres. Each acre produces roughly three tons of grapes – enough to make 3,000 bottles of English wine.

A Taste of the Regions

WALES

Clwyd, Dyfed, Gwynedd, Powys, Gwent, West Glamorgan, Mid Glamorgan, South Glamorgan.

Sweet, tender lamb from the mountains; oats, wheat and barley; soft fruits in the warmer south; fish of all types, from cockles to sea trout; creamy milk and butter; carrots, cabbage and early potatoes. These are the good things of Wales, a country where the cooking is simple and wholesome.

Puffin Island

Bangor

GWYNEDD

Caernarfon

Snowdon

Ffestiniog

CLWYD

Trout

Chester

Wrexham

Butter

Cheese

Little Moreton Hall

Stoke

Harlech

River Dovey

MOUNTAINS

Powis Castle

Welshpool

POWYS

Stafford

Shrewsbury

Ironbridge

Wolverhampton

Salmon

Aberystwyth

River Teifi

CAMBRIAN

Cheese

Welsh
Mountain
Sheep

Builth
Wells

Sgwd-yr-Eira
Waterfall

Hereford

Walks

BRECON

Caver BEACONS

GLAMORGAN

Merthyr
Tydfil

Swansea

Vineyards

Rhondda

Cardiff

Monmouth

Caerphilly

GWENT

Tintern Abbey

Newport

Bristol

A land of breathtaking scenery, with its own lilting language, Wales possesses a terrain that has always presented a challenge to farmers. Those in the north, where the rugged mountains will support little other than oats and sheep, had to scrape a living from the land. In the more affluent south, where the landscape as well as the climate is kinder, the story is different. In the rolling hills dairy and beef cattle do well and it is possible to grow soft fruit, vegetables and crops of wheat and barley, the last of which is mainly used for fattening beef herds. In the warmest parts of the south, there are even vineyards.

Milk, butter, cream and cheese all feature in Welsh cooking. Lamb is popular and so are oats, which appear in many guises. Fishing from the long coastline has had its heyday and the industry which formerly stretched right along the coast is now concentrated in the south. Attempts are being made to revive the shellfish beds in the north, although this is inevitably a gradual process. Clear rivers and deep mountain lakes provide excellent freshwater fish.

The cooking of Wales is that of a region where the living has often been less than easy. People who laboured hard on the land or in the mines and factories concentrated in the industrial south needed sustaining but uncomplicated food that could be quickly prepared at the end of a long day. The thrifty housewife was ingenious in her use of such ingredients as were available, providing nourishing soups and stews as well as mouthwatering home-baking.

CREAMY MILK, SALTY BUTTER

The pastoral country of south Wales, warmed by breezes from the Gulf Stream, and with a high rainfall, has always supported large dairy herds. Even in the mountainous north the dairy tradition exists, and some herds are kept on the lower slopes of the uplands. The country as a whole produces around 1500 million litres of milk a year. Much of the liquid milk goes to London, and the rest is used for cheese, cream, yogurt, ice cream, butter and buttermilk.

Herefords were formerly the predominant breed but these days the Welsh Black is also favoured. Hardy, and mainly concentrated in the north, this is a beef cattle that can provide good-quality milk as well.

Welsh butter is known for its saltiness. The size of a herd of cattle used to be a status symbol among farmers, so few animals were killed off for beef and the dairy herd gradually grew and grew. This naturally led to surpluses of dairy products, including butter, which had then to be well salted in order to preserve it. It is still a salty butter, with a rich, creamy texture, and is delicious spread on scones or teabreads. But if you use it in cooking, you won't need to add much extra salt.

Friesian cattle are immediately recognisable by their black and white markings, and produce about 85% of British milk. The breed comes originally from Holland, but has been developed in various ways in different parts of the world.

A view down into the fields shows a pleasing pattern of straw gathered together and left to dry after the harvest is finished.

The Welsh Black cow is bred mainly for beef. It feeds on grass in the summer, and on hay or silage during the winter. The cattle can be kept on the uplands, which are unsuitable for growing crops.

CHEESES, NEW AND OLD

Caerphilly, a mild, young, salty cheese, which was a favourite lunchtime snack for miners, is probably the best-known cheese of Welsh origins. However, most Caerphilly is now made in the West Country, although a handful of farms in Wales are producing it again, some by totally traditional methods. Welsh creameries instead turn out excellent Red Leicester, Cheddar and Cheshire varieties.

In the past Wales had several home-grown cheeses, which feature in the history books. Although these have disappeared, many new farm cheeses are being produced, but all, so far, on a small, fairly local scale. Llangloffan, for instance, is a creamy, semi-hard cheese which is available plain or flavoured with garlic; Caws Fferm Teifi is made by methods which are 500 years old and is similar in style to Dutch Gouda; and Llanboidy is a hard, full-fat cheese made from the milk of the rare breed of Red Poll cattle. And there are numerous other delicious Welsh cheeses.

Herds of dairy goats and, to a lesser extent, sheep are widespread in Wales and many different sorts of cheese are made from their milk. The traditional cooking of Wales leans heavily on dairy products and cheese crops up in two simple but delicious dishes. Glamorgan sausages, despite their name, contain no meat but are made of cheese, breadcrumbs, herbs and chopped onion or leek, mixed together, formed into sausage shapes, fried and eaten with potatoes (see recipe, page 100). They used to be made with the firm white cheese of Glamorgan, now no longer produced. Welsh rabbit (or rarebit) is a traditional dish that has been adopted nationwide. There are several ways to make it, from simply toasting a slice of cheese on a piece of bread to making a smooth, creamy cheese mixture, perhaps incorporating cream, butter or ale, pouring it on to toast and browning the top under the grill.

SWEET MOUNTAIN SHEEP

The mountains of the north spell sheep, which are the creatures best able to withstand the exposure to wind, rain and cold. The main breed is the Welsh Mountain, which is found throughout Wales. These sheep are the smallest commonly reared in Britain and have smooth

With the increasing interest in self-sufficiency the demand for goats' products such as milk, cheese and yogurt is growing steadily. More than 75,000 goats are kept in Britain, over half of them in herds numbering five or less.

A flock of sheep wends its way home at sunset in the Brecon Beacons. There are well over 3½ million breeding ewes in Wales, and in a year, an efficient upland farm could produce 120 lambs from every 100 ewes.

faces, bright, prominent eyes, small ears and slim, wool-free legs. The rams have curled horns. They are hardy, stocky animals, well suited to mountain life, and produce very fine, soft wool as well as marvellous meat.

Welsh lamb is available nationwide, and a new scheme of marking it clearly has recently been introduced, so it should be easy for shoppers to recognise. The meat is tender and lean, with a rich delicate flavour, which may have a hint of herbs if the flocks have been grazing on the patches of wild thyme and rosemary that grow in the mountains. As Welsh honey tends to have a similarly herby flavour, the two work very successfully together in recipes (see, for example, page 115). Cider and rosemary are other ingredients commonly used to enhance the flavour of the delicious meat.

Hill farmers aim to produce lambs no earlier than April, when the weather starts to improve and the grass begins to sprout again. Most female lambs are kept on the hills to replace older or barren ewes, which are sold to upland farmers to be kept in less harsh conditions. Male lambs are sent to market for meat.

Although the ubiquitous Welsh Mountain sheep predominates, there are also several breeds of sheep

which are restricted to local areas, for instance, two of the Welsh upland breeds are the black-faced Clun Forest and the Kerry Hill, which has a white face with black markings. They are less hardy than hill sheep. Beef cattle, which are a natural spin-off from dairy farming, are found wherever milk is produced. But in many lowland parts of South Wales, flocks of sheep have gradually replaced the herds of cattle.

Many traditional Welsh recipes feature lamb. Mutton hams were made by shepherds, who cured the hind leg of a sheep at home, using salt, sugar and spices, then hung the joint in the chimney to smoke. Lamb and mutton pies were a familiar part of the hiring and livestock fairs that were held throughout Wales. Sometimes the minced meat would be mixed with leek or topped with rowanberry jelly. Cawl was a staple dish using scraps of lamb or bacon and vegetables, cooked together in a broth. The liquid might be served separately, or the whole dish eaten together from a bowl with a special spoon.

Most people probably enjoyed a taste of sweet Welsh lamb only on highdays and holidays. As in so many other parts of the country, the poorer people's staple fare was pork, from the pig kept at the bottom of the garden. Commercial pig farming has declined in Wales in recent years, although it is still carried out in some areas. Poultry farming, particularly of turkeys, is another industry that has faced problems, although it is now being gradually revived.

Salt duck is a peculiarly Welsh way to treat duckling, which is rubbed thoroughly with salt and left for a day or two before cooking. This results in tender meat with a delicious flavour that is not too salty.

GATHERED FROM THE SANDS

Fine salmon are caught in the rivers Teifi, Tywi and Taf in west Wales, where occasionally you will still see coracles, the traditional fisherman's craft. They are light boats, made by stretching hide or canvas over a willow framework. The fishermen went out in pairs in their coracles and caught the fish in nets from the boats. Salmon are also caught in the Severn estuary in special baskets, the design of which has remained the same for centuries. Some of this salmon is smoked in Wales.

The lakes and rivers also provide homes for sea trout, called sewin, brown trout, grayling and red-bellied char, although this last is something of a rarity. A popular way to eat trout, and other fish, is to wrap it in bacon rashers and bake it, or fry it in bacon fat.

Cockles are gleaned from the sands around the beautiful Gower peninsula, and also from some beaches in north Wales. They are mostly gathered by hand, a back-breaking job which can only be done at low tide. Donkeys and ponies are still used to take the wooden carts down to the cockle beds. Some of the fish are cooked and removed from the shells before being sold but many are sold live and can be seen in great heaps on the market stalls of Swansea and Cardiff.

If you buy some or are lucky enough to find fresh cockles elsewhere, wash them well and boil them until the shells open.

Swansea, in common with many other coastal towns of Wales, was once a busy fishing port but now only small catches of cod, sole and hake are landed there. Other sea fish caught off Wales include mullet, bass, plaice and flounder. Herrings and mackerel have been fished at Aberystwyth since medieval times, and were important at many other ports, but today the fishing industry has declined. However, the oyster and mussel beds along the Menai Straits are being revived and now produce good crops. Cardigan Bay is being gradually restocked with lobsters, after overfishing had led to restrictions being placed on the catch. Scallops, clams and crabs are also caught off the Welsh coast.

A food from the sea which is considered a great delicacy in Wales is laver, an edible seaweed, gathered from the rocks. The seaweed is processed commercially into laverbread, a gelatinous purée. It can be eaten coated with oatmeal and fried with bacon, or made into laver sauce to eat with fish or mutton.

PICK YOUR OWN IN THE SOUTH

Fruit and vegetable growing does not lend itself to such a hilly landscape but there are places where horticulture is well established. Carrots, potatoes, peas, cabbage and cauliflower are all grown, with some salads and courgettes produced under glass. Early potatoes are an important crop in Gwynedd, on the Gower peninsula and in Pembrokeshire, now part of Dyfed, although here the rich soils have been depleted by intensive farming and now depend heavily on fertilisers.

Pick-your-own farms flourish in the warmer, flatter south, particularly in Gwent and Glamorgan. Soft fruits, including strawberries, raspberries, red- and blackcurrants, gooseberries, loganberries and blackberries are all on offer, along with tender vegetables such as French and broad beans, sweetcorn and many others. The leek, national symbol of Wales, is not widely grown in the region, but the custom of wearing a leek on 1 March, St David's Day, still survives. It is said to date back to the 7th century when, during a battle against the Saxons, the Welsh troops wore leeks in their helmets to distinguish them from the enemy.

FRESH FROM THE GRIDDLE

Here, as in the north of England and Scotland, oats were the most readily available cereal, widely grown because they are not averse to the cool and wet climate. The village mill also provided wheat and barley flours, and some of these watermills are now being brought back into service to produce nourishing, stone-ground flours.

Tea was always a much-loved meal in Wales, although working families could not indulge in it every day. A lot of the cooking in a Welsh cottage was done on a well-greased griddle, or bakestone, set above the hearth. All kinds of baked goods, including bread, tarts and fruit turnovers, could be produced on the bakestone by a skilled cook, who could even transform her griddle into a primitive oven by inverting a metal pot over it.

Welsh oatcakes are similar to Scottish ones, but thinner, while their pancakes, or *crempog,* are made with buttermilk, then well buttered and stacked up in piles, which are sliced down into portions. They can also be layered with a variety of fillings, sweet or savoury. Welsh cakes are another type of firm griddle cake, served sprinkled with sugar and with a dab of butter in the centre. They are at their best when fresh, although many households still store away a supply to offer to visitors. Traditionally, they were served at inns to weary travellers, while they waited for their supper.

Also on the tea table you might find scones and pikelets, and perhaps a loaf of bara brith, a spicy, speckled fruit bread, best served sliced and spread with Welsh butter. Many cakes are agreeably spicy, with cinnamon and caraway seeds being favourite flavourings.

PURE SPRING WATERS

The influence of the Methodist Church and the temperance movement made a strong mark on Welsh drinking habits and relatively little alcohol is produced. There are a few independent breweries, and mead, from fermented Welsh honey, is made on a small scale. One company in Powys produces a herb-flavoured Welsh whisky and a cream liqueur flavoured with honey. The

---

EARLY POTATOES

The mild coastal slopes of Pembrokeshire rival those of Cornwall and Kent in the race to bring the first of the early potatoes to the markets at the end of May.

Delicately flavoured, these 'first earlies', available until mid-August, are ideal for salads and simple summer dishes, such as Cauliflower and Potato Bake on page 222.

Buy little and often and handle gently to avoid bruising. Scrub or scrape gently before cooking or cook in skins in lightly salted boiling water flavoured with a sprig of fresh mint.

Here are the main varieties of first earlies from Pembrokeshire:

HOME GUARD

Creamy white flesh, more floury than other earlies. Particularly good boiled, served with plenty of butter.

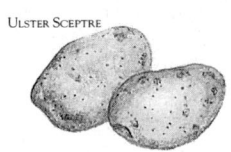

ULSTER SCEPTRE

HOME GUARD

ULSTER SCEPTRE

Excellent cooking quality and firm waxy texture that does not crumble or break when boiled. Also good in salads or chipped.

ARRAN COMET

Very creamy flesh, less waxy than Ulster Sceptre but still firm and can be cooked in the same way.

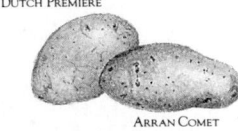

DUTCH PREMIERE

ARRAN COMET

DUTCH PREMIERE

A newcomer to the British scene which is gaining popularity. Pale-yellow flesh, good flavour particularly suitable for chips.

ABOVE

Laver is an edible seaweed packed with minerals and vitamins. The locals eat it as a savoury snack, simply fried or boiled to a purée and spread on slices of fried bread.

RIGHT

A mechanical spinner is used to bring these Pembrokeshire early potatoes to the surface of the ground, then they are gathered up and bagged by hand. The earlier the crop is picked, the lighter the yield – but the higher the price that can be fetched.

FOOD FAIRS AND FESTIVALS

APRIL

Llyn Agricultural Show, Botachu Wyn, Nefyn, Pwllheli, Gwynedd: agricultural show with cattle, sheep, goats, poultry, etc.

MAY

Montgomeryshire Agricultural Show, Feggy Leasone, Welshpool: livestock, ring events and stands.

JUNE

Aberystwyth Agricultural Show, Tanycastell Park, Rhydyfelin, Aberystwyth, Dyfed.

JULY

*Bridgend Show, Waterton, Bridgend: cattle, show jumping, etc.
Royal Welsh Show, Llanelwedd, Builth Wells; livestock.*

AUGUST

*Anglesey Agricultural Show, Mona nr. Llangefni, Anglesey: livestock and horticulture.
Chepstow Agricultural Show, Chepstow Racecourse, Chepstow, Gwent: livestock, horticulture and crafts.*

*Showground, Withybush, Haverfordwest, Dyfed: livestock, horticulture, trade stands and fair.
United Counties Agricultural and Hunters Society Show, Showground, Nantyci, Dyfed: livestock and horticulture.
Vale of Glamorgan Agricultural Show, Penllyne Castle, Cowbridge, South Glamorgan: livestock and horticulture.*

south-facing coastal slopes of Glamorgan have a long history of viniculture; grapes have been grown there for wine since medieval times. Today, a sprinkling of vineyards in Glamorgan and Dyfed produce crisp, dry white wines from German grape varieties.

Filtering down through the hills and mountains of Wales come pure waters, several of which are bottled commercially. Carmarthen water comes from Prysg spring in the Teify valley and is available still or sparkling. Decantae is an extremely pure mineral water, very low in metals and salts, which is bottled at source on Trofarth farm in the foothills of Snowdonia. And Brecon Natural Mineral Water comes from the village of Trap in Brecon Beacons National Park. The carbonated version comes from Carreg spring, while the still water issues from the spring of St David.

Rugged mountains and regular rainfall can cause problems for farmers in the Dovey Valley. But the beauty of the scenery is a great compensation.

also in Northamptonshire and Derbyshire, where a large part of the county's farmland is given over to sheep rearing. However, with these exceptions, sheep farming is not as important in the Midlands as in other parts of the country.

In spite of having such good-quality beef on the doorstep, most butchers' shops in the Midlands concentrate first and foremost on pork products. Throughout the Shires the butchers' windows are full of black puddings, polony, home-cured bacon and hams, sausages, faggots, brawns and, last but by no means least, pork pies. The town of Melton Mowbray, in the heart of Leicestershire's fox-hunting country, is famous for its pork pies. Originally they were eaten after the hunt – or even for breakfast, before it. The bulbous pies have a crisp, hot-water crust and a mouthwatering filling of roughly chopped pork (see recipe, page 148). Commercial production has gone on in Melton Mowbray since the mid-19th century. However, several other manufacturers produce the pies elsewhere, so wherever you live, they should be available.

The rolling, wooded countryside of the Shires provides cover for all sorts of game – pheasant, rabbit and hare amongst others. And to add spice and savour

A window crowded with good things, in this traditional shop in Leominster.

to all things meaty is Worcestershire Sauce, developed almost by accident in the 1830s by two chemists, Mr Lea and Mr Perrins, from a recipe brought back from India by the Governor of Bengal. The exact ingredients and the length of time needed for the sauce to mature in oak barrels are still secret. As well as enhancing casseroles and soups, a dash of the sauce added to tomato juice makes a good hangover cure.

CIDER-MAKING AND BREWING

Hereford & Worcester is second only to Kent as a major

The Nottingham Goose Fair is held every October, but has changed immensely since it started in the 13th century, when hundreds of geese were brought here from miles around to be sold and herded down to London, in time for the Christmas feast.

hop-growing region and the heady, yeasty scent of hops fills the lanes during early autumn. But there are surprisingly few breweries in the area. Instead the main drinks found here are cider and perry, made from fermented pear juice. Both are produced commercially but perry is less widely available than cider. It has a pleasant, mellow flavour, which is not at all sharp.

There are many varieties of apple and pear suitable for making into these delicious alcoholic drinks, and most of them are grown in the surrounding areas. Some farmers make single-variety ciders and perries, mainly for their own use or to sell over the gate, but most of the drinks sold commercially are made with a blend of juices from different varieties.

The abundant fruits of Hereford & Worcester are also used to make concentrated fruit juices. These contain no preservatives, sweeteners, colouring or water, and have a delicious full flavour and aroma. The emphasis is very much on apple and flavours include pure apple – made from Cox's and Russets – as well as apple with blackcurrant, blackberry or plum.

Burton-on-Trent, in Staffordshire, is a town once famous for brewing, but now there are only five breweries left, one of which is a working museum. IPA, found on draught in pubs all over the country, derives from the pale ales once brewed at Burton-on-Trent. Burton pale ales were prized for their brightness and clarity, which came from the natural spring water used in their production. In the 1820s Burton brewed an even paler, hoppier ale for export to India; India Pale Ale (IPA) was so popular that it has been made ever since. Bottled bitters are usually called pale or light ales.

Mild ale is drunk widely in the Midlands, where it is still very popular. Some breweries in the region also produce stout, derived from porter, a dark, well-matured beer which dominated the British beer scene until the late 1800s, when it was superseded by bitter. Real ale brewing is also carried on in many Midlands breweries, and the region has seen the revival of the old custom that was once common in pubs throughout the land – that of home-brewing beer.

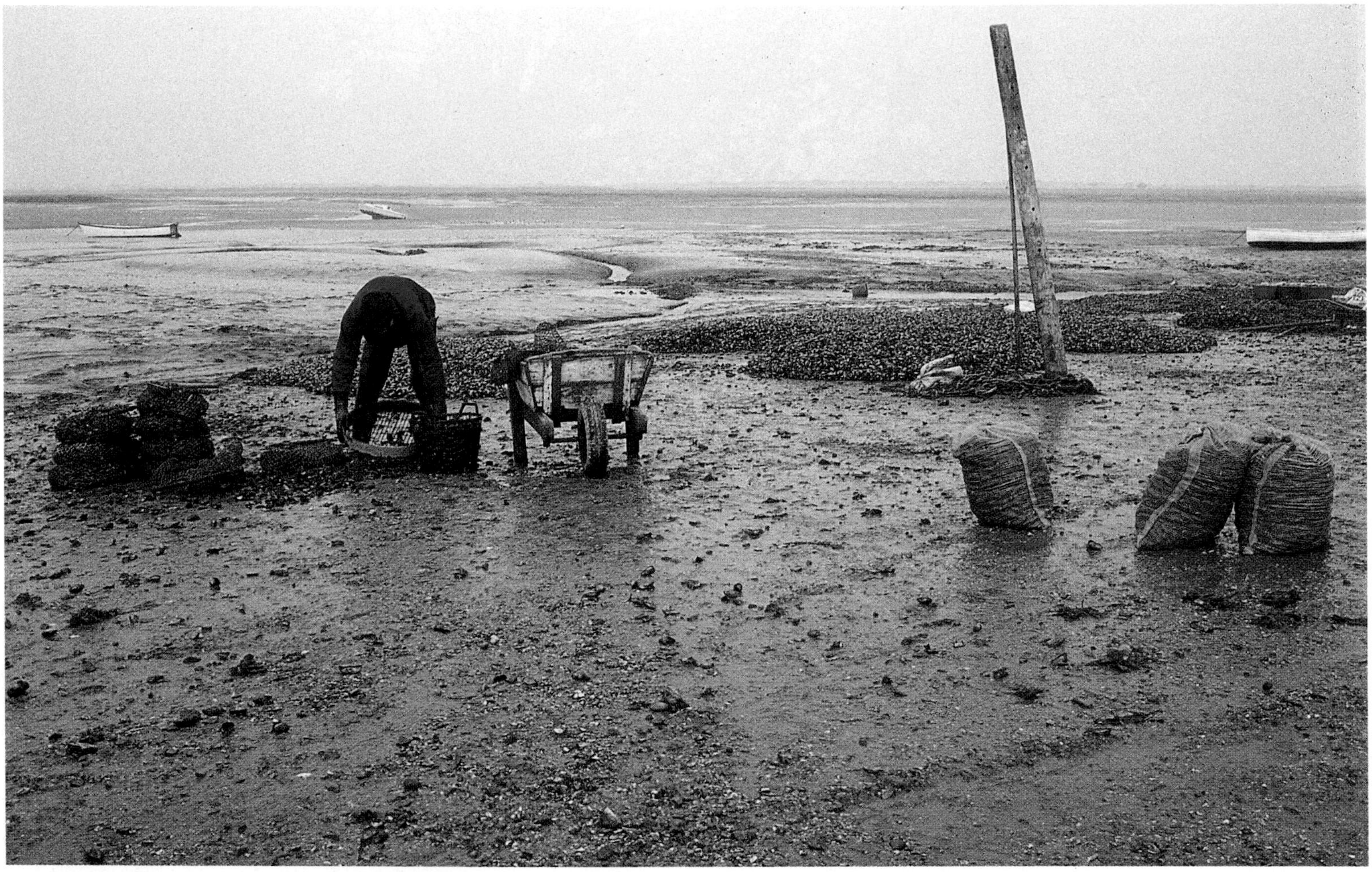

ABOVE
The mussel harvest is arduous work at Brancaster Staithe, Norfolk. Rakes or dredges are sometimes used instead of hand-picking, and the mussels are gathered from established beds in estuaries.

BELOW
Top-quality, fast-growing Pacific oysters are farmed at Butley Orford and are available all year round.

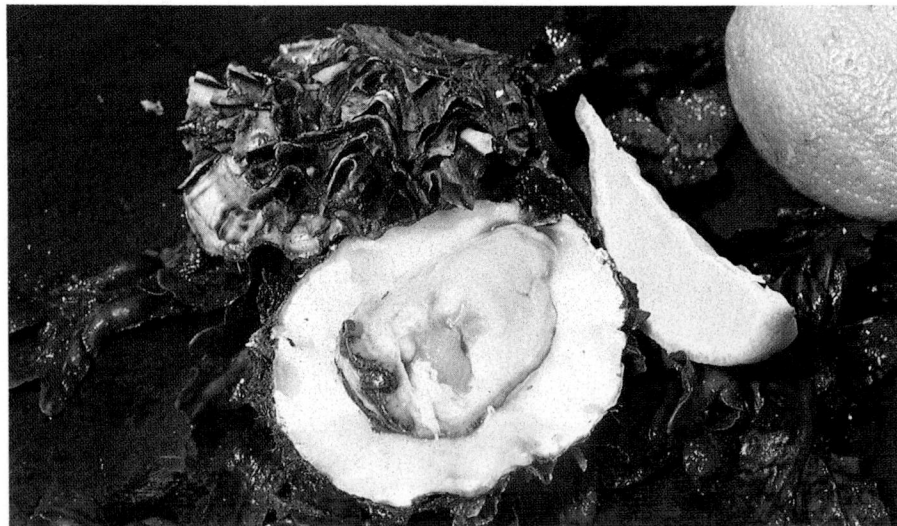

However, the tradition of making smoked herring products – red herrings, bloaters and kippers – has revived to a certain extent. Herrings preserved as 'reds' were essential in the days before refrigeration, but although still produced they are not as popular as they once were. The fish are cured in brine and then smoked for up to six weeks until rock-hard. They have a strong, salty flavour, sometimes likened to ham, and can be soaked before cooking or grilled without soaking. As they keep so well, many are exported to hot countries where storage of fish is a problem.

Bloaters are a different, and very delicious, proposition. They have a short soaking in brine and are slowly smoked over oak, ungutted, for 24 hours. The flavour is mild but slightly gamey, and the flesh pale and tender. The best way to serve them is simply grilled with butter.

Reasonable catches of fish such as plaice, sole, turbot, cod, haddock and skate are landed at ports along the coast, Lowestoft being the largest. Much of this fish is processed and frozen. Sprats, a small and tasty relation of the herring, are always cheap and can sometimes be bought on the beach, straight from the boats at the Suffolk villages of Aldeburgh, Southwold and Dunwich.

Shellfish, too, thrive in eastern waters. Pacific oysters are farmed in the North, for instance at Brancaster or Morston in Norfolk, while in Essex are found the native flat oysters. Sadly, the Colchester oyster beds in Essex, which have the reputation of producing some of the finest oysters in the country, have declined in recent years. However, some oysters are still produced, and there is hope that the crop will revitalise in time.

It's not all a tale of gloom. Pink and brown shrimps, both large and small, are caught in abundance all round the coast. Many fishing villages have developed a speciality over the years. Cromer, in Norfolk, is famous for its crabs. These are smaller than those fished elsewhere, but heavy for their size and packed with meat. The tiny crab boats ply dangerous waters, full of hidden rocks and dangerous tides, to bring home the catch. The crab pots are checked daily, so there is always a fresh supply. Lobsters are caught off the same coast.

Mussels are a cheap, plentiful shellfish which can be used in all sorts of delicious recipes, such as Mussels and Clams with Tomatoes (see recipe, page 204), and they are in season throughout the winter. There are mussel beds all round the East Anglian coast, especially off north Norfolk, and Lincolnshire also benefits from the clean waters of the Wash to produce sweet, plump mussels.

Cockles and whelks are found in great quantities in Norfolk. Stiffkey (pronounced Stookey) is known for 'Stookey Blues', large cockles with grey-blue shells, which are raked out of the sand flats at low tide, using short-handled rakes. They are usually sold boiled and are best eaten well-seasoned with pepper and vinegar. Another north Norfolk village, Wells-next-the-Sea, produces no less than 80 per cent of the nation's whelks, which are caught by fishermen who go miles out to sea and fish with pots baited with herring. Whelks from Wells are commonly found as far afield as London and the Midlands.

Freshwater eels are caught in the Norfolk Broads using traps, but most are exported. Other freshwater fish, such as pike and zander, are found in the county's rivers.

Still on the subject of the sea, samphire is an edible plant which is commonly found around the East Anglian coast and can sometimes be bought on fish stalls in the area. It is fleshy and succulent, and should be eaten lightly boiled and tossed in melted butter.

PICKED FOR PROCESSING

More than a third of the country's entire vegetable crop comes from the eastern counties, including a third of all the peas, half the onions and two-thirds of all the carrots grown. Added to that, a quarter of the soft fruit of England and Wales is grown here, and a fifth of all the orchard fruit. Every county of the region has a special contribution to make to this massive harvest.

The wide, flat fields of Lincolnshire are planted with vegetables as far as the eye can see. There are acres of peas, most of which are destined to be canned or frozen. All the most popular British vegetables are grown here,

---

SHELLFISH FROM THE EASTERN COUNTIES

OYSTERS

Portuguese and Pacific oysters are the main types harvested off the east coast. Eat raw, with a dash of lemon juice, straight from the shell. If served hot, cook lightly. (September to April.)

COCKLES

Usually white or cream in colour, with a circular shell. Sold cooked, shelled and often preserved in brine or vinegar. (Best April to December.)

WHELKS

A brownish or greyish spiral shell, white flesh. Sold boiled, often from stalls. (Best February to July.)

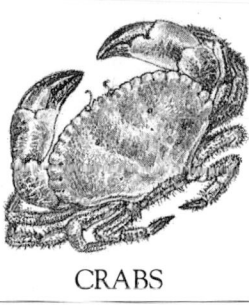

CRABS

Brown crab is the most common variety. Sold boiled and dressed, with meat removed from shell, or undressed. Choose by weight rather than size. Flesh is white and dark. Can be used in recipes or eaten dressed with mayonnaise in salads. (April to December.)

MUSSELS

Dark blue shells, bright yellow flesh. Sold live. Steam open and serve in or out of shell, with a sauce. (September to February.)

LOBSTERS

Usually sold boiled, in the shell, which turns bright scarlet when cooked. The white flesh can be removed from the shell and used in recipes. (April to November.)

SHRIMPS

Brown and pink shrimps are caught in the Wash. Brown shrimps are greyish-brown and have no pointed 'snout'. Usually sold cooked. Shell before eating or using in recipes. (February to October.)

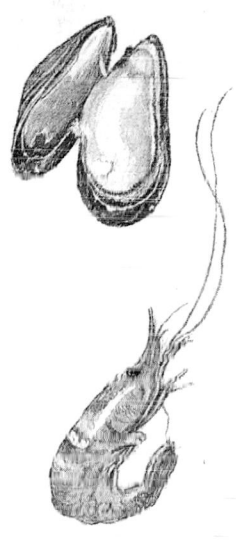

LEFT
A Lincolnshire pea field, in full flower. The crop is planted successively, so that the peas can be harvested in relays from June through to August. Podded, blanched and frozen within 3 hours, they reach the market almost as fresh as when they were picked.

A TASTE OF THE REGIONS

SCOTLAND

HIGHLAND, OUTER HEBRIDES REGION, SHETLAND, ORKNEY, GRAMPIAN, CENTRAL, TAYSIDE, FIFE, LOTHIAN, STRATHCLYDE, BORDERS, DUMFRIES AND GALLOWAY.

Fine and famous foods come from this, the most mountainous region of Britain. Succulent Highland beef and tender lamb, superb salmon, mouthwatering smoked fish, firm potatoes and juicy berries are second to none, as are the traditionally baked cakes, breads and biscuits, and the rich, mellow whiskies.

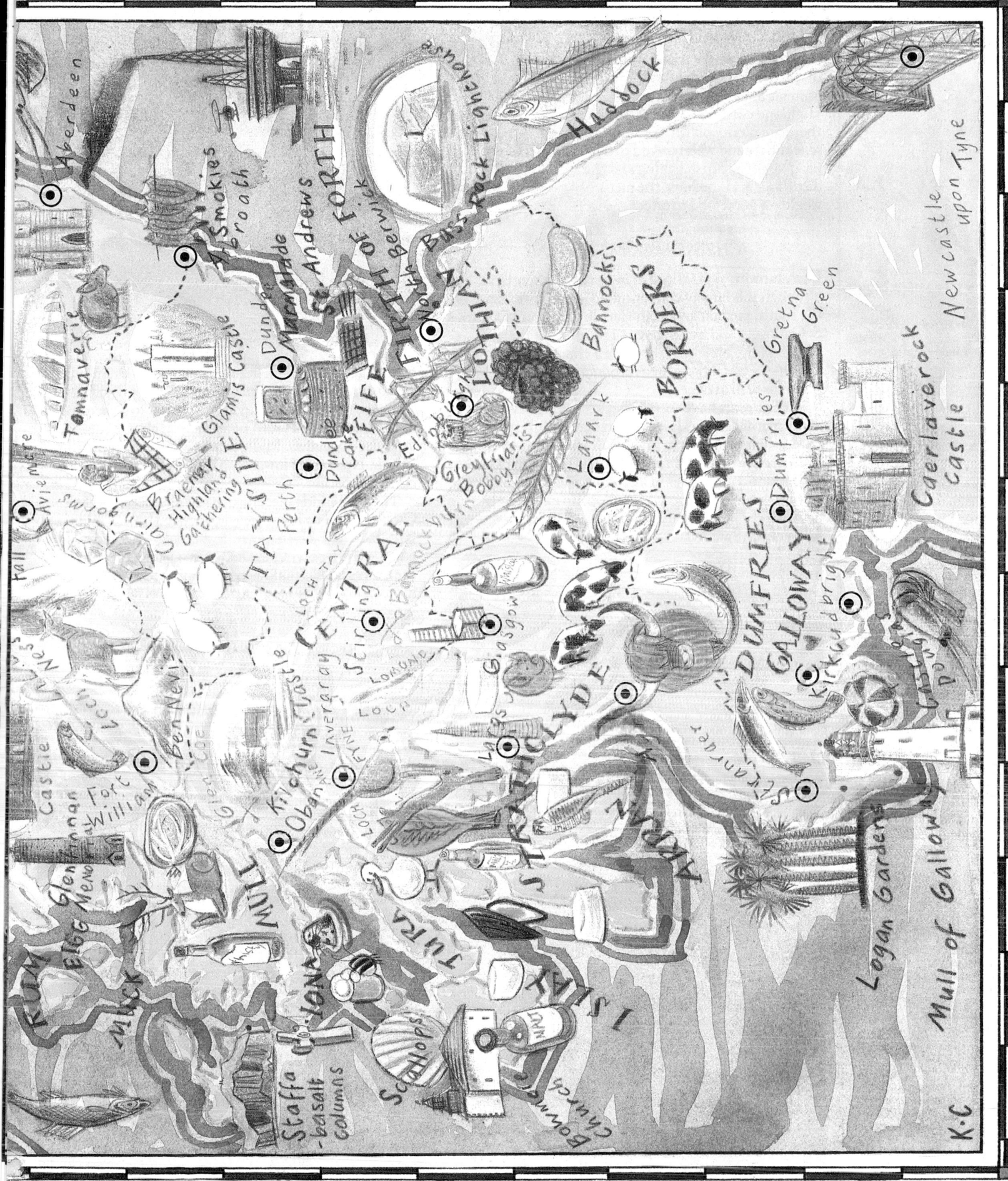

SOUPS & STARTERS

Here you will find the best of British soups – from Scottish cock-a-leekie, Irish potato and parsley soup to Welsh leek soup or London Particular. There are both hot and cold soups and those suitable for a starter or light meal. A rich selection of starters such as pâtés, mousses and dips, made from vegetables, fruit, fish, shellfish and dairy produce provides a great variety of choice.

2. Pour in the stock, add the sage and cloves. Bring to the boil, cover then simmer for 30 minutes, until the parsnip is softened.
3. Remove the sage leaves and cloves, leave to cool slightly, then purée in a blender or food processor.
4. Return to the saucepan and reheat gently with the cream. Season to taste. Serve hot, garnished with the sage or parsley and croûtons.

TO MICROWAVE

 Cut the butter into small pieces and melt in a large bowl on HIGH for 45 seconds. Add the parsnips, apple, stock, sage leaves and cloves, cover and cook on HIGH for 20 minutes, until the parsnip is tender. Complete step 3. Return the soup to the bowl, add the cream and reheat on HIGH for 2–3 minutes without boiling. Complete the remainder of step 4.

TURKEY AND HAZELNUT SOUP

THE EASTERN COUNTIES

Cooked leftovers work well in this recipe if you're using up the remains of the Christmas bird. Just add them to the stock and simmer for 2 to 3 minutes, until hot. Make the soup at other times of year using a Norfolk turkey breast fillet. Chopped hazelnuts add a hint of nuttiness and a hearty texture.

SERVES 4–6 (AS A MEAL)

❋

| 75 g (3 oz) hazelnuts |
| 15 g (½ oz) butter |
| 1 medium onion, skinned and roughly chopped |
| 2.5 ml (½ tsp) paprika |
| 225 g (8 oz) turkey breast fillet, skinned and chopped |
| 900 ml (1½ pints) chicken stock |
| 1 egg yolk |
| 150 ml (5 fl oz) fresh single cream |
| 15 ml (1 tbsp) chopped fresh chervil or 5 ml (1 tsp) dried chervil |
| salt and pepper |
| fresh chervil sprigs, to garnish |

1. Toast the hazelnuts on a sheet of foil under the grill, turning frequently. Put in a blender or food processor and very finely chop.
2. Melt the butter in a saucepan, add the onion and paprika, cover and cook for 5 minutes, until soft.
3. Add the turkey breast and stock and simmer for 5 minutes, until tender. Do not over-cook or the turkey will become rubbery.
4. Allow to cool slightly, then purée in a blender or food processor.
5. Blend the egg yolk with the cream and add to the soup. Return the soup to the pan and reheat without boiling, stirring all the time.

PARSNIP AND APPLE SOUP. A smooth soup with an interesting garnish of diamond-shaped croûtons and fresh sage leaves.

PARSNIP AND APPLE SOUP

THE EASTERN COUNTIES

The velvety texture of a creamy soup is always welcoming, and the unmistakable flavour of parsnips, blended with a hint of tart cooking apple, is very warming. Root crops of all types thrive in fertile East Anglian soil, but parsnips don't reach their peak until after one or two hard frosts.

SERVES 6–8 (AS A STARTER)

❋

| 25 g (1 oz) butter |
| 700 g (1½ lb) parsnips, peeled and roughly chopped |
| 1 Bramley cooking apple, cored, peeled and roughly chopped |
| 1.1 litres (2 pints) chicken stock |
| 4 fresh sage leaves or 2.5 ml (½ tsp) dried sage |
| 2 cloves |
| 150 ml (5 fl oz) fresh single cream |
| salt and pepper |
| fresh sage leaves or parsley and croûtons, to garnish |

1. Melt the butter in a large saucepan, add the parsnips and apple, cover and cook gently for 10 minutes, stirring occasionally.

6. Add the hazelnuts, chopped chervil and season to taste. Serve hot, garnished with sprigs of fresh chervil.

TO MICROWAVE

 Complete step 1. Cut the butter into small pieces and melt in a large bowl on HIGH for 30 seconds. Add the onion and paprika, cover and cook on HIGH for 3–4 minutes, until softened. Add the turkey and the stock, re-cover and cook on HIGH for 5–6 minutes, until tender. Complete step 4. Blend the egg yolk with the cream and add to the soup. Return the soup to the bowl and cook on HIGH for 1–2 minutes without boiling, stirring once. Complete step 6.

COCK-A-LEEKIE SOUP

SCOTLAND

This is a very substantial soup which could also be a main course. It originally contained beef as well as chicken so if you have a small quantity of leftover joint or uncooked beef around add it to the dish. Cooked beef should be added towards the end of cooking time to prevent it becoming tough.

SERVES 4 (AS A MEAL)

❋

15 g (½ oz) butter
275 – 350 g (10–12 oz) chicken (1 large or 2 small chicken portions)
350 g (12 oz) leeks, trimmed
1.1 litres (2 pints) chicken stock
1 bouquet garni
salt and pepper
6 prunes, stoned and halved
fresh parsley sprigs, to garnish

1. Melt the butter in a large saucepan and fry the chicken quickly until golden on all sides.
2. Cut the white part of the leeks into four lengthways and chop into 2.5 cm (1 inch) pieces, reserving the green parts. Wash well. Add the white parts to the pan and fry for 5 minutes, until soft.
3. Add the stock and bouquet garni and season to taste. Bring to the boil and simmer for 30 minutes or until the chicken is tender.
4. Shred the reserved green parts of the leeks, then add to the pan with the prunes. Simmer for a further 30 minutes.
5. To serve, remove the chicken, then cut the meat into large pieces, discarding the skin and bones. Put the meat in a warmed soup tureen and pour over the soup. Serve hot, garnished with parsley sprigs.

SCOTCH BROTH

SCOTLAND

This has been described as the national soup of Scotland and is both hearty and filling. Either cook it slowly for a long time on the hob to tenderise the ingredients or put the meat and water in a pressure cooker, bring to the boil and skim the surface. Add the remaining ingredients, put on the lid, bring to HIGH (15 lb) pressure and cook under pressure for 25 minutes. If made the day before needed, the soup can be allowed to cool so the layer of fat can be removed from the top.

SERVES 4 (AS A MEAL)

❋

700 g (1½ lb) shin of beef, cut into pieces
salt and pepper
1 medium carrot, peeled and chopped
1 medium turnip, peeled and chopped
1 medium onion, skinned and chopped
2 medium leeks, trimmed, chopped and washed
45 ml (3 tbsp) pearl barley
chopped fresh parsley, to garnish

1. Put the meat into a saucepan, cover with 2.3 litres (4 pints) water, season to taste and bring slowly to the boil. Cover and simmer for 1½ hours.
2. Add the vegetables and barley. Continue to simmer, covered, for a further hour or until the vegetables and barley are soft. Skim off any fat and serve the soup hot, garnished with chopped parsley.

COCK-A-LEEKIE SOUP.
The clear golden liquid reveals all the good things that go to make this soup prunes, leeks and juicy mouthfuls of chicken.

flesh, then set aside. Return the bones and strained stock to the pan with the milk. Cover and simmer gently for a further hour.

3. Meanwhile, peel and roughly chop the potatoes, then cook in boiling salted water until tender. Drain well, then mash.

4. Strain the liquid from the bones and return it to the pan with the flaked fish. Add the mashed potato and butter and stir well to give a thick creamy consistency. Adjust the seasoning and garnish with parsley. Serve with crusty bread.

TO MICROWAVE

 Put the haddock, onion and 600 ml (1 pint) boiling water in a large bowl. Cover and cook on HIGH for 10 minutes, until the haddock is cooked. Drain off the liquid and reserve. Remove the bones from the haddock and flake the flesh, then set aside. Return the bones and strained stock to the bowl with the milk, cover and cook on HIGH for 20 minutes. Meanwhile complete step 3. Strain the liquid from the bones and return it to the bowl with the flaked fish. Add the mashed potato and butter and stir well to give a thick creamy consistency. Adjust the seasoning, garnish with parsley and serve with crusty bread.

GOLDEN VEGETABLE SOUP

THE NORTH

Served in larger quantities this hearty soup can make a meal in itself. You can use any other orange or light coloured vegetables (such as potatoes, sweetcorn, yellow courgettes, pumpkins, turnips) that have a firm enough texture not to disintegrate during cooking. Be sparing with the turmeric; it is for colour only and too much will spoil the taste.

SERVES 4 (AS A STARTER)

※

| 25 g (1 oz) butter |
| 1 large carrot, peeled and cut into 4 cm (1½ inch) match sticks |
| 2 celery sticks, cut into 4 cm (1½ inch) match sticks |
| 100 g (4 oz) swede, peeled and cut into 4 cm (1½ inch) match sticks |
| 225 g (8 oz) cauliflower, broken into florets |
| 1 medium onion, skinned and sliced |
| 2.5 ml (½ tsp) ground turmeric |
| 1 litre (1¾ pints) vegetable stock |
| salt and pepper |
| fresh snipped chives, to garnish |

1. Melt the butter in a saucepan, add all the vegetables and cook for 2 minutes, stirring occasionally.

2. Add the turmeric and cook for 1 minute. Pour over the stock and adjust seasoning. Bring to the boil and simmer for 20 minutes. Garnish with snipped chives and serve with crusty brown bread.

CULLEN SKINK. Served as a main course, this traditional, creamily thick soup is hearty enough to satisfy appetites that have been sharpened by the cold.

CULLEN SKINK

SCOTLAND

This classic fish and potato soup is good and filling. The word 'skink' means stock or broth but the strong flavour of the fish means that water and milk can be used for the liquor; there is no need to go to the trouble of making fish stock. For a smoother but less traditional texture you can whizz the soup in a food processor or blender.

SERVES 4 (AS A MEAL)

※

| 1 Finnan haddock, weighing about 350 g (12 oz), skinned |
| 900 ml (1½ pints) boiling water |
| 1 medium onion, skinned and chopped |
| 568 ml (1 pint) fresh milk |
| 700 g (1½ lb) potatoes |
| knob of butter |
| salt and pepper |
| chopped fresh parsley, to garnish |

1. Put the haddock into a medium saucepan, just cover it with the boiling water and bring to the boil again. Add the onion, cover and simmer for 10–15 minutes, until the haddock is tender. Drain off the liquid and reserve.

2. Remove the bones from the haddock and flake the

TO MICROWAVE

Melt the butter in a large bowl on HIGH for 45 seconds, then cook the vegetables, covered, on HIGH for 2 minutes. Add the turmeric and cook on HIGH for 1 minute. Blend in the stock and cook on HIGH for 10 minutes. Garnish and serve.

LONDON PARTICULAR

THE SOUTH-EAST

It's a long time since London was blanketed regularly in thick fogs known as 'pea-soupers'. But that's how this gloriously green soup got its delightful name! And it's still a dish that's perfectly designed to keep out the chill on a misty autumn evening.

SERVES 8 (AS A STARTER)

❊ ☑

15 g (½ oz) butter
50 g (2 oz) streaky bacon rashers, rinded and chopped
1 medium onion, skinned and roughly chopped
1 medium carrot, diced
1 celery stick, chopped
450 g (1 lb) split dried peas
2.3 litres (4 pints) chicken or ham stock
salt and pepper
60 ml (4 tbsp) natural yogurt
chopped grilled bacon and croûtons, to garnish

1. Melt the butter in a large saucepan. Add the bacon, onion, carrot and celery and cook for 5–10 minutes, until beginning to soften.
2. Add the peas and stock and bring to the boil, then cover and simmer for 1 hour, until the peas are soft.
3. Allow to cool slightly, then purée in a blender or food processor until smooth.
4. Return the soup to the pan. Season to taste, add the yogurt and reheat gently. Serve hot, garnished with chopped grilled bacon and croûtons.

TO MICROWAVE

Halve the ingredients. Melt the butter in a large bowl on HIGH for 30 seconds. Add the bacon, onion, carrot and celery, cover and cook on HIGH for 5–7 minutes, until softened. Add the peas and the stock, cover and cook on HIGH for 25–30 minutes, until the peas are soft. Complete step 3. Return the soup to the bowl, season to taste with salt and pepper, stir in the yogurt and reheat on HIGH for 2–3 minutes, without boiling. Garnish with the bacon and croûtons. Serves 4.

LEFT
LONDON PARTICULAR. The underlying flavour of bacon in this recipe is brought out by the garnish of chopped, grilled rashers

RIGHT
GOLDEN VEGETABLE SOUP. A good choice for making the most of a glut. The small pieces of neatly cut vegetables are easy to spoon up.

LIGHT MEALS & SNACKS

The wide variety of British cheeses are ideal for both eating and cooking. When combined with eggs or other ingredients they can be turned into quick, nourishing meals. In this chapter you will find a variety of regional specialities – from Scotch woodcock and pan haggerty to Glamorgan sausages and herrings in oatmeal – as well as new recipes suitable for today's fast living. There's something here for everyone.

EGGS

One of nature's most complete, inexpensive, versatile and nutritious foods, rich in protein, valuable A, D and B Group vitamins and iron. Eggs have many uses in baking, batters and sauces, to bind sweet and savoury mixtures, coat fried food and glaze pastry. There's also a vast range of low-budget main egg dishes.

CHICKEN

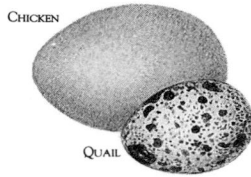

QUAIL

CHICKEN EGGS

White or brown shell, the most widely available type of egg. Chicken eggs are carefully graded for quality and size:
Grade A: perfectly clean, fresh, intact eggs.
Grade B: eggs with slight imperfections, which have been cleaned or preserved in some way.
Free range chicken eggs are from non-battery reared hens.
Size 1: 70 g or over
Size 2: 65–70 g
Size 3: 60–65 g
Size 4: 55–60 g
Size 5: 50–55 g
Size 6: 45–50 g
Size 7: under 45 g
Eggs used in the recipes in this book are size 2 unless otherwise stated.

QUAIL EGGS

A recognised delicacy, these increasingly popular, tiny mottled eggs are available from specialist food shops and good supermarkets. Serve hard-boiled in salad or set in aspic, or poached in a crisp pastry shell for an elegant starter.

GOOSE

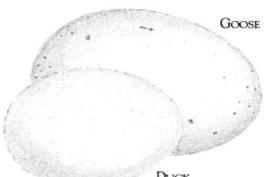

DUCK

GOOSE EGGS

White shell, can weigh up to 300 g (11 oz), slightly oily flavour. Use like duck eggs.

DUCK EGGS

Ivory shell, average weight 75 g (3 oz), rich flavour, available from farm and health food shops. Duck eggs are thin-shelled and often contain more bacteria than other types, so they should be used very fresh and never served soft-boiled. Excellent for baking.

SCOTCH WOODCOCK
SCOTLAND

This savoury dish was popular in Victorian and Edwardian days, when it was served at the end of a meal. With today's trend towards lighter eating habits, savouries have gone out of fashion but this dish is sufficiently tasty to be served as a snack at any time. It's very salty so make sure you have a long cool drink with it.

SERVES 2

2 large slices wholemeal bread
butter for spreading
Gentleman's Relish or anchovy paste for spreading
60–90 ml (4–6 tbsp) fresh milk
2 eggs
pinch cayenne pepper
50 g (1¾ oz) can anchovies, drained

1. Toast the bread, remove the crusts and spread with butter. Cut in half and spread with Gentleman's Relish or anchovy paste.
2. Melt a knob of butter in a saucepan. Whisk together the milk, eggs and cayenne pepper, then pour into the pan and stir slowly over a gentle heat until the mixture begins to thicken. Remove from the heat and stir until creamy.
3. Divide the mixture between the anchovy toasts and top with thin strips of anchovy fillet, arranged in a criss-cross pattern.

TO MICROWAVE

Complete step 1. Melt a knob of butter in a medium bowl on HIGH for 30 seconds. Add the milk, eggs and cayenne pepper and whisk together. Cook on MEDIUM for 2–3 minutes or until the eggs are lightly scrambled, stirring frequently. Complete step 3.

BUBBLE AND SQUEAK
THE SOUTH-EAST

A classic dish of leftover cooked potatoes, cabbage and beef. The name imitates the sounds of cooking, the vegetables and meat first bubbling away as they boiled and later squeaking in the frying pan. Simple and old-fashioned it may be, but it's still an appetising way to deal with the remains of a joint.

SERVES 2

25 g (1 oz) butter
1 medium onion, skinned and finely chopped
450 g (1 lb) potatoes, cooked and mashed
225 g (8 oz) cooked cabbage, finely chopped
4–8 slices cooked beef, chopped
salt and pepper

1. Melt the butter in a large frying pan. Add the onion

and cook for 4–5 minutes, stirring frequently, until softened.
2. Add the potatoes, cabbage and beef. Season to taste. Fry over medium heat for about 15 minutes, stirring frequently, until browned. Serve hot.

CHEESE RAMEKINS
THE WEST

More substantial than a soufflé, these flavoursome ramekins are also a good way of using up odd leftovers of different cheeses. The name comes from the small, round ovenproof container it is baked in, a ramekin dish.

SERVES 4

50 g (2 oz) Double Gloucester cheese, grated
50 g (2 oz) Cheshire cheese, grated
60 ml (4 tbsp) fresh single cream or milk
50 g (2 oz) cooked ham, finely chopped
50 g (2 oz) fresh wholemeal breadcrumbs
few drops of Worcestershire sauce
pinch of ground mixed spice
salt and pepper
2 eggs, separated

1. Put the cheeses into a bowl, then beat in the cream, ham, breadcrumbs, Worcestershire sauce and mixed spice. Season to taste. Grease 4 ramekin dishes and stand on a baking sheet.
2. Beat the egg yolks into the mixture. Whisk the egg whites until stiff, then fold into the mixture.
3. Spoon into the ramekin dishes and bake at 200°C (400°F) mark 6 for 10–15 minutes, until golden and risen. Serve at once.

GLOUCESTER CHEESE AND ALE
THE WEST

Food and drink are combined for a filling snack that was originally served – with more ale to wash it down – after the meat or poultry course of the evening meal at posting houses and inns. Double Gloucester cheese has a stronger flavour than Single Gloucester which is also very difficult to track down in the shops.

MAKES 4

175 g (6 oz) Double Gloucester cheese, thinly sliced
5 ml (1 tsp) prepared English mustard
about 120 ml (4½ fl oz) brown ale
4 thick slices of wholemeal bread

1. Arrange the cheese slices in the bottom of a large shallow ovenproof dish and spread the mustard over the top of them.

2. Pour in enough brown ale to just cover the cheese. Cover with foil, then bake at 190°C (375°F) mark 5 for about 10 minutes, until the cheese has softened.
3. Meanwhile, toast the bread. Pour the warm ale and cheese over the toast and serve immediately.

MOCK CRAB
COUNTRYWIDE

A simple Victorian luncheon dish, cleverly invented to deceive the eye, and even the palate. The 'crab' is in fact finely shredded chicken and grated Red Leicester cheese, and the fishy disguise is made all the more convincing with anchovy flavouring.

SERVES 2

1 hard-boiled egg, the yolk sieved, white chopped

15 g (½ oz) butter

7.5 ml (1½ tsp) prepared English mustard

few drops of anchovy essence

pepper

100 g (4 oz) Red Leicester cheese, grated

2 cooked chicken breast fillets, skinned and finely chopped

lettuce leaves, sliced tomato and cucumber, to garnish

1. Reserve a little of the egg yolk and mix the remainder with the butter, mustard, anchovy essence and pepper to taste.
2. Mix in the cheese with a fork so that it is evenly blended but as many shreds as possible of the cheese remain separate.
3. Mix in the chicken lightly, then taste and adjust the seasoning if necessary. Cover and leave in a cool place for at least 2 hours for the flavours to develop.
4. Serve on a small bed of lettuce, in crab shells if available, garnished with the reserved egg yolk, chopped egg white and a little sliced tomato and cucumber. Accompany with thinly sliced wholemeal bread and butter.

MOCK CRAB Cheaper than the real thing, but just as tasty, serve this savoury concoction in crab shells to complete the deception.

LEFT
GLAMORGAN
SAUSAGES. Crisp and
cheesy 'sausages', which make
a good, economical dish to
serve at any time of day.

RIGHT
BREAKFAST PANCAKES.
Give yourself a weekend treat
with freshly made, well-filled
pancakes.

BREAKFAST PANCAKES

COUNTRYWIDE

There's no need to save pancakes for Shrove Tuesday. They're quick and easy to prepare, and good at any time of day. This breakfast recipe uses a mix of wholemeal flour and oatmeal and makes a welcome change from toast topped with grilled bacon, scrambled eggs and tomato slices.

MAKES 4

❋ ⚡

25 g (1 oz) plain wholemeal flour

25 g (1 oz) medium oatmeal

salt and pepper

4 eggs, beaten

250 ml (9 fl oz) fresh milk

butter for frying

100 g (4 oz) back bacon, grilled and chopped

2 tomatoes, sliced and grilled

1. Put the flour, oatmeal, salt and 15 ml (1 tbsp) egg into a bowl. Gradually add 150 ml (¼ pint) milk to form a smooth batter.
2. Heat a little butter in a 20.5 cm (8 inch) frying pan. When hot, pour in 45 ml (3 tbsp) of the batter, tilting pan to cover base. Cook until pancake moves freely, turn over and cook until golden. Make 4 pancakes.
3. Beat together the remaining eggs, milk and salt and pepper. Scramble in a small saucepan over gentle heat, stirring until the egg starts to set.
4. Place spoonfuls of the egg into the pancakes, add the bacon and tomato slices. Fold the pancakes over. Serve warm as a snack or for breakfast.

TO MICROWAVE

⚡ Complete steps 1 and 2. To scramble the eggs, cook in a medium bowl on HIGH for 3–4 minutes, stirring frequently. Complete step 4.

GLAMORGAN SAUSAGES

WALES

These were the poor man's meatless substitute for the real thing, and are today an interesting dish for vegetarians.

MAKES 8

❋ ⚡

175 g (6 oz) fresh breadcrumbs

100 g (4 oz) Caerphilly cheese, grated

1 small leek, washed and very finely chopped
15 ml (1 tbsp) chopped fresh parsley
large pinch of mustard powder
salt and pepper
2 eggs, separated
about 60 ml (4 tbsp) fresh milk to mix
plain flour for coating
15 ml (1 tbsp) vegetable oil
15 g (½ oz) butter

1. In a large bowl, mix together the breadcrumbs, cheese, leek, parsley and mustard. Season to taste. Add 1 whole egg and 1 egg yolk and mix thoroughly. Add enough milk to bind the mixture together.
2. Divide the mixture into 8 and shape into sausages.
3. Beat the remaining egg white on a plate with a fork until frothy. Dip the sausages into the egg white, then roll in the flour to coat.
4. Heat the oil and the butter in a frying pan and fry the sausages for 5–10 minutes until golden brown. Serve hot or cold.

TO MICROWAVE

☑ Complete steps 1, 2 and 3. Heat a large browning dish on HIGH for 5–8 minutes or according to the manufacturer's instructions. When the browning dish is hot, add 15 ml (1 tbsp) oil and quickly put the sausages into the dish and cook on HIGH for 1½ minutes. Turn the sausages over and cook on HIGH for a further 1 minute.

HAM AND PINEAPPLE TOP KNOT

COUNTRYWIDE

Ham and pineapple are always a favourite combination, and here they make a satisfying snack. The base is a toasted crumpet which soaks up the deliciously gooey topping of Cheddar, hot English mustard and cream.

SERVES 1

1 round ham steak
1 canned pineapple ring, drained
1 crumpet
25 g (1 oz) Cheddar cheese, grated
2.5 ml (½ tsp) mustard powder
15 ml (1 tbsp) fresh single cream
watercress, to garnish

1. Grill the ham steak and pineapple, and toast the crumpet.
2. Mix together the cheese, mustard and cream. Spread on top of the crumpet and grill until golden.
3. Top with the ham steak and pineapple. Garnish with watercress and serve at once.

PAN HAGGERTY

THE NORTH

A warming filling dish at a bargain price. It's a good choice if you're planning an evening at the pub or for satisfying hungry teenage appetites. Use firm fleshed potatoes such as Desirée, Romano or Maris Piper as they will keep their shape and not crumble into mash at the end of the cooking time.

SERVES 4

25 g (1 oz) butter
15 ml (1 tbsp) vegetable oil
450 g (1 lb) potatoes, peeled and thinly sliced
2 medium onions, skinned and thinly sliced
100 g (4 oz) Cheddar or Lancashire cheese, grated
salt and pepper

1. Heat the butter and oil in a large heavy-based frying pan. Remove the pan from the heat and put in layers of potatoes, onions and grated cheese, seasoning well with salt and pepper between each layer, and ending with a top layer of cheese.
2. Cover and cook the vegetables gently for about 30 minutes or until the potatoes and onions are almost cooked.
3. Uncover and brown the top of the dish under a hot grill. Serve straight from the pan.

PAN HAGGERTY. Succulent layers of potatoes, onions and cheese, given a bubbling brown finish under the grill.

MIXED BEAN SALAD
COUNTRYWIDE

Charnwood, or Applewood, cheese is a mature Cheddar variation, smoked and coated with paprika. Cubed, it adds colour and bite to this summertime salad, which mixes fresh French and broad beans with canned kidney beans.

SERVES 4

450 g (1 lb) broad beans
salt and pepper
225 g (8 oz) French beans, trimmed
15 ml (1 tbsp) vegetable oil
150 g (5 oz) natural yogurt
15 ml (1 tbsp) mild wholegrain mustard
15 ml (1 tbsp) lemon juice
397 g (14 oz) can red kidney beans, drained and rinsed
225 g (8 oz) Charnwood or Applewood cheese, cubed
chopped fresh parsley, to garnish

1. Shell the broad beans and cook in boiling salted water for 10 minutes. Add the French beans and continue to cook for 5–10 minutes, until both are tender.
2. Meanwhile, mix together the oil, yogurt, mustard, lemon juice and salt and pepper until well blended.
3. Drain the cooked beans and while still hot, combine with the kidney beans and dressing. Leave to cool.
4. Toss in the cubes of cheese and garnish with chopped fresh parsley just before serving.

TO MICROWAVE

Put the broad beans in a small bowl with 30 ml (2 tbsp) water. Cover and cook on HIGH for 10–12 minutes or until tender. Put the French beans and 15 ml (1 tbsp) water in a small bowl, cover and cook on HIGH for 4–5 minutes, until tender, stirring once. Complete steps 2, 3 and 4.

BACON FROISE
COUNTRYWIDE

An old English dish dating back to the 15th century, froise (or fraize) is a batter-like mixture, which was probably originally cooked in the hot fat that dripped from a spit-roasted joint. It's a tasty economical recipe, delicious served with mushrooms, lightly cooked in a little lemon juice flavoured with black pepper and grilled tomatoes.

SERVES 2

50 g (2 oz) plain flour
1 egg
150 ml (¼ pint) fresh milk
black pepper
4 rashers streaky bacon, rinded and cut into strips
1 egg white
butter for frying
grilled mushrooms and tomatoes, to serve

1. Sift the flour into a bowl. Break in the egg. Gradually add the milk, beating to form a smooth batter. Season with pepper.
2. Gently cook the bacon in a non-stick frying pan until the fat runs and the bacon is crisp. Drain on absorbent kitchen paper.
3. Whisk the egg white until stiff, but not dry, and lightly fold into the batter.
4. Melt a little butter in the frying pan, then, when sizzling, add half the batter and spread out to cover the base of the pan. Cook over a moderate heat until the bottom is a light golden brown and the top is just set.
5. Scatter the bacon over the surface of the batter and cover with the remaining batter. Cook until the top is set, then turn the 'cake' over and brown the other side.
6. Transfer to a warmed plate and cut into wedges. Serve accompanied by mushrooms and tomatoes.

MIXED BEAN SALAD. An attractive mixture of shapes, colours and textures make this an interesting salad. The natural yogurt dressing adds a pleasing sharpness.

MACARONI AND BROCCOLI CHEESE

COUNTRYWIDE

Macaroni Cheese has been popular family fare since Victorian times, when it was fashionable to give a British slant to traditional Italian dishes. This modern version uses British Red Leicester cheese, wholewheat pasta, and broccoli. If you have never used wholewheat pasta before you will find the flavour stronger and nuttier than the plain kind.

SERVES 2

❋ 〽

75 g (3 oz) wholewheat macaroni
salt and pepper
25 g (1 oz) butter
25 g (1 oz) plain flour
300 ml (½ pint) fresh milk
75 g (3 oz) Red Leicester cheese, grated
100 g (4 oz) broccoli florets
15 ml (1 tbsp) fresh wholemeal breadcrumbs

1. Cook the macaroni in 1.1 litres (2 pints) boiling salted water for 15 minutes. Drain.

2. Put the butter, flour and milk in a saucepan. Heat, whisking continuously, until the sauce boils, thickens and is smooth. Simmer for 1–2 minutes.

3. Remove pan from the heat, add most of the cheese and stir until melted. Season to taste.

4. Blanch the broccoli in boiling water for 7 minutes or until tender. Drain well.

5. Put the broccoli in the base of a 900 ml (1½ pint) flameproof serving dish. Cover with the macaroni and cheese sauce. Sprinkle with remaining cheese and breadcrumbs. Brown under a hot grill.

TO MICROWAVE

〽 Put the macaroni in a large bowl. Pour over boiling water to cover the pasta by about 2.5 cm (1 inch). Cover and cook on HIGH for 4 minutes. Stand for 3 minutes. Put the butter, flour and milk in a medium bowl and cook on HIGH for about 4 minutes, until boiling and thickened, whisking frequently. Complete step 3. Cook the broccoli in a large bowl in 45 ml (3 tbsp) water on HIGH for 3½ minutes. Drain well. Complete step 5.

MACARONI AND BROCCOLI CHEESE. Substantial and very nourishing, this crisply topped supper dish is sure to become a firm favourite.

MAIN COURSES

In this chapter is a superb collection of main course recipes – including lamb, beef, veal, pork, poultry and game, fish and shellfish. There are main course meals for everyday, dishes to serve when entertaining and substantial vegetarian recipes to enjoy at any time.

LAMB

CROWN ROAST

THE SOUTH-EAST

A spectacular dinner party dish. Some supermarkets now stock prepared crown roasts, or ask your butcher in advance to prepare one for you. If you're doing it, make sure that only the best ends of neck are chined, that is, the backbone sawn through so that the joint can be carved more easily. The cutlet bones must be left in one piece. Use a well-flavoured variety of apple for the filling such as Discovery or Jonagold.

SERVES 6

2 best end necks of lamb, each with 6 cutlets, chined
15 g (½ oz) butter
1 medium onion, skinned and chopped
3 celery sticks, chopped
2 eating apples, cored and chopped
100 g (4 oz) fresh breadcrumbs
30 ml (2 tbsp) chopped fresh mint
grated rind and juice of ½ lemon
1 egg
salt and pepper
30 ml (2 tbsp) plain flour
450 ml (¾ pint) lamb or beef stock
mint sprigs, to garnish

1. Trim each cutlet bone to a depth of 2.5 cm (1 inch).
2. Bend the joints around, fat side inwards, and sew together using strong cotton or fine string to form a crown. Cover the exposed bones with foil.
3. Melt the butter in a saucepan and cook the onion, celery and apples until brown. Stir in the breadcrumbs, mint, lemon rind and juice and egg. Season to taste and cool, then fill the centre of the joint with the stuffing and weigh.
4. Place the joint in a small roasting tin. Roast at 180°C (350°F) mark 4 for 25 minutes per 450 g (1 lb) plus 25 minutes. Baste occasionally and cover with foil if necessary.

PARSON'S VENISON.
Cooked to a turn, to leave just a hint of juicy pinkness in the centre. The stuffing helps to keep the meat moist.

5. Transfer the roast to a warmed serving dish and keep warm. Drain off all but 30 ml (2 tbsp) of the fat in the roasting tin, then add the flour and blend well. Cook for 2-3 minutes, stirring continuously. Add the stock and boil for 2-3 minutes. Adjust the seasoning and serve hot with the joint. Garnish with sprigs of mint.

TO MICROWAVE

⊡ Complete steps 1 and 2. To prepare stuffing, put the butter, onion, celery and apples in a large bowl. Cover and cook on HIGH for 7-8 minutes, until softened. Complete step 3. Cook, uncovered, on HIGH for 10 minutes per 450 g (1 lb). Turn round halfway through cooking. Wrap crown in foil and stand for 10 minutes before serving.

GUARD OF HONOUR

Like Crown Roast, this is prepared from two best ends of neck. Trim as above but interlace the bones, fat side outwards, to form an arch. Fill the cavity with the stuffing, as above, and fasten with strong cotton or fine string.

PARSON'S VENISON

COUNTRYWIDE

Not venison at all but a leg of lamb, given a richer, fuller flavour reminiscent of game. The boned joint is stuffed with a savoury mushroom mixture, then marinated and cooked in a heady concoction of wine and port, seasoned with spices.

SERVES 4-6

| 25 g (1 oz) butter |
| 1 small onion, skinned and finely chopped |
| 100 g (4 oz) mushrooms, chopped |
| 100 g (4 oz) cooked ham, chopped |
| 30 ml (2 tbsp) snipped fresh chives |
| salt and pepper |
| 1.8-2 kg (4-4½ lb) leg of lamb, skinned and boned |
| 200 ml (7 fl oz) dry red wine |
| 75 ml (3 fl oz) port |
| 6 juniper berries, crushed |
| 1.25 ml (¼ tsp) ground allspice |
| 45 ml (3 tbsp) red wine vinegar |
| 1 bay leaf |
| 1.25 ml (¼ tsp) freshly grated nutmeg |

1. Melt half the butter in a saucepan, add the onion and mushrooms and cook, stirring frequently, until the onion is soft but not browned. Stir in the ham and chives and season to taste. Leave to cool.
2. Season the lamb inside and out with pepper, then spread onion mixture over inside. Roll up tightly and tie securely. Place in a large glass bowl or casserole.
3. To make the marinade, mix remaining ingredients, except butter, pour over lamb, cover and leave in a cool place for 24 hours, turning occasionally.
4. Remove the meat from the marinade, drain and dry. Reserve the marinade. Melt the remaining butter in a flameproof casserole. Add the meat and brown on all sides over medium to high heat.
5. Pour in the marinade, bring almost to the boil, cover and roast at 180°C (350°F) mark 4 for 1¾-2 hours, until the meat is tender, basting occasionally with marinade.
6. Transfer meat to a warmed plate. Skim fat from surface of liquid, then boil rapidly until reduced. Remove bay leaf, adjust seasoning and serve with meat.

LEFT
CROWN ROAST OF LAMB. A joint to carry triumphantly to the table, standing up proudly from a bed of buttery baby vegetables. Little paper ruffs add to the finishing decorative touch.

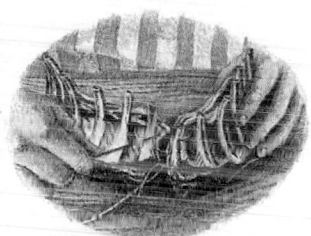

Bend the joints around, fat side inwards, and sew together using strong cotton or fine string to form a crown.

NEW LAMB CUTS

The traditional roasting joints, leg (sold on the bone whole or as the fillet half and the knuckle or shank end) and shoulder (sold on the bone whole or as the blade or knuckle half) are now especially popular boned and rolled for easy carving – they may also be sold ready-stuffed.

Boning large cuts means that the butcher is able to remove some of the fat during the process and produce joints of uniform size, which also makes calculating servings easier.

Smaller boneless lamb cuts include best end neck fillets (see Gloucestershire Squab Pie, page 119) and prime steak cut from the leg (see recipe, page 121) or chump end of the loin.

Ready-cubed boneless lamb is ideal for kebabs and lean lamb mince makes delicious rissoles and lamb burgers (see page 122).

LAMB CUTLETS REFORM

THE SOUTH-EAST

Reform sauce is mouth-wateringly piquant and deliciously seasoned with herbs and spices. It was invented in the 1830s by the great French chef Alexis Soyer. At the time he was Chef de Cuisine of the Reform Club in London's Pall Mall, a favourite meeting place for politicians after Parliament. The club still exists, with Lamb Cutlets Reform a popular item on the menu.

This recipe is a simplified version of the traditional one, and omits ingredients such as hard-boiled egg white and cooked tongue which would make the sauce too elaborate for modern tastes.

SERVES 4

15 g (½ oz) butter
1 small onion, skinned and finely chopped
1 medium carrot, finely sliced
50 g (2 oz) lean ham, cut into thin strips
60 ml (4 tbsp) red wine vinegar
45 ml (3 tbsp) port
568 ml (1 pint) lamb or chicken stock
2 cloves
2 blades of mace
1 bay leaf
4 juniper berries, crushed
pinch of dried thyme
8 lamb cutlets, each weighing about 75 g (3 oz)
50 g (2 oz) cooked ham, finely minced
50 g (2 oz) fresh breadcrumbs
1 egg, beaten
15 ml (1 tbsp) cornflour

1. To make the Reform sauce, melt the butter in a medium saucepan, then add the onion, carrot and ham strips and cook gently until just turning brown. Add the vinegar and port and boil rapidly until almost all the liquid evaporates.
2. Remove the pan from the heat and add the stock, cloves, mace, bay leaf, juniper berries and thyme. Stir well, return to the heat and bring to the boil. Lower the heat and simmer gently for about 30 minutes.
3. Meanwhile, trim the cutlets to remove most of the surrounding fat. Scrape the bone absolutely clean to within 2.5 cm (1 inch) of the 'eye' of the meat.
4. Mix the minced ham and breadcrumbs together. Brush each cutlet with beaten egg and coat with the ham and breadcrumb mixture. Cover and chill until required.
5. Blend the cornflour with about 30 ml (2 tbsp) water and add to the sauce. Stir well and bring the sauce to the boil, stirring continuously. Simmer until thickened.
6. Grill the cutlets for about 4 minutes on each side, until golden brown. Arrange the cutlets on a warmed serving dish and garnish each one with a cutlet frill. Reheat the sauce gently and serve separately.

BREAST OF LAMB WITH MINT STUFFING

THE SOUTH-EAST

An inexpensive cut with a good flavour, breast of lamb can be rather fatty, so be sure to trim it well.

SERVES 6

2 lamb breasts, each weighing about 900 g (2 lb), boned
15 g (½ oz) butter
1 medium onion, skinned and finely chopped
1 egg, beaten
30 ml (2 tbsp) milk
100 g (4 oz) fresh wholemeal breadcrumbs
60 ml (4 tbsp) chopped mixed fresh mint and parsley
salt and pepper
pinch of sugar

1. Flatten the meat and remove excess fat.

2. Melt the butter in a medium frying pan and fry the onion until soft but not brown. In a separate bowl, beat the egg with the milk and mash in the breadcrumbs. Mix together the onion, herbs and eggy-bread mixture and season to taste with the salt and pepper and sugar.
3. Divide the mixture between the two breasts of lamb and spread it out evenly, then roll up the meat as tightly as possible and secure well with strong cotton or fine string. Cover with foil and roast at 230°C (450°F) mark 8 for 40 minutes. Remove the foil so that the meat can brown and roast for a further 15 minutes.

A WELSH WAY WITH LAMB

WALES

Although Welsh lamb is delicious served plain, adding sweet and spicy ingredients makes it a truly flavoursome dish.

SERVES 6

1 leg or shoulder of lamb, weighing about 1.4 kg (3 lb)

salt and pepper

5 ml (1 tsp) ground ginger

45–60 ml (3–4 tbsp) honey

fresh rosemary sprigs

300 ml (½ pint) dry cider

1. Weigh the lamb joint, then put it into a roasting tin and sprinkle with salt and pepper and the ground ginger. Pour over the honey (heated if it is very stiff), put the rosemary on top and pour round the cider.
2. Roast at 220°C (425°F) mark 7 for 30 minutes, then reduce the heat to 200°C (400°F) mark 6 and continue to roast until the lamb is tender, allowing 20 minutes per 450 g (1 lb). Baste several times during the cooking, and if the top looks as if it is getting too dark – the honey is inclined to scorch – protect it with foil. If necessary, add a little more cider. The cider and honey form the gravy and nothing more is needed. Skim off any excess fat.

LAMB CUTLETS REFORM. It's the savoury sauce which really makes this dish. The cutlets are coated in a tasty mixture of minced ham and breadcrumbs, which forms a crispy coating when grilled.

LAMB WITH CHERRIES
THE SOUTH-EAST

Juicy red cherries from the orchards of Kent add a slight sharpness to this unusual casserole. Flavours and textures blend deliciously as the ingredients cook together in red wine.

SERVES 6

225 g (8 oz) streaky bacon rashers, rinded and chopped

15 g (½ oz) butter

1.4 kg (3 lb) boneless leg or shoulder of lamb, cut into 4 cm (1½ inch) cubes

1 medium onion, skinned and sliced

1 medium carrot, sliced

1 celery stick, sliced

1 garlic clove, skinned and sliced

568 ml (1 pint) dry red wine

bouquet garni

freshly grated nutmeg

salt and pepper

450 g (1 lb) fresh red cherries, stoned

1. In a large frying pan, fry the bacon in its own fat until browned. Add the butter to the pan and fry the lamb, a little at a time, until browned. Remove from the pan with the bacon and put in the casserole.
2. Fry the onion, carrot, celery and garlic in the fat remaining in the pan for about 5 minutes, until lightly browned. Add the vegetables to the casserole.
3. Pour over the wine and add the bouquet garni, pinch of nutmeg and salt and pepper. Cover and bake at 150°C (300°F) mark 3 for about 2½ hours, until tender.
4. Thirty minutes before the end of the cooking time, stir the cherries into the casserole and continue to cook until the meat is tender and the cherries soft. Serve hot with courgettes and new potatoes.

IRISH STEW
NORTHERN IRELAND

A simple dish of lamb, potatoes and onions, well flavoured with herbs. If any other ingredients are added, the result is not an authentic Irish stew. Use a deep casserole to hold the layers of meat and vegetables, and allow for long slow cooking so that the liquid is thickened and enriched. Use a firm potato such as the Romano or Maris Piper varieties.

SERVES 4

700 g (1½ lb) middle neck of lamb, cut into cutlets and trimmed

2 medium onions, skinned and sliced

450 g (1 lb) old potatoes, thinly sliced

15 ml (1 tbsp) chopped fresh parsley

5 ml (1 tsp) dried thyme

salt and pepper

chopped fresh parsley, to garnish

1. Make layers of meat, vegetables, herbs and salt and pepper in a deep casserole, ending with a top layer of potato to make a neat 'lid'.

LAMB WITH CHERRIES. Plump fruits are a pleasing addition to this comforting casserole, which gets its mellow flavour from bacon, herbs and spices.

2. Pour in 300 ml (½ pint) water and cover with greaseproof paper or foil and then the casserole lid. Bake at 170°C (325°F) mark 3 for about 2 hours or until the meat and vegetables are tender. Serve hot, garnished with parsley.

PORTMANTEAU
LAMB CHOPS

THE SOUTH-EAST

This dish is so called because it resembles the travelling bag known as a portmanteau when stuffed with chicken livers and mushrooms, which complement the flavour of the lamb. Use chops which are thick enough to hold the stuffing.

SERVES 4

4 thick lamb loin chops

40 g (1½ oz) butter

100 g (4 oz) chicken livers, thawed if frozen and finely chopped

100 g (4 oz) mushrooms, finely chopped

salt and pepper

1 egg, beaten

50 g (2 oz) fresh wholemeal breadcrumbs

fresh parsley sprigs, to garnish

1. Using a sharp, pointed knife, make a horizontal cut in each chop, working from the outside fat edge to the bone, to form a pocket.
2. To make the stuffing, melt 15 g (½ oz) of the butter in a frying pan, add the chicken livers and mushrooms and fry for 4–5 minutes, until soft but not brown. Season to taste.
3. Leave the stuffing to cool slightly, then spoon into the cavity in the chops and secure the open edges with wooden cocktail sticks.
4. Dip the chops in the beaten egg, then in the breadcrumbs to coat thoroughly.
5. Put the chops in a roasting tin. Melt the remaining butter and pour over the chops. Bake at 200°C (400°F) mark 6 for 15 minutes, then turn and bake for a further 15 minutes, until golden brown. Serve hot, garnished with parsley sprigs.

LAMB
AND BARLEY STEW

THE SOUTH-EAST

Lamb from the Weald of Kent is particularly tasty and pearl barley is a good bulking ingredient to use in stews and casseroles. It will keep for up to 18 months in an air-tight container.

SERVES 4–6

1.4 kg (3 lb) boned leg or shoulder of lamb, trimmed of fat and cubed

30 ml (2 tbsp) plain wholemeal flour

salt and pepper

3 streaky bacon rashers, rinded and chopped

25 g (1 oz) butter

2 medium onions, skinned and chopped

2 medium carrots, sliced

100 g (4 oz) turnip or swede, peeled and diced

2 celery sticks, diced

30 ml (2 tbsp) pearl barley

10 ml (2 tsp) mixed chopped fresh herbs, such as thyme, rosemary, parsley, basil

300 ml (½ pint) lamb or beef stock

chopped fresh parsley, to garnish

PORTMANTEAU LAMB CHOPS. Inviting parcels, filled with a rich, savoury stuffing, and oven-baked until golden brown.

1. Toss the lamb in the flour, seasoned with salt and pepper.
2. Dry fry the bacon in a large flameproof casserole. Add the butter and the lamb and fry until browned all over, stirring. Remove the lamb and the bacon from the casserole with a slotted spoon and set aside.
3. Add the onions, carrots, turnip or swede and celery to the casserole and fry for 5–10 minutes, until beginning to brown.
4. Return the lamb to the casserole, add the pearl barley and herbs and pour in the stock.
5. Bring to the boil, then cover and simmer for 2 hours, stirring occasionally to prevent sticking, until the lamb is tender.
6. Serve hot, sprinkled with chopped parsley.

and keep warm.
3. Add the wine to the roasting tin, stirring in any sediment from the bottom of the tin. Stir in the redcurrant jelly. Bring to the boil, then stir in the remaining soured cream and boil for 2–3 minutes, until thickened slightly.
4. Thickly slice the lamb and serve with the sauce spooned over. Accompany with new boiled potatoes and courgettes.

TO MICROWAVE

 Complete step 1. Put the lamb in a shallow dish and spoon over the garlic mixture. Cook, uncovered, on HIGH for 3 minutes. Cover and cook on MEDIUM for 10–15 minutes, rearranging twice, until cooked to your liking. Transfer the lamb to a warmed serving dish. Stir the remaining soured cream, the wine and redcurrant jelly into the dish. Cook on HIGH for 1–2 minutes, stirring occasionally, until hot. Complete step 4.

BROWN RAGOO OF LAMB

COUNTRYWIDE

The strange name of this dish comes from the French word ragoût, meaning a thick meat or poultry stew, enriched with a well-flavoured stock and also containing plenty of mixed vegetables. It is an example of France's influence on British cooking. Carrots, onions and mushrooms are always easy to find, and you can substitute peas for the broad beans if necessary.

SERVES 6

25 g (1 oz) butter
900 g (2 lb) leg of lamb, cut into 2.5 cm (1 inch) cubes
12 small onions, skinned
3 carrots, cut into quarters
4 cloves
1 medium onion, skinned
3 fresh parsley sprigs
2 fresh thyme sprigs
2 bay leaves
small fresh rosemary sprig
750 ml (1¼ pints) lamb or beef stock
salt and pepper
100 g (4 oz) button mushrooms
175 g (6 oz) broad beans, cooked
squeeze of lemon juice
chopped fresh parsley, to garnish

1. Melt the butter in a large, heavy-based frying pan, add the lamb in batches and cook until an even golden brown. Transfer to a casserole dish using a slotted spoon. Add the small onions and the carrots to the frying pan and fry until lightly browned. Transfer to the casserole dish.

LAMB FILLET WITH REDCURRANT SAUCE.
The sharpness of redcurrants is the perfect foil for thick, succulent slices of lamb, which need only simple vegetables to accompany.

LAMB FILLET WITH REDCURRANT SAUCE

COUNTRYWIDE

Try this idea next time you're cooking for a special occasion. Tender lamb fillet is coated with a garlic and mustard mixture before roasting. The savoury pan juices are used as the basis of a scrumptious red wine and soured cream sauce, which is poured over the thickly sliced meat to serve.

SERVES 3

90 ml (6 tbsp) fresh soured cream
1 garlic clove, skinned and crushed
5 ml (1 tsp) wholegrain mustard
salt and pepper
450 g (1 lb) lamb fillet
30 ml (2 tbsp) dry red wine
15 ml (1 tbsp) redcurrant jelly

1. Mix 30 ml (2 tbsp) of the soured cream with the garlic and mustard. Season to taste.
2. Put the lamb fillet in a roasting tin and spoon the garlic mixture all over. Roast at 180°C (350°F) mark 4 for 30 minutes, until tender and cooked to your liking. Transfer the lamb to a warmed serving dish

OPPOSITE
GLOUCESTERSHIRE SQUAB PIE. A golden pastry crust sliced open to reveal a delectable filling of juicy lamb and apple slices.

2. Stick the cloves in the onion and add to the casserole with the herbs and stock. Season to taste and bring to the boil.

3. Cover tightly and bake at 180°C (350°F) mark 4 for about 2½ hours, stirring occasionally.

4. Remove the onion stuck with cloves from the casserole, then stir in the mushrooms, broad beans and lemon juice and continue to cook for 10 minutes.

5. Using a slotted spoon, lift the meat and vegetables from the casserole, arrange on a large serving plate and keep warm. Boil the liquid until it is reduced to about 400 ml (14 fl oz). Pour some of the sauce over the meat and vegetables. Garnish with chopped parsley and serve with the rest of the sauce handed separately. Accompany with boiled or mashed potatoes.

GLOUCESTERSHIRE SQUAB PIE

THE WEST

You'd be forgiven for thinking this dish might contain young pigeons, otherwise known as squabs, but this pie has always been made with lamb. If you can buy it locally in the Cotswolds the flavour will be delicious set off by the sharp apple and spices.

SERVES 4
✳

225 g (8 oz) plain flour

salt and pepper

50 g (2 oz) butter

50 g (2 oz) lard

700 g (1½ lb) lamb neck fillets, sliced into 12 pieces

1 large cooking apple, peeled, cored and sliced

450 g (1 lb) onions, skinned and thinly sliced

1.25 ml (¼ tsp) ground allspice

1.25 ml (¼ tsp) grated nutmeg

150 ml (¼ pint) lamb or beef stock

fresh milk, to glaze

1. Put the flour and a pinch of salt in a bowl. Rub in the butter and lard until the mixture resembles fine breadcrumbs. Add enough cold water and mix in to form a firm dough. Knead lightly until smooth, then chill until required.

2. Place half the lamb in the base of a 900 ml (1½ pint) pie dish. Arrange half the apple slices and half the onion slices over the top. Sprinkle over the allspice and nutmeg and season to taste. Repeat the layers, then pour over the stock.

3. Roll out the pastry to fit the dish and use to cover the pie, moistening the edges so the pastry is well sealed. Use any pastry trimming to decorate.

4. Brush the pastry with milk and bake at 200°C (400°F) mark 6 for 20 minutes. Reduce the temperature to 180°C (350°F) mark 4 and cook for a further 1 hour 15 minutes. Cover the pastry if it shows signs of becoming too brown. Serve hot.

SPANISH ONION · RED ONION · SHALLOT

Onions, garlic and leeks, members of the same family, all have their own individual flavouring qualities. Most onions can be obtained through the year, garlic is most commonly available dried, and leeks enjoy a long season.

SPANISH ONION

British grown despite the name, these are large, sweet and mild. Use cooked when less pronounced flavour is required; delicious stuffed (see recipe, page 217) in a tart or as sauce for lamb.

RED ONION

Of Italian origin. Particularly attractive sliced raw into rings and added to salads for colour as well as flavour.

GARLIC

Very pungent, use sparingly. Cut into slivers to flavour roast lamb, chop finely or crush in garlic press or with knife blade for soups, casseroles and stuffings. Also available as powder and salt.

SHALLOT

Smaller and less pungent than most onions, delicious in subtle sauces for fish and steak, or glazed as an accompanying vegetable (see recipe, page 228).

SPRING ONION

Cropped before bulb forms fully. Excellent in salads, for garnish, or finely chopped to give mild flavour.

LEEK · SPRING ONION · GARLIC

LEEK

Available August to May. National vegetable of Wales. Less strong-flavoured than onions, delicious braised or puréed as an accompanying vegetable; baby leeks can be shredded raw in salads. Leeks are excellent in soups (see recipes, pages 83, 87) and casseroles, or to make a creamy flan (page 211).

SHEPHERD'S PIE
THE NORTH

Few seemingly simple and traditional dishes have so much controversy about their names. There are those who hold that it is shepherd's pie when made with lamb and cottage pie when made with beef – and vice versa. Some people say it should be made with raw meat, others with cooked. This version has more flavoursome ingredients than some recipes and tastes excellent.

SERVES 4

✳ ⩘

450 g (1 lb) minced lamb
1 large onion, skinned and chopped
1 bay leaf
50 g (2 oz) mushrooms, sliced
2 carrots, sliced
25 g (1 oz) plain wholemeal flour
300 ml (½ pint) lamb or beef stock
15 ml (1 tbsp) tomato purée
salt and pepper
700 g (1½ lb) potatoes, peeled and chopped
25 g (1 oz) butter
60 ml (4 tbsp) fresh milk
50 g (2 oz) Lancashire cheese, crumbled

OXFORD JOHN STEAKS WITH CAPER SAUCE. Generous, tender steaks need only the simplest cooking. The mouthwateringly sharp capers add a refreshing bite to the sauce.

1. Dry fry the lamb with the onion, bay leaf, mushrooms and carrots for 8–10 minutes.
2. Add the flour and cook, stirring, for 1 minute. Gradually blend in the stock and tomato purée. Cook, stirring, until the mixture thickens and boils.
3. Cover and simmer gently for 25 minutes. Remove the bay leaf and season to taste. Spoon into a 1.7 litre (3 pint) ovenproof serving dish.
4. Meanwhile, cook the potatoes in boiling salted water for 20 minutes, until tender. Drain well. Mash with the butter and milk and mix well. Pile on to the mince mixture and sprinkle over the cheese.
5. Bake at 200°C (400°F) mark 6 for 15–20 minutes. Serve hot with a green vegetable.

TO MICROWAVE

⩘ Dry fry the lamb, onion, bay leaf, mushrooms and carrots in a 1.7 litre (3 pint) shallow heatproof dish, covered, on HIGH for 8 minutes. Add the flour and cook on HIGH for 1 minute. Gradually blend in the stock and tomato purée, then cook on HIGH for 5 minutes, stirring occasionally. Cook the potatoes in a large bowl in 150 ml (¼ pint) water for 15 minutes. Complete steps 4 and 5.

OXFORD JOHN STEAKS WITH CAPER SAUCE
THE SOUTH-EAST

At Oxford's indoor market there are butchers who have for years supplied the colleges with high quality meat. A speciality is Oxford John, the local name for a lamb leg steak. It's a tender cut that just needs gentle frying before serving with a piquant sauce.

SERVES 4

✳

4 lamb leg steaks, each weighing about 175 g (6 oz)
salt and pepper
25 g (1 oz) butter
5 ml (1 tsp) plain flour
300 ml (½ pint) lamb or beef stock
30 ml (2 tbsp) drained capers
15 ml (1 tbsp) vinegar from the capers

1. Season the lamb steaks to taste. Heat the butter in a frying pan and fry the steaks gently for 10–15 minutes, turning occasionally, until browned on both sides. Remove from the pan with a slotted spoon and transfer to a warmed dish.
2. Stir to loosen any sediment at the bottom of the pan, then stir in the flour and cook for 1–2 minutes. Gradually add the stock, stirring all the time, then cook until the sauce thickens, boils and is smooth. Add the capers and vinegar and simmer for 1–2 minutes.
3. Return the lamb steaks to the pan and simmer for 5 minutes or until the lamb is cooked to your liking. Serve hot.

LAMB AND WATERCRESS BAKE

COUNTRYWIDE

Methods of watercress cultivation have improved so that it is now available all year round. Bought vacuum-packed, it keeps unopened for up to five days, but wilts quickly when exposed to the air. If you buy watercress in bunches, store them upside down, with the leaves plunged into cold water.

SERVES 4–6

450 g (1 lb) minced lamb
2 large onions, skinned and finely chopped
2 bunches watercress, trimmed and finely chopped
10 ml (2 tsp) dried oregano
105 ml (7 tbsp) plain flour
300 ml (½ pint) lamb or chicken stock
50 ml (2 fl oz) dry white wine
25 g (1 oz) butter
salt and pepper
568 ml (1 pint) fresh milk
175 g (6 oz) Lancashire cheese, crumbled
225 g (8 oz) oven-ready lasagne verdi

1. Brown the lamb well in its own fat in a large saucepan. Pour off excess fat. Add the onion and cook for 5 minutes, stirring occasionally. Add the watercress, oregano and 30 ml (2 tbsp) of the flour. Cook for 1–2 minutes, then gradually stir in the stock and wine and season with salt and pepper. Bring to the boil, then simmer gently, uncovered, for 45 minutes, stirring occasionally.
2. Put the butter, remaining flour and milk in a saucepan. Heat, whisking continuously, until the sauce thickens, boils and is smooth. Simmer for 1–2 minutes. Remove the pan from the heat and stir in 100 g (4 oz) of the cheese, stir until melted and season with salt and pepper.
3. Layer the mince mixture with the uncooked lasagne in a fairly deep ovenproof serving dish. Spoon over the cheese sauce. Sprinkle over remaining cheese.
4. Bake at 190°C (375°F) mark 5 for about 40 minutes, until browned. Serve hot straight from the dish.

TO MICROWAVE

The cheese sauce can be prepared in the microwave. Put the butter, remaining flour and milk in a medium bowl and stir together. Cook on HIGH for 5–6 minutes, until the sauce has boiled and thickened, whisking frequently. Complete the sauce as in step 2.

CHUMP CHOPS WITH BLACKCURRANT SAUCE

COUNTRYWIDE

Make the most of the superb sharpness of blackcurrants during their summer season. They are particularly good with lamb, because their natural acidity acts as a foil to the lamb's fattiness. The easiest way to remove fresh blackcurrants from their stalks is to run a fork down the stem.

SERVES 4

4 lamb chump chops, each weighing about 225 g (8 oz)
1 medium onion, skinned and chopped
15 ml (1 tbsp) chopped fresh rosemary
15 ml (1 tbsp) chopped fresh parsley
grated rind of 1 lemon
300 ml (½ pint) apple and blackcurrant juice
15 ml (1 tbsp) blackcurrant jelly
50 g (2 oz) blackcurrants, stripped
30 ml (2 tbsp) fresh soured cream

1. Dry fry the chops in a large non-stick frying pan until brown and sealed on both sides.
2. Add the onion, rosemary, parsley and lemon rind, lightly fry for 2 minutes, then pour in the apple and blackcurrant juice. Simmer gently, covered, for 20–25 minutes until the chops are tender.
3. Remove the chops from the pan, put on to a warmed serving plate and keep hot.
4. Add the blackcurrant jelly and most of the blackcurrants to the pan, then boil the juices to reduce by half. Add the soured cream and reheat gently, then pour over the chops. Serve garnished with the remaining blackcurrants. Accompany with creamed potatoes and sliced carrots.

LAMB AND WATERCRESS BAKE. A sustaining variation of lasagne. The smooth, cheesy topping conceals the mouthwatering layers of meat sauce and pasta.

LAMB KEBABS IN SPICY YOGURT DRESSING

COUNTRYWIDE

A good dish for the end of summer, when corn-on-the-cob comes into the shops. The kebabs can be grilled, or cooked outdoors on a barbecue. A few hours in the marinade helps tenderise them, as well as adding flavour and moisture.

SERVES 4

1 large corn-on-the-cob
salt and pepper
8 shallots
150 g (5 oz) natural yogurt
1 garlic clove, skinned and crushed
2 bay leaves, crumbled
15 ml (1 tbsp) lemon juice
5 ml (1 tsp) ground allspice
15 ml (1 tbsp) coriander seeds
700 g (1½ lb) boned leg of lamb, trimmed and cut into 2.5 cm (1 inch) cubes
225 g (8 oz) courgettes, topped and tailed and cut into 0.5 cm (¼ inch) slices
4 tomatoes, halved
lemon wedges, to garnish

1. Blanch the corn in boiling salted water for 1 minute, drain well, cut into 8 pieces and set aside. Blanch the shallots in boiling salted water for 1 minute, skin and set aside.
2. To make the marinade, pour the yogurt into a shallow dish and stir in the garlic, bay leaves, lemon juice, allspice, coriander seeds and salt and pepper.
3. Thread the lamb cubes on to eight skewers with the courgettes, tomatoes, corn and shallots. Place in the dish, spoon over the marinade, cover and leave for 2–3 hours, turning occasionally to ensure even coating.
4. Grill the kebabs for about 15–20 minutes, turning and brushing with the marinade occasionally. To serve, spoon remaining marinade over the kebabs and garnish with lemon wedges. Accompany with boiled rice.

MINTED LAMB BURGERS WITH CUCUMBER

COUNTRYWIDE

Lamb and mint were made for each other, and the flavours marry perfectly in these quick burgers. When buying cucumbers, feel the stalk end and only buy if it is firm. Don't peel the cucumber, as both appearance and flavour are improved if the skin is left on.

SERVES 4

450 g (1 lb) minced lamb
1 small onion, skinned and finely chopped
100 g (4 oz) fresh breadcrumbs
finely grated rind of ½ lemon
45 ml (3 tbsp) chopped fresh mint
1 egg, beaten
salt and pepper
30 ml (2 tbsp) plain flour
½ cucumber, cut into 5 cm (2 inch) long wedges
6 spring onions, trimmed and cut into 1 cm (½ inch) pieces
200 ml (7 fl oz) lamb or chicken stock
15 ml (1 tbsp) dry sherry

1. Mix the lamb, onion, breadcrumbs and lemon rind with 15 ml (1 tbsp) of the chopped mint and egg. Season.
2. Shape into 8 burgers with floured hands, then completely coat in the flour.
3. Dry fry the burgers in a large heavy-based non-stick frying pan for about 6 minutes, until lightly browned, turning once. Add the cucumber and spring onions.
4. Pour in the stock and sherry, then add the remaining mint and salt and pepper to taste. Bring to the boil, cover and simmer gently for about 20 minutes or until the meat is tender. Skim off any excess fat before serving, and taste and adjust seasoning. Serve with boiled new potatoes.

TO MICROWAVE

 Heat a large browning dish on HIGH for 5–8 minutes or according to the manufacturer's instructions. Meanwhile, complete steps 1 and 2. Add 10 ml (2 tsp) oil to the browning dish, then quickly add the burgers and cook on HIGH for 2 minutes. Turn over and cook on HIGH for 2–3 minutes or until browned. Add the cucumbers, spring onions, 150 ml (¼ pint) stock, the sherry and the remaining mint. Cook on HIGH for 4–5 minutes or until the liquid is boiling and slightly reduced. Skim off any excess fat and season. Serve with boiled new potatoes.

MARINATED LAMB WITH ONION PUREE

COUNTRYWIDE

Even a short soak in a piquant marinade improves the flavour of everyday chops. Go easy on the sage – just a hint is all that's needed, as the flavour can be overpowering.

SERVES 4

45 ml (3 tbsp) vegetable oil
15 ml (1 tbsp) white wine vinegar
1.25 ml (¼ tsp) dried sage
1 garlic clove, skinned and crushed
4 lamb chump chops, each about 225 g (8 oz), trimmed
2 medium onions, skinned and finely chopped
30 ml (2 tbsp) plain flour
300 ml (½ pint) fresh milk
1 clove
30 ml (2 tbsp) fresh single cream
salt and pepper
fresh sage sprigs, to garnish

1. To make the marinade, whisk together the oil, vinegar, sage and crushed garlic.
2. Place the chops flat in a shallow dish. Pour over the marinade, cover and leave to marinate in a cool place for 1 hour.
3. Remove the chops from the marinade and place under a hot grill. Cook for 7–10 minutes on each side.
4. Meanwhile, put the marinade and chopped onions

in a small saucepan. Cover and cook over low heat for about 10–15 minutes, until onions are soft.
5. Stir in the flour, then gradually stir in the milk. Add the clove. Bring to the boil, stirring occasionally, and simmer for 2 minutes. Discard the clove, transfer to a blender or food processor and purée until smooth. Return the sauce to the rinsed-out pan. Add the cream and salt and pepper to taste and reheat gently. Arrange the chops on a warmed serving dish and garnish with sprigs of sage. Serve the onion purée separately.

TO MICROWAVE

 Complete steps 1, 2 and 3. Meanwhile, put the marinade and chopped onions in a medium bowl. Cover and cook on HIGH for 7–10 minutes, until softened. Stir in the flour, milk and the clove. Cook on HIGH for 2–3 minutes until boiling and thickened, whisking frequently. Discard the clove. Transfer the sauce to a blender or food processor and purée until smooth. Transfer the purée to a heatproof serving bowl and cook on HIGH for 2 minutes or until hot. Stir in the cream and salt and pepper to taste. Complete the remainder of step 5.

LOIN OF LAMB WITH APRICOT AND HERB STUFFING

COUNTRYWIDE

A fruity stuffing goes well with lamb and here no-soak dried apricots save time. Ask the butcher to bone the loin for you, then it's simple to roll and tie it into a neat joint.

SERVES 6

15 g (½ oz) butter
1 medium onion, skinned and finely chopped
30 ml (2 tbsp) chopped fresh thyme or mint
75 g (3 oz) fresh wholemeal breadcrumbs
salt and pepper
100 g (4 oz) no-soak dried apricots, finely chopped
1 egg, beaten
1.6 kg (3½ lb) loin of lamb, boned
fresh thyme or mint sprigs, to garnish

1. Melt the butter in a large frying pan. Add the onion and fry for 5 minutes, until softened. Stir in thyme or mint, breadcrumbs and seasoning. Set aside to cool.
2. Add the apricots to the mixture with the egg and mix well together.
3. Lay the meat out flat, fat side down, and spread the stuffing over the lamb.
4. Roll up the meat to enclose the stuffing and tie with strong cotton or fine string at regular intervals. Put the joint in a roasting tin and bake at 180°C (350°F) mark 4 for about 1 hour or until cooked to your liking.
5. To serve, remove the string and carve into thick slices. Garnish with sprigs of fresh thyme or mint.

BEEF

ROAST BEEF AND YORKSHIRE PUDDING

THE NORTH

The North may claim it for its own but all over Britain this is recognised as a traditional dish, especially for Sunday lunch time. Using semi-skimmed instead of whole milk will produce the same effect as using half milk and half water in the Yorkshire pudding. Keep the meat warm, resting under a tent of foil, until you are ready to carve it.

* ALLOW 175 g (6 oz) OFF THE BONE PER PERSON; 225–350 g (8–12 oz) ON THE BONE PER PERSON

SERVES 4–8

sirloin, rib, rump or topside*
25 g (1 oz) beef drippings (optional)
salt and pepper
5 ml (1 tsp) mustard powder (optional)
Prepared English mustard or horseradish sauce, to serve
For the Yorkshire pudding
100 g (4 oz) plain flour
pinch of salt
1 egg
200 ml (7 fl oz) fresh milk
For the gravy
10 ml (2 tsp) plain flour
300 ml (½ pint) beef stock

1. Weigh the meat and calculate the cooking time: for rare beef allow 15 minutes per 450 g (1 lb) plus 15 minutes; for medium beef allow 20 minutes per 450 g (1 lb) plus 20 minutes; and for well-done beef allow 25 minutes per 450 g (1 lb) plus 25 minutes. Put the meat into a shallow roasting tin, preferably on a roasting rack, with the thickest layer of fat uppermost and the cut sides exposed to the heat. Add drippings if the meat is lean. Season the meat with pepper and mustard powder, if wished.

2. Roast at 180°C (350°F) mark 4 for the calculated time, basting occasionally with the juices from the tin. Forty-five minutes before the end of the cooking time, cover the joint with foil and place on the bottom shelf of the oven. Increase the oven temperature to 220°C (425°F) mark 7.

3. To make the Yorkshire pudding, mix the flour and a pinch of salt in a bowl, then make a well in the centre and break in the egg.

4. Add half the milk and, using a wooden spoon, gradually work in the flour. Beat the mixture until it is smooth, then add the remaining milk and 100 ml (3 fl oz) water. Beat until well mixed and the surface is covered with tiny bubbles.

5. Put 30 ml (2 tbsp) fat from the beef into a baking tin and place in the oven at 220°C (425°F) mark 7 until the fat is very hot.

6. Pour in the batter and return to the oven to cook for 40–45 minutes, until risen and golden brown. Do not open the oven door for 30 minutes.

7. After 30 minutes, transfer the cooked meat to a warmed serving plate and leave to rest for 20 minutes, covered, before carving.

8. To make the gravy, the meat juices alone may be used. For a thicker gravy, skim some of the fat from the surface and place the tin over moderate heat. Sprinkle the flour into the tin and stir it into the pan juices, scraping up the brown sediment. Cook over high heat, stirring constantly, until the flour has browned slightly. (When the meat is carved, any juices from the meat can be added to the gravy.) Add up to 300 ml (½ pint) of beef stock to the tin and stir well. Bring it to the boil, simmer for 2–3 minutes and season to taste. Pour into a sauce boat or jug.

9. Serve the carved beef with the Yorkshire pudding, cut into portions. Accompany with the gravy and mustard or horseradish sauce.

VARIATION

For individual Yorkshire Puddings or Popovers, use 50 g (2 oz) plain flour, a pinch of salt, 1 egg and 150 ml (¼ pint) milk and water mixed. Cook for 15–20 minutes. This quantity will fill 12 patty tins.

BEEF WELLINGTON. An impressive dish, using a fine cut of meat. The pastry casing is crisply browned, while the meat within stays moist and juicy.

BEEF WELLINGTON

THE SOUTH-EAST

The Duke of Wellington was a highly prominent statesman and soldier of the nineteenth century. This dish, however, bears his name not because he was a great gourmet but because the finished joint was thought to resemble one of the brown shiny military boots which were called after him.

SERVES 8

1.4 kg (3 lb) fillet of beef
pepper
15 ml (1 tbsp) vegetable oil
40 g (1½ oz) butter
225 g (8 oz) button mushrooms, sliced
175 g (6 oz) smooth liver pâté
368 g (13 oz) packet frozen puff pastry, thawed
1 egg, beaten, to glaze

1. Trim and tie up the fillet at intervals so it retains its shape. Season to taste with pepper. Heat the oil and 15 g (½ oz) of the butter in a large frying pan, add the meat and fry briskly on all sides. Press down with a wooden spoon while frying to seal well.
2. Roast at 220°C (425°F) mark 7 for 20 minutes, then set the beef aside to allow it to cool and remove the string.
3. Meanwhile, cook the mushrooms in the remaining butter until soft; leave until cold, then blend with the pâté.
4. On a lightly floured surface, roll out the pastry to a large rectangle about 33×28 cm (13×11 inches) and 0.5 cm (¼ inch) thick.
5. Spread the pâté mixture down the centre of the pastry. Place the meat on top in the centre. Brush the edges of the pastry with the egg.
6. Fold the pastry edges over lengthways and turn the parcel over so that the join is underneath. Fold the ends under the meat on a baking sheet.
7. Decorate with leaves cut from the pastry trimmings. Brush with the remaining egg and bake at 220°C (425°F) mark 7 for 50–60 minutes, depending how well done you like your beef, covering with foil after 25 minutes. Allow the Beef Wellington to rest for 10 minutes before serving.

BEEF WELLINGTON
Tie the beef fillet at regular intervals.

Fold the pastry edges over to cover the meat.

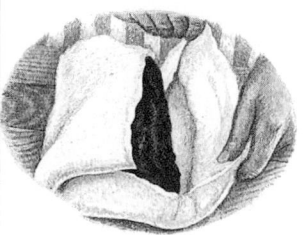

BEEF CUTS

We all enjoy traditional British beef dishes using cuts like sirloin, rib or topside for Roast Beef and Yorkshire (see recipe, page 124) or silverside for boiled beef (see recipes, opposite). However, today's demand is increasingly for quick-cooking cuts which are ready-trimmed for convenience and economy, and lean for health, often labelled according to fat content (e.g. less than 5%, 10% or 15%).

For a roasting joint, boneless rib, or a combination of rolled and boned back and top rib, and rolled top rump are good choices.

New small beef cuts include specially tenderised quick-grill as well as flash-fry steak, and thin slices of beef such as topside for making beef olives (see recipe, page 129).

Trimmed steak for braising and stewing is sold cubed or sliced. Extra lean mince is available fine-textured for hamburgers and coarse-cut for dishes like shepherd's pie.

Beef cuts often have different names in different parts of the country but are becoming increasingly standardised.

SPICED BEEF
NORTHERN IRELAND AND THE MIDLANDS

If the meat has not had a prolonged salting it may not need soaking, so check with your butcher when buying. Leisurely simmering ensures that the silverside is meltingly tender and a spicy mixture spread over it before roasting keeps the joint moist as it takes on a delicious flavour.

SERVES 6

1.8 kg (4 lb) salted rolled silverside
1 medium onion, skinned and sliced
4 medium carrots, sliced
1 small turnip, peeled and sliced
8 cloves
100 g (4 oz) dark soft brown sugar
2.5 ml (½ tsp) mustard powder
5 ml (1 tsp) ground cinnamon
juice of 1 lemon

1. If necessary, soak the meat in cold water for several hours or overnight, then rinse. Tie up the meat to form a neat joint and put in a large saucepan or flameproof casserole with the vegetables.
2. Cover with water and bring slowly to the boil. Skim the surface, cover and simmer for 3–4 hours, until tender. Leave to cool completely in the liquid for 3–4 hours.
3. Drain the meat well, then put into a roasting tin and stick the cloves into the fat. Mix together the remaining ingredients and spread over the meat.
4. Bake at 180°C (350°F) mark 4 for 45 minutes to 1 hour, until tender, basting from time to time. Serve hot or cold.

BOILED BEEF AND CARROTS
THE SOUTH-EAST

Immortalised by the old music hall song, this is a truly traditional Cockney dish. The length of time the meat is soaked depends on how salty it is; check with the butcher. The greyish colour turns an appetising pink when cooked.

SERVES 6

1.6 kg (3½ lb) lean salted silverside or brisket of beef
bouquet garni
6 black peppercorns, lightly crushed
2 small onions, skinned and quartered
8 cloves
2 small turnips, peeled and quartered
2 celery sticks, chopped
1 leek, trimmed, chopped and washed
18 small carrots

1. If necessary, soak the meat in cold water for several hours or overnight, then rinse. Tie up into a neat joint.
2. Place the beef in a large saucepan, add just enough

SPICED BEEF. A handsome joint makes a pleasant change from the Christmas turkey. The meat has a tangy, mustard-flavoured crust, which darkens to a mouthwatering brown during cooking.

BOILED BEEF AND
CARROTS. Look for carrots
which still have some of their
feathery foliage, and leave the
stems on while they cook for a
pretty effect. Long, slow
cooking ensures that the meat
is beautifully tender.

water to cover and bring slowly to the boil. Skim the
surface, add the bouquet garni, peppercorns, onions,
each quarter stuck with a clove, turnip, celery and leek.
Lower the heat and simmer very gently for about
2 hours.

3. Add the small carrots and simmer gently for a further
30–40 minutes or until the carrots are tender.

4. Carefully transfer the beef and small carrots to a
warmed serving plate and keep warm.

5. Skim the fat from the surface of the cooking liquor,
then strain. Boil the liquid to reduce slightly, then pour
into a warmed sauceboat or jug.

6. Serve the beef surrounded by the carrots, with the
sauce handed separately. Accompany with peas and
mashed potatoes or dumplings.

BRAISED BEEF WITH CHESTNUTS AND CELERY

COUNTRYWIDE

*An unusual casserole, which dates from the eighteenth
century. Make it in the late autumn and winter when both
celery and fresh chestnuts are available. It's well worth
spending the extra time needed to shell the chestnuts, as they
do add a very special flavour to the finished dish.*

SERVES 6

✳

18 fresh chestnuts, skins split

15 g (½ oz) butter

15 ml (1 tbsp) vegetable oil

2 bacon rashers, rinded and chopped

900 g (2 lb) stewing steak, cubed

1 medium onion, skinned and chopped

15 ml (1 tbsp) plain flour

300 ml (½ pint) brown ale

300 ml (½ pint) beef stock

pinch of freshly grated nutmeg

finely grated rind and juice of 1 orange

salt and pepper

3 celery sticks, chopped

chopped fresh parsley, to garnish

1. Cook the chestnuts in simmering water for about
7 minutes. Peel off the thick outer skin and thin inner
skin while still warm, removing from the water one at a
time.

2. Heat the butter and oil in a flameproof casserole,
add the bacon and beef in batches and cook, stirring
occasionally, until browned. Remove the meat with a
slotted spoon.

3. Add the onion to the casserole and fry, stirring,
until softened. Drain off most of the fat. Return the
meat to the casserole, sprinkle in the flour and cook,
stirring, for 1–2 minutes.

4. Stir in the brown ale, stock, nutmeg, orange juice
and half the rind. Season to taste. Bring to the boil, stir
well to loosen the sediment, then add the chestnuts.
Cover tightly with foil and a lid and bake at 170°C
(325°F) mark 3 for about 45 minutes.

5. After 45 minutes baking time, add the celery to the
casserole and continue baking for about 1 hour until the
meat is tender. Serve with the remaining orange rind
and the parsley sprinkled over the top.

2. Add the onions and mushrooms to the pan, adding more oil if necessary, and fry until softened. Season to taste, add the flour and stir well so that the flour absorbs the fat.

3. Return the meat to the pan, pour in the stout and add the bay leaf and brown sugar. Stir well to mix.

4. Cover and cook gently, either on top of the stove or in the oven at 180°C (350°F) mark 4 for about 2½ hours or until the meat is tender.

BEEF POCKETS STUFFED WITH MUSHROOMS

SCOTLAND

Mushrooms make marvellous stuffings and as a year-round crop are always available. Ginger wine is an English speciality which appeals to the British palate's desire for strong positive flavours. Even this small quantity makes a significant difference to the recipe.

SERVES 4

| 4 thick-cut steaks, each weighing 175 g (6 oz) |
| salt and pepper |
| 15 g (½ oz) butter |
| 175 g (6 oz) mushrooms, finely chopped |
| 1 garlic clove, skinned and crushed |
| 1 large onion, skinned and finely chopped |
| 15 ml (1 tbsp) chopped fresh parsley |
| 15 ml (1 tbsp) ginger wine |
| 15 ml (1 tbsp) fresh wholemeal breadcrumbs |
| 15 ml (1 tbsp) fresh double cream |

1. Using a sharp, pointed knife, make a horizontal cut in each steak without cutting all the way through. Season to taste.

2. Melt the butter in a medium saucepan and lightly cook the mushrooms, garlic and onion for 5 minutes, until softened. Remove from the heat.

3. Add the parsley, ginger wine, breadcrumbs and cream. Mix together well.

4. Generously fill each pocket of the steaks with the stuffing.

5. Grill the steaks for 5–15 minutes, until the meat is cooked to taste (see page 131 for times). Serve at once with new potatoes and broccoli.

TO MICROWAVE

 Complete step 1. Melt the butter in a shallow dish on HIGH for 30 seconds. Add the mushrooms, garlic and onion and cook on HIGH for 7 minutes. Complete steps 3 and 4. Preheat a large browning dish on HIGH for 5–8 minutes or according to manufacturer's instructions. Quickly put the steaks in the browning dish and cook on HIGH for 2 minutes. Turn and cook on HIGH for 3–5 minutes, until cooked to taste. Serve with new potatoes and broccoli.

BEEF IN STOUT. Leave this stew to simmer gently until the meat is meltingly tender. The stout lends a good depth of flavour.

BEEF POCKETS STUFFED WITH MUSHROOMS To form pocket, make horizontal cut in steak without cutting all the way through.

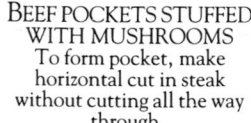

BEEF IN STOUT

NORTHERN IRELAND

This is a simple dish but one that's packed with goodness. Stout gets its dark colour and bitterness from the roasted malt or barley used in its brewing. It makes a delicious gravy when used in a casserole, and a touch of sugar brings out the flavour even more.

SERVES 4–6

| 15 g (½ oz) butter |
| about 15 ml (1 tbsp) vegetable oil |
| 900 g (2 lb) stewing steak, cut into 5 cm (2 inch) cubes |
| 4 medium onions, skinned and sliced |
| 225 g (8 oz) button mushrooms, halved |
| salt and pepper |
| 30 ml (2 tbsp) plain flour |
| 300 ml (½ pint) stout |
| 1 bay leaf |
| 5 ml (1 tsp) soft dark brown sugar |

1. Heat the butter and oil in a large flameproof casserole and cook the meat for 10 minutes, until browned all over. Remove the meat from the pan with a slotted spoon.

HEREFORD BEEF OLIVES

THE MIDLANDS

Hereford cattle produce some of the best beef in Britain, very tender with excellent flavour. Choose a snug-fitting dish for this recipe so the sauce does not evaporate.

SERVES 4

※

75 g (3 oz) streaky bacon rashers, rinded and finely chopped

1 small onion, skinned and chopped

10 ml (2 tsp) chopped fresh parsley

100 g (4 oz) fresh breadcrumbs

50 g (2 oz) shredded beef suet

1.25 ml (¼ tsp) dried mixed herbs

1 egg, size 6

1 lemon

salt and pepper

8 thin slices topside beef, weighing about 700 g (1½ lb)

15 ml (1 tbsp) prepared English mustard

45 ml (3 tbsp) seasoned flour

25 g (1 oz) butter

30 ml (2 tbsp) vegetable oil

450 ml (¾ pint) beef stock

2 medium onions, skinned and sliced

1. Mix the bacon with the onion, parsley, breadcrumbs, suet, herbs and egg. Add the grated rind of ½ of the lemon and 5 ml (1 tsp) juice and season.
2. Put the meat between greaseproof paper and beat out with a meat mallet or rolling pin.
3. Spread mustard thinly over the meat, then divide stuffing equally between the pieces. Roll up and secure with strong cotton or fine string. Toss in seasoned flour.
4. Heat the butter and oil in a shallow flameproof casserole into which all the beef olives will just fit. Brown them well, then remove from the pan.
5. Stir the remaining seasoned flour into the pan residue and brown lightly. Gradually stir in stock and bring to boil. Season to taste, then return meat to pan.
6. Scatter the onions over the meat. Cover and bake at 170°C (325°F) mark 3 for 1½ hours or until tender.

BEEF HARE

COUNTRYWIDE

Although chuck steak is a tougher cut, it should be lean and not too fatty. When cooked slowly and cleverly spiced it comes up meltingly tender and, in this recipe, has a gamey flavour rather like hare.

SERVES 4

※

plain flour, to coat

salt and pepper

freshly grated nutmeg

900 g (2 lb) chuck steak, cut into 7.5×2.5 cm (3×1 inch) strips

5 ml (1 tbsp) celery seeds

8 cloves

1 medium onion, skinned and quartered

1 small young parsnip, peeled and grated

150 ml (¼ pint) dry red wine

1. Season the flour with salt and pepper and plenty of nutmeg, then toss the meat in it to coat, shaking off any excess.
2. Pack the meat into a deep 900 ml (1½ pint) ovenproof earthenware dish, scattering celery seeds in between the layers.
3. Stick 2 cloves into each onion quarter, then arrange the onion and parsnip on top of the meat. Pour in the wine, cover tightly and leave for about 2 hours.
4. Place in an oven at 220°C (425°F) mark 7 and immediately reduce the temperature to 170°C (325°F) mark 3. Bake for 2¼ hours or until the beef is tender.

HEREFORD BEEF OLIVES. Juicy rolls of succulent beef, wrapped round a herby filling and braised slowly in a well-seasoned stock.

DORSET JUGGED STEAK

THE WEST

This traditional Dorset dish was often prepared to be eaten on days when the fair came to town since it is good tempered enough to wait until the revellers come home, although the forcemeat balls should not be cooked for too long. Jugging is a method of slow cooking which retains all the flavours of the meat while mingling them with those of the other ingredients.

SERVES 4

700 g (1½ lb) stewing steak, cut into 2.5 cm (1 inch) cubes

25 g (1 oz) plain wholemeal flour

1 medium onion, skinned and sliced

4 cloves

salt and pepper

150 ml (¼ pint) port

about 450 ml (¾ pint) beef stock, to cover

225 g (8 oz) sausagemeat

50 g (2 oz) fresh wholemeal breadcrumbs

30 ml (2 tbsp) chopped fresh parsley

15 ml (1 tbsp) redcurrant jelly

1. Toss the meat in the flour, shaking off excess, and put into an ovenproof casserole.
2. Add the onion and cloves and season to taste. Pour in the port and just enough stock to cover the meat.
3. Cover the casserole and bake at 170°C (325°F) mark 3 for about 3 hours, until the meat is tender.
4. Meanwhile, mix together the sausagemeat, breadcrumbs and parsley and season to taste. With floured hands, form the mixture into 8 balls.
5. Forty minutes before the end of the cooking time, stir the redcurrant jelly into the casserole. Add the forcemeat balls and cook, uncovered, until the forcemeat balls are cooked and slightly brown. Skim off any excess fat and serve hot.

DORSET JUGGED STEAK. Chunks of steak and succulent forcemeat balls are cooked together in a port-enriched gravy, flavoured with just a hint of cloves.

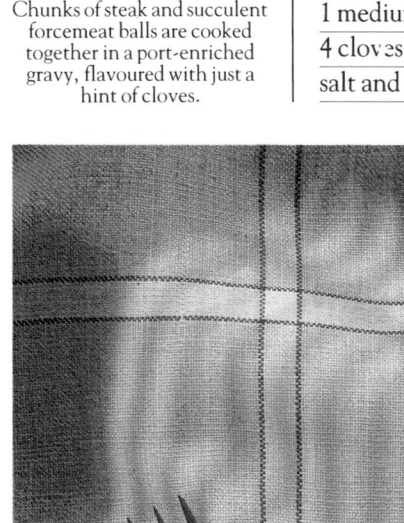

CELERIAC AND MUSTARD BEEF
COUNTRYWIDE

It's easier to ask your butcher to cut the slices of silverside, rather than attempting to do it yourself. That way you need only buy as much as you need to make this juicy variation on beef olives. Bat the slices out until paper-thin so that they will be perfectly tender when cooked.

SERVES 4

8 thin slices silverside, about 700 g (1½ lb) total weight
3 medium carrots, grated
1 medium onion, skinned and thinly sliced
175 g (6 oz) celeriac, grated and sprinkled with lemon juice
75 ml (5 tbsp) wholegrain mustard
75 ml (5 tbsp) chopped fresh parsley
salt and pepper
15 g (½ oz) butter
30 ml (2 tbsp) vegetable oil
30 ml (2 tbsp) plain flour
300 ml (½ pint) beef stock
60 ml (4 tbsp) Madeira or medium sherry
extra chopped fresh parsley, to garnish

1. Put the meat between 2 sheets of dampened greaseproof paper and bat out with a meat mallet or rolling pin.
2. Place all the vegetables in a saucepan. Cover with cold water and bring to the boil. Drain immediately.
3. Stir half the mustard and half the parsley into the vegetable mixture and season to taste.
4. Spoon a little of the vegetable mixture on to each slice of beef. Fold in the edges and roll up to enclose the filling. Secure with wooden cocktail sticks or tie neatly with strong cotton or fine string.
5. Heat the butter and oil in a large frying pan, add the beef rolls and brown quickly. Transfer to a 2 litre (3½ pint) ovenproof casserole with a slotted spoon.
6. Stir the flour into the frying pan. Cook, stirring, for 1–2 minutes, then gradually add the stock, Madeira, remaining mustard and parsley. Bring to the boil.
7. Pour the sauce over the beef, cover the casserole and bake at 180°C (350°F) mark 4 for about 1½ hours or until the beef is tender. Garnish with chopped parsley and serve hot. Accompany with boiled rice and seasonal vegetables.

STILTON STEAKS
THE MIDLANDS

Stilton is the only British cheese to have its name protected by copyright, which means that it can only be produced in the three counties of Derbyshire, Nottinghamshire and Leicestershire. It's a rich, creamy cheese, immediately recognisable with its pattern of blue veins, and has a distinctive mellow flavour.

SERVES 4

100 g (4 oz) Stilton cheese, crumbled
25 g (1 oz) butter, softened
50–75 g (2–3 oz) shelled walnut pieces, finely chopped
pepper
4 sirloin or fillet steaks, each weighing about 100–175 g (4–6 oz), trimmed

1. Put the cheese in a bowl and mash with a fork. Add the butter and walnuts and mix in. Season to taste.
2. Put the steaks on the grill rack and season with plenty of pepper. Put under a preheated hot grill and cook for 2–10 minutes on each side, according to the thickness of the steaks and how well done you like them (see page 131 for times).
3. Remove the steaks from under the grill, sprinkle the cheese and nut mixture evenly over them and press down with a palette knife. Grill for 1 further minute or until the topping is melted and bubbling. Serve hot, accompanied with boiled new potatoes and a mixed salad.

STILTON STEAKS. The mouthwateringly savoury cheese topping gets an unexpected crunchiness from finely chopped walnuts. Simple accompaniments are all that's needed to complete the meal.

STRIPS OF BEEF IN
WHISKY SAUCE. The
creamy sauce has a deliciously
boozy flavour, and the dish is
very quick to cook.

STRIPS OF BEEF IN
WHISKY SAUCE

SCOTLAND

*This quick-cooking dish requires prime meat. Whisky
liqueur will reduce to a sweet glistening glaze.*

SERVES 4

15 g (½ oz) butter

700 g (1½ lb) sirloin steak, cut into strips

1 large onion, skinned and chopped

75 ml (3 tbsp) whisky liqueur such as Drambuie

75 ml (3 fl oz) fresh double cream

salt and pepper

1. Melt the butter in a medium frying pan. Add the
beef strips and onion and cook for 5–10 minutes, until
the beef is brown and cooked to taste.

2. Stir in the liqueur and cream. Heat gently to reduce
slightly. Serve at once with vegetables and brown rice.

TO MICROWAVE

Preheat a large browning dish on HIGH for
8–10 minutes or according to manufacturer's
instructions. Quickly put the butter, beef and onions in
the browning dish. Cook on HIGH for 5–7 minutes,
until meat is cooked to taste, stirring frequently. Stir in
the liqueur and season to taste. Cook on HIGH for
1 minute, then stir in the cream and serve.

MEAT BALLS IN
TOMATO SAUCE

COUNTRYWIDE

*There's an Italian influence here. Serve these meat balls with
spaghetti as a change from Bolognese sauce.*

SERVES 4

150 g (5 oz) crustless wholemeal bread

150 ml (¼ pint) fresh milk

25 g (1 oz) butter

20 ml (4 tsp) plain wholemeal flour

200 ml (7 fl oz) beef stock

397 g (14 oz) can tomatoes, sieved with their juice

pinch of sugar

2.5 ml (½ tsp) dried thyme

salt and pepper

1 large onion, skinned and finely chopped

450 g (1 lb) lean minced beef

5 ml (1 tsp) paprika

15 ml (1 tbsp) vegetable oil

1. Crumble the bread into a bowl, pour over the milk
and leave to soak for about 30 minutes.
2. Meanwhile, put 15 g (½ oz) of the butter, flour and
stock in a saucepan. Heat, whisking continuously, until
the sauce thickens, boils and is smooth.
3. Add the tomatoes, sugar and thyme. Season to taste
and simmer, covered, for 30 minutes.
4. Put the onion and the mince in a bowl and add the
soaked bread together with any remaining milk and
paprika. Season to taste. Using floured hands, shape
the mixture into 16 balls.
5. Heat the oil and remaining butter in a frying pan,
add the meat balls, a few at a time, and fry until
browned all over.
6. Place the meat balls in a single layer in a shallow
ovenproof serving dish and pour over the sauce. Cover
and bake at 180°C (350°F) mark 4 for about 30 minutes.
Serve hot, over spaghetti.

TO MICROWAVE

Complete step 1. Meanwhile, put half the butter,
flour and stock in a large bowl and cook on HIGH for

3–4 minutes, whisking frequently until boiling and thickened. Add the tomatoes, sugar and thyme. Season to taste, cover and cook on HIGH for 15 minutes, stirring occasionally. Meanwhile, complete steps 4 and 5. Place the meatballs in a shallow dish, pour over the sauce, cover and cook on HIGH for 14 minutes or until cooked. Serve with freshly cooked spaghetti.

TEVIOTDALE PIE

SCOTLAND

Originating in the Borders where good meat is taken for granted, this dish is a kind of suet pie which makes a small amount of meat go a long way. Vegetables can be incorporated with the meat under the suet crust, making it a true one-pot meal if liked.

SERVES 4

450 g (1 lb) lean minced beef
1 medium onion, skinned and chopped
300 ml (½ pint) beef stock
5 ml (1 tsp) Worcestershire sauce
salt and pepper
225 g (8 oz) self-raising flour
25 g (1 oz) cornflour
75 g (3 oz) shredded beef suet
about 300 ml (½ pint) fresh milk

1. Put the meat in a large saucepan, preferably non-stick, over medium heat and cook in its own fat until beginning to brown. Add the onion and cook for a further 5 minutes until softened.
2. Add the stock and Worcestershire sauce. Season to taste and simmer for 15–20 minutes.
3. Put the self-raising flour, cornflour and suet in a bowl, then gradually stir in the milk to form a thick batter. Season well.
4. Put the meat in a 1.1 litre (2 pint) pie dish. Cover with the batter mixture. Bake at 180°C (350°F) mark 4 for about 30–35 minutes, until risen and browned.

BEEF IN WINE WITH WALNUTS

COUNTRYWIDE

Ground walnuts add an interesting texture to this tasty casserole. Buy walnut pieces, which are cheaper than halves. Shin of beef is a good value cut which can be left cooking in a low oven for hours without spoiling.

SERVES 6

✳

900 g (2 lb) shin of beef, trimmed and cut into 2.5 cm (1 inch) cubes
150 ml (¼ pint) dry red wine

3 medium parsnips, peeled
15 ml (1 tbsp) vegetable oil
15 g (½ oz) butter
1 small onion, skinned and finely chopped
1 garlic clove, skinned and crushed
5 ml (1 tsp) ground allspice
30 ml (2 tbsp) plain flour
150 ml (¼ pint) beef stock
50 g (2 oz) shelled walnut pieces, ground
salt and pepper
chopped walnuts, to garnish

1. Put the beef in a bowl with the wine and mix well. Cover and leave to marinate overnight, stirring occasionally.
2. Cut the parsnips into 5 cm (2 inch) lengths, about 1 cm (½ inch) wide. Drain the meat from the marinade, reserving the marinade. Heat the oil and butter in a large frying pan, add the beef, a few pieces at a time, and brown quickly. Transfer to an ovenproof casserole with a slotted spoon.
3. Add the onion and garlic to the frying pan and fry until beginning to brown. Stir in the allspice, flour, reserved marinade, stock and walnuts. Bring to the boil, stirring constantly
4. Pour into the casserole and add the parsnips. Season lightly to taste. Cover and bake at 170°C (325°F) mark 3 for 2½–3 hours or until the meat is really tender.
5. Serve hot, straight from the casserole, sprinkled with the chopped walnuts. Accompany with boiled rice and a green salad.

BEEF IN WINE WITH WALNUTS. Soaking the meat overnight in red wine guarantees a fine flavour and tender result in this casserole, which also uses chunks of parsnip.

MEAT LOAF WITH
ONION SAUCE. An
economical recipe, to serve
hot one day, cold the next.
The loaf has a good, firm
texture and plenty of flavour.

MEAT LOAF WITH
ONION SAUCE

COUNTRYWIDE

A tasty and economical dish that's good served hot with the onion sauce, or cold with pickles and chutney. Do choose good quality mince, as if the meat is too cheap it will tend to be fatty and lacking in flavour.

SERVES 4

25 g (1 oz) butter
2 medium onions, skinned and finely chopped
5 ml (1 tsp) paprika
450 g (1 lb) lean minced beef
75 g (3 oz) fresh breadcrumbs
1 garlic clove, skinned and crushed
60 ml (4 tbsp) tomato purée
15 ml (1 tbsp) chopped fresh mixed herbs or 5 ml (1 tsp) dried
salt and pepper
1 egg, beaten
15 g (½ oz) plain wholemeal flour
300 ml (½ pint) fresh milk

1. Grease a 900 ml (1½ pint) loaf tin, then line the base with greased greaseproof paper. Set aside.
2. Melt 15 g (½ oz) of the butter in a frying pan. Add half of the onions and cook until softened. Add the paprika and cook for 1 minute, stirring. Remove from the heat.

3. Add the beef, breadcrumbs, garlic, tomato purée and herbs. Season to taste. Stir thoroughly until evenly mixed, then bind with the beaten egg.
4. Spoon the mixture into the loaf tin, level the surface and cover tightly with foil. Stand the tin in a roasting tin and pour in water to a depth of 2.5 cm (1 inch). Bake the meat loaf at 180°C (350°F) mark 4 for 1½ hours.
5. Meanwhile, melt the remaining butter in a saucepan. Add the rest of the onion and cook over low heat, stirring occasionally, for 10 minutes until soft but not coloured. Add the flour and cook over low heat, stirring, for 1–2 minutes.
6. Remove the pan from the heat and gradually stir in the milk, stirring after each addition to prevent lumps forming. Bring to the boil slowly and continue to cook, stirring continuously, then simmer for 2–3 minutes until thick and smooth. Simmer very gently for a further 2–3 minutes. Add salt and pepper to taste. To serve, turn out the meat loaf on to a warmed serving plate and peel off the lining paper. Serve with the hot onion sauce. Accompany with creamed potatoes and courgettes.

TO MICROWAVE

Complete step 1 using a 900 ml (2 pint) loaf dish. Melt 15 g (½ oz) of the butter on HIGH in a large bowl for 30 seconds. Add half of the onions and the paprika, cover and cook on HIGH for 5–7 minutes, until the onions are softened. Complete step 3. Spoon into the loaf dish, stand on a roasting rack, cover with kitchen paper and cook on MEDIUM for 25 minutes or until cooked. Leave to stand for 5 minutes. Meanwhile, complete the recipe.

VEAL

SCOTCH COLLOPS

Collop is another word for escalope, the thick slice of meat off the bone which is cut across the grain. Collops may be beef, lamb or venison, as well as veal, and should always be flattened before use. A rolling pin will do less damage to the meat fibres than a meat mallet.

SERVES 4

4 veal escalopes, each weighing 175 g (6 oz), halved

40 g (1½ oz) butter

1 small onion, skinned and chopped

175 ml (6 fl oz) dry white wine

400 ml (14 fl oz) veal or chicken stock

5–10 ml (1–2 tsp) mushroom ketchup

about 15 ml (1 tbsp) lemon juice

10 ml (2 tsp) plain flour

salt and pepper

pinch of ground mace

crisp bacon rolls, fried button mushrooms, lemon twists and parsley sprigs, to garnish

1. Flatten each veal escalope between two sheets of greaseproof paper with a rolling pin or meat mallet.
2. Melt 25 g (1 oz) of the butter in a large frying pan, add the veal and cook for about 2 minutes on each side. Transfer to a warmed serving plate and keep warm.
3. Add the onion to the pan and cook for about 3 minutes, stirring frequently, until softened but not browned. Stir in the wine and boil until almost evaporated. Stir in the stock, mushroom ketchup and lemon juice. Bring to the boil and simmer until reduced to 225 ml (8 fl oz).
4. Work the flour into the remaining butter, then gradually whisk into the stock to thicken slightly. Season with salt, pepper and mace, taste and add more mushroom ketchup and lemon juice, if necessary.
5. Arrange the collops, overlapping each other, on the serving dish and spoon some sauce down the centre. Garnish with bacon rolls, mushrooms, lemon twists and parsley. Serve remaining sauce separately.

VEAL WITH COURGETTES

Courgettes are grown in Britain, from seed, sown under glass early in the year. Strips of veal, combined with the crispness of the courgettes and the sharpness of grapefruit, makes this a special dish.

SERVES 4

2 grapefruits

30 ml (2 tbsp) vegetable oil

450 g (1 lb) veal fillet in one piece, very thinly sliced

15 g (½ oz) butter

450 g (1 lb) courgettes, thinly sliced

salt and pepper

1. Using a potato peeler, pare rind off one grapefruit. Cut into julienne strips. Squeeze juice and reserve.
2. Using a serrated knife, peel the remaining grapefruit, removing all skin and pith. Thinly slice the flesh and reserve.
3. Heat the oil in a large frying pan. Add the veal slices, a few at a time, and fry for 2–3 minutes until well browned on both sides. Transfer to a warmed serving dish. Cover and keep warm in a low oven.
4. Add the butter to the pan then fry the courgettes for 2–3 minutes until beginning to brown. Add the julienne strips and 90 ml (6 tbsp) of the reserved juice.
5. Bring to the boil then simmer for 4–5 minutes or until the liquid is well reduced. Stir in the reserved flesh and season with salt and pepper to taste.
6. Spoon the contents of the pan over the veal and serve immediately.

VEAL CUTS

Veal is a naturally very lean, tender meat, with virtually no fat or gristle, and many veal cuts contain less than 5% fat.

Veal escalope, cut across the grain of the meat, is one of the most popular cuts (see recipes, pages 137, 139).

Cutlets and rump steaks, good with a creamy mushroom sauce, or with apples, are new additions to the veal range.

Veal braising steak, or pie veal as it is traditionally called, makes a delicious blanquette (see recipe, right) and veal mince is perfect for Veal and Ham Pie and light-textured meatballs.

VEAL AND HAM PIE. A lovely firm, meaty filling, with its surprise centrepiece of hard-boiled egg, is baked in a rich, golden crust.

VEAL AND HAM PIE

COUNTRYWIDE

This raised meat pie with a row of hard-boiled eggs at its centre is traditional British picnic food. The hot-water crust should not be allowed to cool completely before lining the tin. This type of pastry is particularly good for pies as it absorbs the delicious juices inside while keeping its crisp crust outside.

SERVES 8–10

450 g (1 lb) minced veal

100 g (4 oz) boiled ham, minced

30 ml (2 tbsp) chopped fresh parsley

2.5 ml (½ tsp) ground mace

1.25 ml (¼ tsp) ground bay leaves

finely grated rind of 1 lemon

2 medium onions, skinned and finely chopped

salt and pepper

100 g (4 oz) lard, plus extra for greasing tin

350 g (12 oz) plain wholemeal flour

1 egg yolk

3 eggs, hard-boiled and shelled

10 ml (2 tsp) powdered aspic jelly

1. Grease a 1.4 litre (2½ pint) loaf tin and line the base with greased greaseproof paper.
2. Put the first 7 ingredients in a bowl, 5 ml (1 tsp) salt and 1.25 ml (¼ tsp) pepper. Mix well to combine.
3. Put the lard and 200 ml (7 fl oz) water in a saucepan and gently heat until the lard has melted. Bring to the boil, remove from the heat and tip in the flour with 2.5 ml (½ tsp) salt. Beat well to form a soft dough.
4. Beat the egg yolk into the dough. Cover with a damp tea towel and rest in a warm place for 20 minutes, until

the dough is elastic and easy to work. Do not allow the dough to cool.
5. Pat two-thirds of the pastry into the base and sides of the prepared tin, making sure it is evenly distributed. Press in half of the meat mixture and place the eggs down the centre. Fill with the remaining meat mixture.
6. Roll out the remaining pastry for the lid. Cover the pie with the pastry and seal the edges. Use the pastry trimmings to decorate the top, then make 1 large hole in the centre of the pie.
7. Bake at 180°C (350°F) mark 4 for 1½ hours. If necessary, cover the pastry with foil towards the end of cooking to prevent overbrowning. Leave to cool for 3–4 hours.
8. Make up the aspic jelly to 300 ml (½ pint) with water. Cool for about 10 minutes.
9. Pour the liquid aspic through the hole in the top of the pie. Chill the pie for about 1 hour. Leave to stand at room temperature for about 1 hour before removing from the tin.

VEAL BLANQUETTE

THE SOUTH-EAST

Veal is a delicate, tender meat which is not fatty. It should look moist and be a good deep pink colour. This simple recipe provides a creamy sauce which enhances the flavour of the meat without masking it.

SERVES 4–6

✳ at the end of step 3

700 g (1½ lb) pie veal, trimmed and cubed

2 medium onions, skinned and chopped

2 medium carrots, chopped

squeeze of lemon juice

bouquet garni

salt and pepper

25 g (1 oz) butter

45 ml (3 tbsp) plain flour

1 egg yolk

30–45 ml (2–3 tbsp) fresh single cream

4–6 streaky bacon rashers, rinded, rolled and grilled

chopped fresh parsley, to garnish

1. Put the meat, onions, carrots, lemon juice and bouquet garni and seasonings into a large saucepan with enough water to cover. Cover and gently simmer for about 1 hour, until the meat is tender.
2. Strain off the cooking liquid, reserving 568 ml (1 pint) and keep the meat and vegetables warm.
3. Melt the butter in a pan, stir in the flour and cook gently for 1 minute. Remove from the heat and gradually stir in the reserved liquid. Return to the heat, slowly bring to the boil and continue cooking, stirring, until the sauce thickens.
4. Adjust the seasoning, remove from the heat and when slightly cooled stir in the egg yolk and cream. Add the meat and vegetables and reheat without boiling for 5 minutes. Serve garnished with the bacon rolls and parsley.

VEAL ESCALOPES IN MUSHROOM SAUCE

COUNTRYWIDE

Veal is the best choice for this dish, as it has a tenderness and subtle flavour that's hard to beat. If you can't find veal, however, slices of turkey or pork fillet or tenderloin can be used instead. Fromage frais adds smoothness to the sauce.

SERVES 4

4 veal escalopes, each weighing 175 g (6 oz)	
2 slices cooked ham, halved	
50 g (2 oz) butter	
1 stick celery, chopped	
1 eating apple, peeled and chopped	
25 g (1 oz) Cheddar cheese, grated	
1 small onion, skinned and chopped	
100 g (4 oz) button mushrooms, sliced	
25 g (1 oz) plain flour	
300 ml (½ pint) fresh milk	
salt and pepper	
30 ml (2 tbsp) fromage frais	
celery leaves, to garnish	

1. Put each escalope between a sheet of greaseproof paper and beat till thin with a meat mallet or rolling pin.

2. Place a ham slice on each escalope.
3. Melt 15 g (½ oz) of the butter in a large frying pan and lightly fry the celery and apple for 3–4 minutes. Stir in the cheese.
4. Place some of the stuffing on each escalope and roll up, securing with wooden cocktail sticks or fine string or strong cotton.
5. Melt the remaining butter in the pan. Add the veal rolls, brown on all sides and cook for 10 minutes. Remove from the pan, place on a warmed serving plate and keep hot.
6. Add the onion and mushrooms to the pan and cook about 5 minutes, until softened. Stir in the flour and cook for 2 minutes, then gradually add the milk, stirring continuously, until the sauce thickens, boils and is smooth. Simmer for 1–2 minutes. Season to taste.
7. Stir in the fromage frais. Pour the sauce over the escalopes and garnish with celery leaves. Serve at once.

TO MICROWAVE

Complete steps 1 and 2. Melt half the butter in a shallow dish on HIGH for 30 seconds. Add the celery and apple and cook on HIGH for 3 minutes. Stir in the cheese. Complete step 4. Melt remaining butter in the same dish on HIGH for 1 minute, add the veal and cook on HIGH for 3½–4 minutes. Complete the remainder of step 5. Add the onion and mushrooms to the dish, cook on HIGH for 5–7 minutes, then stir in the flour and milk. Cook on HIGH for 4–5 minutes, until boiling and thickened, stirring frequently. Season to taste. Complete step 7.

PORK

ROAST PORK WITH APPLES
COUNTRYWIDE

Crisp crackling is one of the best things about roast pork. To make sure that yours is good and crunchy, score deeply through the skin with a sharp knife, following the natural grain of the meat, then rub in butter and coarse salt before roasting. Baked apples make a delicious accompaniment.

SERVES 6–8

1.6 kg (3½ lb) loin of pork
40 g (1½ oz) butter
coarse salt
fresh rosemary sprig
6 large Cox's Orange Pippin apples, cored
salt and pepper
150 ml (¼ pint) dry white wine (optional)
150 ml (¼ pint) chicken stock
fresh watercress sprigs, to garnish

1. Score the pork rind all over with a sharp knife. Rub with the butter, then sprinkle with coarse salt.
2. Place the rosemary on a rack in a roasting tin, put the pork on top and roast at 180°C (350°F) mark 4 for 2 hours.
3. Season the apples to taste inside and make a shallow cut through the skin around the apples about one third of the way down. Place in a tin or dish and baste with some of the fat from the pork. Cook on a lower shelf for the last 30 minutes of the cooking time.
4. Keep the pork warm on a rack. Drain off most of the fat from the roasting tin, leaving the meat juices. Stir in the wine, if using, loosening the sediment at the bottom of the pan. Boil until almost completely evaporated. Stir in the stock and boil for 2–3 minutes. Strain into a sauceboat.
5. Arrange the apples around the pork, garnish with watercress and serve accompanied by the gravy.

OPPOSITE
ROAST PORK WITH
APPLES. A sprig of rosemary,
placed under the joint during
cooking, imparts a subtle
flavour. Whole baked apples
are an attractive and unusual
alternative to apple sauce.

LEFT
LIKKY PIE. A flavoursome
sauce, enriched with cream
and eggs, is used in the filling
of this pie, which also
contains leeks and tender
cubes of pork.

PORK FILLET IN MUSTARD CREAM SAUCE

THE WEST

A rich dish combining the best of the West – pork, mustard and cream. Take care when flattening the pork not to use the indented side of a meat mallet or it will look battered.

SERVES 4

700 g (1½ lb) pork fillet or tenderloin, cut into 1.25 cm (½ inch) slices

15 g (½ oz) butter

15 ml (1 tbsp) vegetable oil

1 garlic clove, skinned and crushed

150 ml (¼ pint) medium-dry white wine

150 ml (5 fl oz) fresh soured cream

50 ml (2 tbsp) mild wholegrain mustard

salt and pepper

1. Slightly flatten each piece of pork with a rolling pin or meat mallet.
2. Heat the butter and oil in a large frying pan and fry the garlic for 1 minute without browning it. Add the meat and brown on both sides.
3. Push the meat to one side of the pan and pour in the wine. Stir to loosen any sediment at the bottom of the pan, then add the soured cream and mustard. Mix the meat into the sauce and cook for 2–3 minutes, stirring. Season with salt and pepper. Serve hot.

LIKKY PIE

THE WEST

This feast-day dish, more grammatically known as Leek Pie, has a delicate subtle flavour.

SERVES 4

✳ before step 5

225 g (8 oz) leeks, trimmed, sliced and washed

salt and pepper

450 g (1 lb) lean boneless pork, cut into 2.5 cm (1 inch) cubes

150 ml (¼ pint) fresh milk

75 ml (3 fl oz) fresh single cream

2 eggs, lightly beaten

212 g (7½ oz) packet frozen puff pastry, thawed

1. Parboil the leeks in salted water for about 5 minutes. Drain well. Fill a 1.1 litre (2 pint) pie dish with the leeks and pork. Season to taste and pour in the milk.
2. Cover with foil and bake at 200°C (400°F) mark 6 for about 1 hour. (Don't worry if it looks curdled.)
3. Stir the cream into the eggs, then pour into the dish. Allow the pie to cool.
4. Roll out the pastry on a lightly floured surface to 5 cm (2 inches) wider than the dish. Cut a 2.5 cm (1 inch) strip from the outer edge and use to line the dampened rim of the pie dish. Dampen the pastry rim with water, cover with the pastry lid and seal the edges well, then knock up and flute. Make a hole in the centre of the pie and use pastry trimmings to decorate.
5. Bake at 220°C (425°F) mark 7 for about 25–30 minutes, until risen and golden brown.

PORK CUTS

*Boneless prime
pork roasting joints – leg, loin
and shoulder – can contain as
little as 12% fat and are easy to
carve and serve.*

*Smaller boneless pork cuts
include pork fillet or tenderloin
(see recipes, pages 141, 145,
148); shoulder, chump and loin
chops for grilling, frying and
braising; shoulder, loin or leg
steaks which are excellent
braised (see page 143) or cut
into strips for stir-fried dishes.*

*Cubed pork is useful for pies and
casseroles, and pork mince is
delicious in stuffed vegetables
(see recipe, page 147).*

*Cured small pork cuts include
smoked and unsmoked bacon
chops (see recipes, pages 149,
150) – look for the British
Charter Quality Bacon Mark
(see page 151).*

*Also available are ham steaks in
a variety of cures including low-
salt, and thick-cut gammon
rashers and steaks.*

POT ROAST OF PORK AND RED CABBAGE

THE EASTERN COUNTIES

*Pork shoulder is an economical cut that is good for pot
roasting. Cabbage and apple are traditional
accompaniments to pork. Here they are cooked with the
meat and take on a delicious flavour from the juices.*

SERVES 4

45 ml (3 tbsp) red wine vinegar
450 g (1 lb) red cabbage, shredded
225 g (8 oz) cooking apple, peeled, cored and sliced
15 ml (1 tbsp) demerara sugar
15 ml (1 tbsp) plain flour
salt and pepper
700 g (1½ lb) boneless pork shoulder, rinded
chopped fresh parsley, to garnish

1. Bring a large saucepan of water with 15 ml (1 tbsp) of
the vinegar to the boil. When boiling, add the cabbage
and bring back to the boil, then drain well.
2. Place the apple slices and the cabbage in an
ovenproof casserole just wide enough to hold the pork
joint.
3. Add the sugar, the remaining vinegar and the flour.
Season to taste and stir together well.
4. Slash the fat side of the joint several times and
sprinkle with salt and pepper. Place on top of the
cabbage and cover the casserole.
5. Bake at 190°C (375°F) mark 5 for about 1¾ hours or
until the pork is tender. Serve the pork sliced on a
warmed serving platter, surrounded by cabbage.
Garnish with chopped parsley and serve the remaining
cabbage in a serving dish. Accompany with mashed
potatoes.

SOMERSET HONEYED PORK STEW

THE WEST

*Pork lends itself to sweet sauces with a touch of tartness
which counteract the rich flavour of the meat. Pork and
honey go particularly well together. Try to buy Somerset or
other regional honey which has a strong flavour and scent
which recalls the flowers on which the bees have feasted.*

SERVES 4–6

450 g (1 lb) lean belly pork, rinded, boned and cut into chunky cubes
225 g (8 oz) dried black-eye or haricot beans, soaked overnight in cold water
15 ml (1 tbsp) clear honey
568 ml (1 pint) chicken stock
300 ml (½ pint) apple juice

OPPOSITE
PORK STEAKS WITH
PEPPERS. *The interesting
blend of flavours in this bright
and colourful dish cuts
through the richness of the
pork. It is ideal for family
suppers and special occasions
alike.*

1 medium onion, skinned and stuck with a few whole cloves
bouquet garni
3 medium carrots, peeled and sliced
2 leeks, trimmed, sliced and washed
2 celery sticks, sliced
30 ml (2 tbsp) Worcestershire sauce
15 ml (1 tbsp) tomato purée
salt and pepper

1. Cook the pork in a flameproof casserole over a brisk
heat until the fat runs.
2. Drain the beans and add to the pork with the honey,
stock, apple juice, onion and bouquet garni. Slowly
bring to the boil, then cover and simmer for 1 hour or
until the beans are just becoming tender.
3. Add the carrots, leeks and celery to the casserole
with the Worcestershire sauce and tomato purée,
season to taste. Continue simmering for a further
15–30 minutes or until the beans are really tender.
Discard the bouquet garni before serving. Accompany
with crusty bread.

PORK CHOPS WITH CHEESE AND BEER

THE WEST

*This substantial savoury dish combines good home-produced
ingredients. Rutland cheese is an unusual mixture made
from Cheddar, beer, garlic and parsley. If you can't find it,
use plain Cheddar and add garlic and parsley to the mixture.*

SERVES 4

❋ ⊿

4 loin chops, each weighing 175 g (6 oz)
100 g (4 oz) Rutland cheese, grated
5 ml (1 tsp) prepared English mustard
45 ml (3 tbsp) brown ale
tomato halves and watercress sprigs, to garnish

1. Grill the chops under a moderate grill for
7–10 minutes depending on the thickness. Turn over
and grill for 7–10 minutes, until cooked through.
2. Mix together the cheese, mustard and brown ale.
Spread over the chops and grill until the cheese has
melted. Transfer to a warm serving plate and garnish
with tomato halves and watercress sprigs.

TO MICROWAVE

⊿ Remove the fat from the chops. Preheat a large
browning dish on HIGH for 5–8 minutes or according to
manufacturer's instructions. Quickly put the chops in
the browning dish. Cook on HIGH for 5 minutes, turn
over and cook on HIGH for 5 minutes. Stand, covered,
for 5 minutes. Mix together the cheese, mustard and
brown ale, then spread over the chops. Cook on HIGH
for 2 minutes. Complete the remainder of step 2.

FLAVOURED CHEESES

Flavouring cheeses with herbs and spices, and by smoking, is a time-honoured practice. Now some of Britain's best-loved traditional cheeses have been given a new look and taste with some really imaginative flavourings. Choose from these attractively named cheeses, which convey all that's best in British.

RUTLAND

Again from the Vale of Belvoir, Medium flavoured Cheddar with beer, garlic and parsley. Perfect for a ploughman's lunch or Welsh rarebit.

WINDSOR RED

Medium flavoured Cheddar marbled with ruby red elderberry wine from Merrydown in East Sussex. Made in the Vale of Belvoir in the Midlands, home of several fine flavoured cheeses. Serve it with a glass of port, to conclude a special meal.

APPLEWOOD

From Ilchester in Somerset. Medium flavoured Cheddar is treated with natural applewood smoke extract and coated with paprika. Delicious eaten with dessert apples or a wedge of apple pie.

COTSWOLD

Also from the Vale of Belvoir Golden, close-textured Double Gloucester is flavoured with chopped chives and onion. Excellent with crusty bread or in sandwiches. See also Mixed Vegetable Ring (page 215).

WEDMORE

Another Somerset cheese. A semi-hard cheese made from unpasteurised cows' milk, with a band of chopped chives running through it. Available from the farm and a few specialist cheese shops.

SAGE LANCASHIRE

Semi-soft, crumbly, buttery Lancashire cheese flavoured with dried sage. This makes a very tasty salad, or try it in the soufflés on page 92.

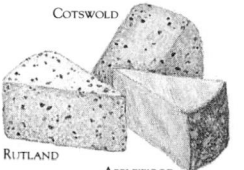

PORK STEAKS WITH PEPPERS

COUNTRYWIDE

A quick and easy dish with a piquant sauce that makes itself. Sweet peppers are grown under glass on a small scale in Britain and these are available from May to October. Choose fresh, bright peppers with firm, unwrinkled skin. Store for a few days if necessary in the salad drawer of the fridge.

SERVES 4

15 ml (1 tbsp) vegetable oil

15 g (½ oz) butter

1 medium onion, skinned and chopped

2.5 cm (1 inch) piece fresh root ginger, peeled and finely grated

1 garlic clove, skinned and crushed

4 boneless pork loin steaks, each weighing 150 g (5 oz)

1 red pepper, seeded and thinly sliced

1 green pepper, seeded and thinly sliced

45 ml (3 tbsp) dry sherry

30 ml (2 tbsp) soy sauce

150 ml (¼ pint) unsweetened pineapple juice

salt and pepper

1. Heat the oil and butter in a large frying pan, add the onion, ginger and garlic and gently fry for 5 minutes, until soft. Push to one side of the pan.
2. Add the steaks and brown on both sides, then add the remaining ingredients and mix thoroughly together.
3. Cover tightly and simmer gently for 8–10 minutes, until the steaks are tender and the peppers are soft. Transfer the steaks and peppers to warmed serving plates. Bring the remaining liquid in the pan to the boil and boil for 2–3 minutes until reduced slightly. Spoon over the steaks and serve with boiled rice.

PORK IN PLUM SAUCE. Fruit works well in offsetting the fattiness of pork, and here the juice from plums, simmered in rosé wine, is used to make an interesting sauce.

the garlic, juniper berries and sage. The milky cooking juices will look curdled, so rub the sauce through a sieve or liquidise in a blender or food processor until smooth. Taste and adjust the seasoning.

4. Carve the pork into thick slices. Pour a little of the sauce over the slices and serve the remaining sauce separately. Garnish with sprigs of sage. Accompany with boiled new potatoes and a green salad.

PORK IN PLUM SAUCE

COUNTRYWIDE

There are many varieties of plum and one type or another should be available from late July through to October. Monarch, a large, black cooking plum, in season from mid-September, would be a good choice, or the widely grown Victoria, which comes into the shops a little earlier, could be used instead. And damsons, if you happen to find them, can also be substituted.

SERVES 4

✳ ◿

450 g (1 lb) plums
300 ml (½ pint) rosé wine
salt and pepper
25 g (1 oz) plain wholemeal flour
700 g (1½ lb) pork fillet or tenderloin, trimmed and cubed
25 g (1 oz) butter
1 large onion, skinned and chopped
175 g (6 oz) white cabbage, shredded
30 ml (2 tbsp) natural yogurt

1. Simmer the plums in the wine for 5 minutes, until tender. Strain, reserving the juice. Remove the stones from the plums and purée half in a blender or food processor.
2. Season the flour, then coat the pork cubes.
3. Melt the butter in a large saucepan or flameproof casserole and lightly fry the onion and cabbage for 3–4 minutes. Add the meat and fry until brown on all sides.
4. Pour in the reserved plum juice and puréed plums, then simmer, uncovered, for 10–15 minutes, until tender. Just before serving add the remaining plums and yogurt and reheat gently.

TO MICROWAVE

◿ Put the plums and wine in a large bowl and cook on HIGH for 3–4 minutes. Complete the remainder of step 1 and step 2. Melt the butter in a large bowl on HIGH for 45 seconds. Add the onion and cabbage and cook on HIGH for 7 minutes, stirring occasionally. Add the pork and cook on HIGH for 3 minutes. Pour in 200 ml (7 fl oz) plum juice and the puréed plums and cook on HIGH for 3–4 minutes, until boiling, stirring occasionally. Cook on LOW for 7–8 minutes, until the pork is tender. Stir in the remaining plums and yogurt. Stand, covered, for 5 minutes.

BRAISED PORK

COUNTRYWIDE

It may seem odd to cook pork in milk but in fact the richness of the milk, coupled with long, slow cooking, produces mouth-wateringly tender results. Loin is a particularly lean cut and can be rather dry if roasted, but this recipe keeps it moist and succulent. And the use of garlic, juniper and sage makes the dish delightfully aromatic.

SERVES 6

15 ml (1 tbsp) vegetable oil
25 g (1 oz) butter
1 kg (2¼ lb) loin of pork, rinded
2 garlic cloves, skinned
1 large onion, skinned and chopped
568 ml (1 pint) fresh milk
5 juniper berries
4 fresh sage sprigs, plus extra for garnish
salt and pepper

1. Heat the oil and the butter in a large saucepan or flameproof casserole into which the meat will just fit. Fry the pork, garlic and onion for about 15 minutes, until the pork is browned on all sides. Add the milk, juniper berries and sage. Season to taste.
2. Bring to the boil, cover and simmer for 1½–2 hours, until the pork is tender and cooked through, turning and basting from time to time.
3. Transfer the pork to a warmed serving dish. Discard

PORK FILLET IN WINE AND CORIANDER

COUNTRYWIDE

Coriander seeds quickly lose their mild, orangy flavour when ground, so try to buy whole seeds to crush yourself.

SERVES 4

※

---

700 g (1½ lb) pork fillet or tenderloin, trimmed and cut into 1.25 cm (½ inch) slices

15 g (½ oz) butter

15 ml (1 tbsp) vegetable oil

1 small green pepper, seeded and sliced into rings

1 medium onion, skinned and chopped

15 g (½ oz) plain flour

15 ml (1 tbsp) coriander seeds, ground

150 ml (¼ pint) chicken stock

150 ml (¼ pint) dry white wine

salt and pepper

---

1. Place the pork between 2 sheets of greaseproof paper and flatten with a mallet or rolling pin until thin.
2. Melt the butter and oil in a large saucepan, add the pork and brown on both sides. Add the pepper and onion and lightly cook for 8–10 minutes, until softened.
3. Stir in the flour and coriander and cook for 1 minute. Gradually add the stock and wine, stirring until the sauce thickens, boils and is smooth. Season to taste. Simmer gently for 5–10 minutes, until the pork is tender and cooked through.

TO MICROWAVE

Complete step 1. Put the butter in a shallow dish and cook on HIGH for 30 seconds. Stir in the pepper and onion and cook on HIGH for 5 minutes. Stir in the flour and coriander and cook on HIGH for 1 minute. Gradually add the stock and wine. Cook on HIGH for 4–5 minutes, stirring frequently, until boiling and thickened. Add the pork and cook on HIGH for 5 minutes, until boiling, stirring occasionally. Cook on LOW for 4 minutes, until the pork is tender and cooked through. Stand, covered, for 5 minutes before serving.

PORK FILLET IN WINE AND CORIANDER. Gently spiced, and given a full-bodied flavour with white wine, this dish needs only plain boiled rice as an accompaniment.

CHICKEN PARCELS. The tasty filling is a simple yet delicious way to use up cooked chicken leftovers.

onion is transparent. Stir in the flour and curry powder and cook, stirring, for 1 minute. Remove from the heat and gradually stir in the stock. Bring to the boil, stirring continuously, then simmer for 2–3 minutes, until thickened.

2. Reduce the heat, add the lemon juice and chicken and season to taste. Leave to cool.

3. When the chicken mixture is cool, roll out the pastry on a lightly floured surface to a 35.5 cm (14 inch) square. Using a sharp knife, cut into 4 squares.

4. Place the pastry on dampened baking sheets, then spoon the chicken mixture on to the pastry, leaving a border round the edges. Brush the edges of each square lightly with water. Fold each square in half and seal and crimp the edges to make a parcel.

5. Make 2 small slashes on the top of each parcel. Brush with beaten egg to glaze.

6. Bake at 220°C (425°F) mark 7 for 15–20 minutes or until the pastry is golden brown. Serve with a mixed salad or Brussels sprouts.

CHICKEN PARCELS
COUNTRYWIDE

These neat puff pastry pasties are filled with a lovely, spicy mixture of chicken chunks, carrots and onion. They are perfect picnic food as they can be made in advance and eaten cold in the fingers, but are also good served hot with accompanying vegetables.

SERVES 4

※

15 g (½ oz) butter
1 small onion, skinned and chopped
2 medium carrots, diced
15 ml (1 tbsp) plain wholemeal flour
5 ml (1 tsp) mild curry powder
300 ml (½ pint) chicken stock
5 ml (1 tsp) lemon juice
225 g (8 oz) boneless cooked chicken, chopped
salt and pepper
368 g (13 oz) packet frozen puff pastry, thawed
beaten egg, to glaze

1. Melt the butter in a large saucepan, add the onion and carrots, cover and cook for 4–5 minutes, until the

CHICKEN WITH GRAPES, LEMON AND CREAM
COUNTRYWIDE

Everyday chicken takes on a note of luxury, in this pretty dish with its garnish of seedless green grapes. The creamy sauce is well flavoured with lemon and herbs, and the recipe is ready in little more than 30 minutes from start to finish.

SERVES 4

15 g (½ oz) butter
15 ml (1 tbsp) vegetable oil
4 chicken breast fillets, skinned, each weighing about 100 g (4 oz)
150 ml (¼ pint) chicken stock
finely grated rind and juice of 1 lemon
5 ml (1 tsp) fresh chopped rosemary or 2.5 ml (½ level tsp) dried
salt and pepper
150 ml (5 fl oz) fresh single cream
225 g (8 oz) seedless green grapes, halved

1. Heat the butter and oil in a large frying pan, add the chicken and cook quickly until lightly browned on both sides.

2. Reduce the heat and add the stock, lemon rind and juice and rosemary. Season to taste, cover and simmer gently for about 10 minutes, until the chicken is tender.

3. Remove the chicken from the pan, cover and keep warm. Boil the cooking juices to reduce a little. Add the chicken, cream and grapes and heat through gently, then adjust seasoning. Serve with noodles or boiled rice.

TO MICROWAVE

☑ Put the butter and oil in a large shallow dish and cook on HIGH for 45 seconds, until melted. Add the chicken, stock, lemon rind and juice, rosemary and seasoning. Cover and cook on HIGH for 6–8 minutes or until the chicken is tender. Remove the chicken from the dish and keep warm. Cook the sauce, uncovered, on HIGH for 3 minutes to reduce slightly, then add the chicken, cream and grapes. Cook on HIGH for 2 minutes. Season to taste and serve.

STIR-FRIED CHICKEN WITH COURGETTES

COUNTRYWIDE

The ancient Chinese art of stir-frying has been a welcome addition to British cooking techniques. It's a speedy, healthy way to cook, as the food is only over the heat for a few minutes and so keeps much of its bite, colour and vitamins.

SERVES 4

☑

30 ml (2 tbsp) vegetable oil

1 garlic clove, skinned and crushed

450 g (1 lb) chicken breast fillets, skinned and cut into thin strips

450 g (1 lb) courgettes, cut into thin strips

1 red pepper, seeded and cut into thin strips

45 ml (3 tbsp) dry sherry

15 ml (1 tbsp) soy sauce

60 ml (4 tbsp) natural yogurt

pepper

1. Heat the oil in a large frying pan or a wok and fry the garlic for 1 minute. Add the chicken and cook for 3–4 minutes, stirring continuously.
2. Add the courgettes and pepper and continue to cook for 1–2 minutes, until the chicken is cooked and the vegetables are tender but still crisp.
3. Stir in the sherry and soy sauce and cook for 1 minute, until hot. Stir in the yogurt and season to taste with pepper. Serve immediately with boiled rice or noodles.

TO MICROWAVE

☑ Put all of the ingredients, except the yogurt, in a large bowl or browning dish. Cook on HIGH for 6–8 minutes, stirring frequently. Stir in the yogurt and serve immediately with boiled rice or noodles.

STIR-FRIED CHICKEN WITH COURGETTES. Beautifully bright, the vegetables keep all their crispness as well as their colour. Succulent strips of chicken are mingled with a soy and sherry sauce.

CHICKEN AND BLUE CHEESE SALAD

COUNTRYWIDE

Blue Cheshire is rich and creamy with an excellent flavour. Other blue cheeses, such as Shropshire Blue or Stilton, could also be used in this recipe. Radishes bought fresh, with the leaves still attached, should be eaten as soon as possible. If pre-packed, however, they will keep for a day or two in the fridge.

SERVES 4

250 g (9 oz) boneless cooked chicken, diced

75 g (3 oz) brown rice, cooked

100 g (4 oz) Blue Cheshire cheese, cubed

50 g (2 oz) radishes, sliced

25 g (1 oz) sultanas

2 celery sticks, sliced

1 Cox's eating apple, cored and diced

15 ml (1 tbsp) lemon juice

150 g (5 oz) natural yogurt

30 ml (2 tbsp) mayonnaise

fresh watercress sprigs and red apple slices, to garnish

1. Mix the chicken, rice, cheese, radishes, sultanas and celery together in a large bowl.
2. Coat the apple in lemon juice, then add to the salad.
3. Mix together the yogurt and mayonnaise and fold into the salad mixture. Cover and chill until ready to serve. Serve in a large salad bowl, garnished with watercress and apple slices.

CHICKEN WITH TARRAGON MAYONNAISE

COUNTRYWIDE

It is important to use fresh tarragon in this dish: dried tarragon is a poor substitute.

SERVES 6

6 chicken breast fillets, skinned

2 celery sticks, trimmed and sliced

200 ml (7 fl oz) dry white wine

30 ml (2 tbsp) chopped fresh tarragon

salt and pepper

300 ml (½ pint) lemon mayonnaise

fresh tarragon sprigs, to garnish

1. Put the chicken breasts in a large frying pan. Add the celery, wine, tarragon, salt and pepper. Cover and simmer for 20–30 minutes until tender. Leave to cool.
2. When cool, strain the juices into a pan and boil rapidly until reduced to 90 ml (6 tbsp). Leave to cool.
3. Arrange the chicken on a serving plate. Stir the reduced marinade into the mayonnaise and spoon over the chicken. Serve, garnished with tarragon.

SALMAGUNDI

· THE NORTH

Salmagundi has been a popular cold dish for centuries, often incorporating other cold meats, fish and a variety of vegetables. This recipe can be made using chicken only and leaving out the duck. Select firm-textured vegetables and arrange the ingredients in ever-widening circles to create an attractive effect.

SERVES 8

1 oven-ready duckling, weighing about 2.3 kg (5 lb), thawed if frozen

salt and pepper

1 oven-ready chicken, weighing about 2 kg (4½ lb), thawed if frozen

450 g (1 lb) carrots, cut into 0.5 cm (¼ inch) wide strips

450 g (1 lb) potatoes, peeled

150 ml (¼ pint) vegetable oil

75 ml (5 tbsp) lemon juice

pinch of mustard powder

pinch of sugar

450 g (1 lb) shelled peas, cooked

1 cucumber, sliced

225 g (8 oz) tomatoes, thinly sliced

4 celery sticks, thinly sliced

4 eggs, hard-boiled (optional)

mayonnaise (optional)

slices of stuffed olives and radishes, to garnish

1. Weigh the duckling, prick the skin all over with a skewer or sharp fork and sprinkle with salt. Place breast-side down on a rack or trivet in a roasting tin. Roast in the top of the oven at 200°C (400°F) mark 6, basting occasionally, for 20 minutes per 450 g (1 lb).
2. Weigh the chicken and sprinkle with salt and pepper. Place in a shallow roasting tin and roast below the duck on the lowest shelf of the oven for 20 minutes per 450 g (1 lb) plus 20 minutes. Cool both for 1–2 hours or until cool enough to handle.
3. Using a sharp knife, make a slit along each side of the breastbone of both the chicken and duck. Remove and discard the skin.
4. Carefully remove all the flesh from the carcasses of both birds. Discard the carcasses and cut the flesh of the birds into thin strips, about 5 cm (2 inches) long.
5. Cook the carrots in boiling salted water for 8 minutes or until just tender. Drain and rinse in cold water. Cook the potatoes in boiling salted water for 15 minutes until tender. Drain and leave to cool, then dice finely.
6. Make the dressing by whisking the oil, lemon juice, mustard and sugar together with salt and pepper to taste.
7. Choose a large oval platter for making up the salmagundi. Place the potato and peas in the bottom of the dish to give a flat base. Arrange the carrot strips or a layer of cucumber on top, following the oval shape of the platter.

8. Pour over a little dressing. Next, arrange a layer of cucumber or carrot, slightly inside the first layer so that it may be easily seen.

9. Top with more layers of chicken meat, peas, tomato slices, celery and duck meat. Make each layer smaller than the previous one so that the lower layers can all be seen. Sprinkle each one with dressing. Continue layering until all the ingredients are used.

10. If using the eggs, shell and halve them, then top each half with a little mayonnaise, if used. Garnish with a few radish slices and stuffed olives, arranged round the edge of the dish.

TO MICROWAVE

☑ Weigh the duckling. Prick the skin all over with a skewer or sharp fork. Place breast-side down on a microwave roasting rack, standing in a dish. Cover with a split roasting bag to prevent spitting. Cook on HIGH for 8 minutes per 450 g (1 lb), turning over halfway through cooking. Leave to cool. Drain the fat from the dish. Weigh the chicken and stand on the roasting rack. Cover with a split roasting bag and cook on HIGH for 8 minutes per 450 g (1 lb). Leave to cool. Complete steps 5 and 6, then complete the recipe from step 3.

SALMAGUNDI. A stunning salad, that uses cold cooked chicken, duck and vegetables. Definitely a dish to make when you're feeding a crowd.

RABBIT CASSEROLE WITH DUMPLINGS. Celery, leek, carrot and bacon add flavour, while herby dumplings give substance to this heart-warming dish.

1. Fry the bacon in a flameproof casserole until the fat runs. Add the rabbit and fry gently until browned. Add the celery, leeks, bay leaf and carrots and mix well. Sprinkle in the wholemeal flour and stir well. Cook for 1 minute, then remove from the heat and gradually add the stock. Bring to the boil, stirring continuously. Season to taste.
2. Cover and bake at 170°C (325°F) mark 3 for about 1½ hours or until the rabbit is tender.
3. To make the dumplings, mix the self-raising flour, suet, chives and salt and pepper together. Add enough cold water to make a soft dough.
4. Twenty to twenty-five minutes before the end of the cooking time, shape the dough into 12 balls and place on top of the casserole. Cover again and bake until the dumplings are well risen and cooked through. Serve immediately with runner beans.

RABBIT IN THE DAIRY

COUNTRYWIDE

Young rabbit is a tender, white meat, which tastes rather like chicken and should not be swamped with strong herbs. This recipe uses milk to enhance the delicacy of flavour, and is deliberately left pale.

SERVES 4

✳ ⬚

1 small celery stick, finely chopped
1 small onion, skinned and finely chopped
25 g (1 oz) cooked ham, finely chopped
8 rabbit joints
salt and pepper
2 bay leaves
300 ml (½ pint) fresh milk

1. Put the celery, onion and ham in an ovenproof casserole. Place the pieces of rabbit on top, season to taste and add the bay leaves.
2. Bring the milk to the boil, then pour over the rabbit. Cover tightly and bake at 170°C (325°F) mark 3 for about 2 hours, until the rabbit is tender. Accompany with broad beans or carrots and boiled new potatoes.

TO MICROWAVE

⬚ Complete step 1. Bring the milk to the boil and pour over the rabbit. Cover and cook on HIGH for 10 minutes, then on MEDIUM for 45 minutes or until the rabbit is tender.

RABBIT CASSEROLE WITH DUMPLINGS

THE EASTERN COUNTIES

Country families were always glad to get their hands on a fresh rabbit to help stretch the week's food. And rabbit still makes a cheap meal, served in a well-flavoured casserole with plenty of vegetables. Dumplings are an East Anglian favourite – to be called a 'Norfolk dumpling' just means you are delightfully plump!

SERVES 4

✳

100 g (4 oz) streaky bacon rashers, rinded and chopped
4 rabbit portions
4 celery sticks, chopped
2 leeks, trimmed, sliced and washed
1 bay leaf
225 g (8 oz) carrots, sliced
30 ml (2 tbsp) plain wholemeal flour
568 ml (1 pint) chicken stock
salt and pepper
75 g (3 oz) self-raising flour
40 g (1½ oz) shredded beef suet
15 ml (1 tbsp) snipped fresh chives

OFFAL

LAMBS' LIVER AND MUSHROOMS

COUNTRYWIDE

A dish that's quick to put together but good enough to serve to guests. Simply fry the lambs' liver and mushrooms for a few minutes before adding tomatoes and an all-important dash of Worcestershire sauce. A flourish of soured cream stirred in at the end of cooking makes the result into something a bit special.

SERVES 3

| 15 g (½ oz) butter |
| 1 medium onion, skinned and sliced |
| 450 g (1 lb) lambs' liver, cut into strips |
| 15 ml (1 tbsp) plain flour |
| 100 g (4 oz) button mushrooms |
| 150 ml (¼ pint) beef stock |
| 4 tomatoes, skinned and roughly chopped |
| 30 ml (2 tbsp) Worcestershire sauce |
| salt and pepper |
| 150 ml (5 fl oz) fresh soured cream |

1. Melt the butter in a large frying pan and gently fry the onion for 5 minutes, until softened.
2. Coat the liver strips with the flour and add to the pan with the mushrooms. Fry for 5 minutes, stirring well, then add the stock and bring to the boil.
3. Stir in the tomatoes and Worcestershire sauce. Season to taste, then simmer for 3–4 minutes. Stir in the soured cream, and reheat without boiling. Serve hot with ribbon noodles.

TO MICROWAVE

Cut the butter into small pieces and melt in a large bowl on HIGH for 30 seconds. Add the onion, cover and cook on HIGH for 5–7 minutes, until softened. Coat the liver in the flour and add to the bowl with the mushrooms. Cover and cook on HIGH for 2–3 minutes or until the liver just changes colour, stirring once. Add the stock, tomatoes, Worcestershire sauce and salt and pepper, re-cover and cook on HIGH for 2–3 minutes or until boiling, stirring once. Stir in the soured cream and serve immediately.

LAMBS' LIVER AND MUSHROOMS. Meltingly tender liver and juicy mushrooms make a mouthwatering combination. Serve with a bed of ribbon noodles.

OFFAL

Offal is extremely tasty, economical and nutritious. Liver and kidney are rich sources of iron and important vitamins; sweetbreads, tripe, heart and brains contribute valuable protein. In the North they're particularly adventurous with offal.

LIVER

Britain's most popular offal. Calves' is a delicacy; less expensive lambs' is excellent with bacon, onions and robust herbs (see Liver with Sage, right). Stronger tasting ox and pigs' liver is best cooked long and slowly or minced in pâtés and faggots (see recipe, right).

KIDNEYS

Calves' and lambs' are delicious grilled, fried or braised. Ox and pig kidney lend superb flavour to meat puddings and pies (see Steak and Kidney Pie, page 130).

HEART

Lambs' and pigs' hearts are best stuffed and casseroled (see recipe, page 180).

SWEETBREADS

These come from calves and lambs. Calves' are most delicate, lambs' most widely available.

BRAINS

Sold in 'sets'; lamb's serves 1; calf's or ox 2. Prepare as sweetbreads.

TRIPE

Ox stomach lining. Sold dressed (bleached), tripe is stewed with onions (see recipe, page 182), cooked in milk or crumbed and fried.

TONGUE

Sliced ready-cooked ox tongue is probably most familiar. Tongue is also delicious hot with caper, herb or Cumberland sauce (see recipe, page 165).

OXTAIL

Oxtail needs long, slow cooking to produce rich gravy (see recipe, page 180) and also makes one of Britain's favourite soups.

TROTTERS

Calves' and pigs' feet produce protein-rich jelly. Calves' feet are traditionally used to make aspic.

WELSH FAGGOTS

WALES

These are also known as 'poor man's goose' or 'savoury duck' and are a traditional, filling and economical dish. The word faggots is a corruption of fegato, the Italian for liver.

SERVES 4

450 g (1 lb) pigs' liver
2 medium onions, skinned
75 g (3 oz) shredded beef suet
100 g (4 oz) fresh breadcrumbs
5 ml (1 tsp) finely chopped fresh sage or 2.5 ml (½ tsp) dried sage
salt and pepper
300 ml (½ pint) boiling beef stock

1. In a food processor or blender, finely chop the liver with the onions. Stir in the suet, breadcrumbs and sage. Season to taste.
2. Roll the mixture into 12 balls and place them in a well-greased, shallow ovenproof dish.
3. Pour the stock into the dish, cover and bake at 180°C (350°F) mark 4 for about 30 minutes, until the juices run clear. Uncover and continue cooking for 10 minutes. Traditionally faggots are served with a purée of dried peas.

TO MICROWAVE

Complete steps 1 and 2. Pour 150 ml (¼ pint) boiling stock into the dish, cover and cook on HIGH for 12–14 minutes or until cooked through. Uncover and brown under a hot grill.

LIVER WITH SAGE

COUNTRYWIDE

Calves' liver, with its meltingly tender texture, would be ideal in this dish, but it's not always easy to find and tends to be pricey. Lambs' liver also gives excellent results. If you can, use fresh sage; the flavour is not as subtle with dried.

SERVES 4

25 g (1 oz) butter
1 medium onion, skinned and chopped
30 ml (2 tbsp) chopped fresh sage or 5 ml (1 tsp) dried
450 g (1 lb) liver, sliced
25 g (1 oz) plain wholemeal flour
300 ml (½ pint) fresh milk
salt and pepper

1. Melt the butter in a medium saucepan and fry the onion and sage for 3 minutes. Coat the liver in the flour, then add to the pan and cook for 3 minutes on one side. Turn over and cook for a further 3 minutes.
2. Gradually stir in the milk and bring to the boil,

stirring, until the sauce thickens, boils and is smooth. Season to taste. Cook for 1–2 minutes. Serve with jacket potatoes or rice and a green vegetable.

TO MICROWAVE

Melt the butter in a shallow dish on HIGH for 45 seconds. Add the onions and sage and cook, covered, on HIGH for 5 minutes. Add the liver coated in flour and cook, covered, on HIGH for 2 minutes, then turn and cook on HIGH for a further 2 minutes. Gradually add the milk and cook on HIGH for 4–5 minutes, until boiling and thickened, stirring frequently. Serve with jacket potatoes or rice and a green vegetable.

STIR-FRIED LIVER WITH CABBAGE AND CARAWAY

COUNTRYWIDE

Take a tip from the Chinese and try stir-frying to keep vegetables crisp and meat moist. It takes just a few minutes from start to finish to cook this inexpensive dish, in which apple and caraway seeds add to the flavour.

SERVES 4

450 g (1 lb) lambs' liver, thinly sliced
15 g (½ oz) butter
15 ml (1 tbsp) vegetable oil
350 g (12 oz) green cabbage, finely shredded
1 large onion, skinned and chopped
1 Discovery or Crispin apple, quartered, cored and thinly sliced
15 ml (1 tbsp) caraway seeds
30 ml (2 tbsp) cider vinegar
15 ml (1 tbsp) demerara sugar

1. Cut the liver into narrow 5 cm (2 inch) strips.
2. Heat the butter and oil in a large deep frying pan or wok. Brown the liver a few pieces at a time, stirring all the time – don't overcook them, the centres should be juicy. Remove with a slotted spoon.
3. Stir the cabbage and onions into the pan. Stir over a high heat for 4–5 minutes, until the vegetables begin to soften.
4. Add the apple, caraway seeds, vinegar and sugar. Continue to cook, stirring, over a moderate heat for 1–2 minutes. Return the liver to the pan, season and reheat very quickly. Serve immediately.

TO MICROWAVE

Complete step 1. Put the butter and oil in a large bowl and cook on HIGH for 2 minutes or until melted and hot. Add the liver and cook on HIGH for 2 minutes or until it just changes colour, stirring once. Remove with a slotted spoon. Add the onion, cover and cook on HIGH for 2 minutes, then add the cabbage, apple, caraway seeds, vinegar and sugar. Cover and continue to cook on HIGH for 2 minutes or until the cabbage is softened. Add the liver, re-cover and cook on HIGH for 2 minutes or until hot. Season and serve immediately.

CHICKEN LIVERS IN SHERRY CREAM SAUCE

COUNTRYWIDE

Rich chicken livers have a very moist, crumbly texture. This dish can be served in small quantities as a starter, or as a main course. If grapes are not available, substitute with 25 g (1 oz) sultanas.

SERVES 2

225 g (8 oz) chicken livers, thawed if frozen

25 g (1 oz) plain flour

salt and pepper

25 g (1 oz) butter

75 ml (3 fl oz) sherry

50 ml (2 fl oz) chicken stock

50 g (2 oz) black or green seedless grapes, halved

150 ml (5 fl oz) fresh soured cream

1. Coat the livers in well-seasoned flour.
2. Melt the butter in a medium frying pan and fry the livers with any remaining flour for about 4 minutes, stirring once or twice. Gradually stir in the sherry and stock and simmer for 1–2 minutes.
3. Add the grapes and soured cream. Heat through gently and serve hot with brown rice.

TO MICROWAVE

Complete step 1. Melt the butter in a large shallow dish on HIGH for 45 seconds. Add the livers with any remaining flour and cook on HIGH for 2 minutes, stirring occasionally. Gradually add the sherry and stock and cook on HIGH for 3 minutes, stirring occasionally. Add the grapes and cream and cook on HIGH for 1 minute. Serve hot with brown rice.

CHICKEN LIVERS IN SHERRY CREAM SAUCE. Extremely quick to make, this is an ideal – and very tasty – supper dish.

flour, the stock, red wine, tomato purée, lemon rind and bay leaves and season well. Bring to the boil and replace the meat. Cover and simmer for 3 hours, then skim well.

3. Stir the carrots and parsnips into the casserole. Re-cover the casserole and simmer for a further ½ hour, until the meat is quite tender.

4. Skim all fat off the surface of the casserole, adjust seasoning and garnish with parsley. Accompany with plain boiled or mashed potatoes and crisply cooked winter cabbage.

STUFFED HEARTS

THE NORTH

This traditional recipe for lambs' hearts was originally called Love in Disguise, one of the many fancy names given to offal dishes to mask their origins. The fresh, zesty stuffing ingredients complement the meaty taste of their casings.

SERVES 4

✳ ⩘

| 4 lambs' hearts |
| 40 g (1½ oz) butter |
| 1 small onion, skinned and chopped |
| 50 g (2 oz) fresh wholemeal breadcrumbs |
| finely grated rind of 1 lemon |
| 15 ml (1 tbsp) chopped fresh sage or 2.5 ml (½ tsp) dried |
| pinch of freshly grated nutmeg |
| salt and pepper |
| 1 egg yolk |
| 30 ml (2 tbsp) plain flour |
| 450 ml (¾ pint) chicken stock |
| 45 ml (3 tbsp) dry sherry |
| chopped fresh sage and grated lemon rind, to garnish |

1. Wash the hearts thoroughly under running cold water. Trim and remove any ducts.

2. Melt 15 g (½ oz) of the butter in a large frying pan and lightly fry the onion for about 5 minutes, until softened. Remove from the heat and stir in the breadcrumbs, lemon rind, sage and nutmeg. Season to taste. Bind with the egg yolk and mix well.

3. Fill the hearts with the stuffing and sew up neatly with strong cotton or fine string. Coat them in the flour.

4. Heat the remaining butter in a flameproof casserole and brown the hearts well. Pour over the stock and sherry, season well and bring to the boil.

5. Cover and bake at 150°C (300°F) mark 2 for about 2 hours or until tender. Serve the hearts sliced and pour the skimmed juices over. Garnish with the sage and lemon rind. Accompany with mashed potatoes and red cabbage with pears (see recipe, page 228).

TO MICROWAVE

⩘ Complete steps 1, 2, 3 and 4. Transfer to a large bowl, cover and cook on MEDIUM for 1 hour or until tender. Complete the remainder of step 5.

BRAISED OXTAIL. The meat has a flavour all its own that's unbeatable. A really sustaining casserole, best served in the coldest months to keep the chill at bay.

BRAISED OXTAIL

COUNTRYWIDE

Cook long and cook slow – that's the rule for oxtail. And all those hours spent simmering will be amply repaid when you taste the rich tender meat and juices. If you cook it the day before, the cooled fat is much easier to remove.

SERVES 4

✳

| 2 small oxtails, total weight about 1.4 kg (3 lb), trimmed and cut into pieces |
| 30 ml (2 tbsp) plain flour |
| salt and pepper |
| 15 g (½ oz) butter |
| 15 ml (1 tbsp) vegetable oil |
| 2 large onions, skinned and sliced |
| 900 ml (1½ pints) beef stock |
| 150 ml (¼ pint) dry red wine |
| 15 ml (1 tbsp) tomato purée |
| finely grated rind of ½ lemon |
| 2 bay leaves |
| 225 g (8 oz) carrots, thickly sliced |
| 450 g (1 lb) parsnips, peeled and cut into chunks |
| chopped fresh parsley, to garnish |

1. Coat the oxtail pieces in the flour, seasoned with salt and pepper. Heat the butter and oil in a large flameproof casserole and brown the oxtail pieces, a few at a time. Remove with a slotted spoon.

2. Add the onions to the casserole and fry for 5 minutes, until lightly brown. Stir in any remaining

CREAMED SWEETBREADS

COUNTRYWIDE

Sweetbreads, although considered a great delicacy, are not always readily available, so you may have to order them from your butcher. Soaking helps to keep them white. The sauce is deliberately kept fairly mild, so that the delicate flavour of the sweetbreads can be enjoyed to the full.

SERVES 4

450 g (1 lb) sweetbreads
1 small onion, skinned and chopped
1 medium carrot, chopped
few fresh parsley stalks
1 bay leaf
salt and pepper
40 g (1½ oz) butter
60 ml (4 tbsp) plain flour
300 ml (½ pint) fresh milk
squeeze of lemon juice
chopped fresh parsley, to garnish

1. Rinse and soak the sweetbreads in cold water for 2 hours. Drain and remove any fat attached.
2. Put the sweetbreads, vegetables, herbs and salt and pepper in a saucepan with water to cover, then simmer gently for about 15 minutes, until the sweetbreads are tender. Drain, reserving 300 ml (½ pint) of the cooking liquid, and keep hot.
3. Put the butter, flour, milk and reserved stock in a saucepan. Heat, whisking continuously, until the sauce thickens, boils and is smooth. Simmer for 1–2 minutes. Season to taste and add the lemon juice.
4. Add the sweetbreads to the sauce and simmer gently for 5–10 minutes. Garnish with parsley and serve at once with new potatoes and a green vegetable.

TO MICROWAVE

Put the sweetbreads, vegetables, herbs and salt and pepper in a medium bowl with 300 ml (½ pint) water. Cover and cook on HIGH for 8–10 minutes or until cooked. Remove the sweetbreads and vegetables with a slotted spoon and set aside while cooking the sauce. Add the butter, flour and milk to the cooking liquid and cook on HIGH for 5–6 minutes, until boiling, whisking frequently. Add the sweetbreads and vegetables, cover and cook on HIGH for 2–3 minutes to reheat. Add lemon juice and salt and pepper to taste. Complete step 4.

CREAMED SWEETBREADS. Beautifully tender and served in a simple sauce, sweetbreads make an appetising and unusual dish.

TRIPE AND ONIONS
THE NORTH

Lancashire claims to be the home of tripe and onions, an inexpensive and filling dish. Tripe is the stomach linings of an ox; the first stomach's lining is called blanket, the second honeycomb and the third thick seam. They all taste the same, only the appearance is different. Tripe is always sold dressed and parboiled.

SERVES 4

✳

450 g (1 lb) dressed tripe, washed
3 medium onions, skinned and sliced
568 ml (1 pint) fresh milk
pinch of grated nutmeg
1 bay leaf (optional)
salt and pepper
25 g (1 oz) butter
45 ml (3 tbsp) plain flour
chopped fresh parsley, to garnish

1. Put the tripe in a saucepan and cover with cold water. Bring to the boil, then drain and rinse under running cold water. Cut into 2.5 cm (1 inch) pieces.
2. Put the tripe, onions, milk, nutmeg, bay leaf (if using) and salt and pepper into the rinsed out pan. Bring to the boil, cover and simmer for about 2 hours, until tender. Strain off the liquid and reserve 600 ml (1 pint).
3. Melt the butter in a saucepan, stir in the flour and cook gently for 1 minute, stirring. Remove pan from the heat and gradually stir in the reserved cooking liquid. Bring to the boil and continue to cook, stirring, until the sauce thickens.
4. Add the tripe and onions and reheat. Adjust the seasoning and serve sprinkled with parsley.

BRAISED KIDNEYS IN PORT
COUNTRYWIDE

Tender lambs' kidneys are quick to cook and at their best when served in a richly flavoured sauce.

SERVES 3

✳

8 lambs' kidneys
25 g (1 oz) butter
1 medium onion, skinned and sliced
100 g (4 oz) mushrooms, sliced
45 ml (3 tbsp) plain flour
150 ml (¼ pint) port
150 ml (¼ pint) chicken stock
15 ml (1 tbsp) chopped fresh parsley
bouquet garni
salt and pepper

1. Skin the kidneys, then cut each one in half lengthways. Snip out the cores with scissors.
2. Heat the butter in a large frying pan or flameproof casserole and fry the onion for 3–4 minutes, until softened. Add the mushrooms and fry for a further 3–4 minutes.
3. Stir in the kidneys and cook for 5 minutes, stirring occasionally.
4. Stir in the flour, then gradually stir in the port and stock. Slowly bring to the boil. Stir in the parsley and bouquet garni. Season to taste.
5. Cover and simmer for 15 minutes, stirring occasionally. Remove the bouquet garni and serve hot with boiled rice or mashed potatoes and a mixed salad.

TO MICROWAVE

Put the butter and onion in a large bowl. Cover and cook on HIGH for 5–7 minutes, until the onion is softened, stirring occasionally. Meanwhile, complete step 1. Stir in the mushrooms and the kidneys to the softened onion, re-cover and cook on HIGH for 3–4 minutes, until the kidneys just change colour. Sprinkle in the flour, then gradually add the port, stock, parsley, bouquet garni and salt and pepper. Re-cover and cook on HIGH for 7–8 minutes or until the kidneys are tender, stirring occasionally. Complete the remainder of step 5.

TONGUE AND MUSHROOM SUPPER
COUNTRYWIDE

Don't think of tongue just as a cold meat – it's delicious in hot dishes, too. Choose cooked sliced ox tongue for this recipe, in which onions and mushrooms, plus a creamy egg mixture, keep the meat from drying out during cooking.

SERVES 4

15 g (½ oz) butter
30 ml (2 tbsp) chopped fresh parsley
1 small onion, skinned and chopped
100 g (4 oz) mushrooms, sliced
15 ml (1 tbsp) chopped gherkins
100 g (4 oz) sliced tongue, quartered
salt and pepper
15 ml (1 tbsp) plain flour
2 eggs, beaten
150 ml (¼ pint) fresh milk
65 ml (2½ fl oz) fresh single cream

1. Melt the butter in a saucepan and lightly fry the parsley, onion and mushrooms for 3 minutes, then stir in the gherkin.
2. Grease a 20.5 cm (8 inch) flan dish and put the tongue in the base. Cover with the onion and mushroom mixture, then season to taste.

BRAISED KIDNEYS IN PORT
Cut kidneys in half, then use sharp knife to cut out the core.

CREAMED KIDNEYS IN WINE. Use wine and cream to add flavour and a silky texture to inexpensive kidneys, and the result is a dish that's in a class of its own.

3. Blend the flour with the eggs and beat in the milk and cream. Pour into the dish.
4. Bake at 190°C (375°F) mark 5 for 40 minutes. Serve hot or cold with mashed potatoes and sliced beetroot.

TO MICROWAVE

 Melt the butter in a small bowl on HIGH for 30 seconds. Add the parsley, onion and mushrooms and cook on HIGH for 4 minutes. Put the gherkins and tongue in a 20.5 cm (8 inch) glass flan dish and add the mushroom mixture. Complete step 3. Cook on HIGH for 15 minutes, then stand, covered, for 5 minutes. Complete the remainder of step 4.

CREAMED KIDNEYS IN WINE
COUNTRYWIDE

Use lambs' kidneys, which are the smallest available and always juicy and tender, in this very speedy dish.

SERVES 4

25 g (1 oz) butter
12 lambs' kidneys, cored and halved
225 g (8 oz) mushrooms, sliced
3 celery sticks, diced
1 medium onion, skinned and finely chopped
25 g (1 oz) plain flour
300 ml (½ pint) dry red wine
5 ml (1 tsp) mustard powder
salt and pepper
150 ml (5 fl oz) fresh double cream

1. Melt the butter in a medium saucepan. Add the kidneys, mushrooms, celery and onion and fry gently for 10 minutes, until tender.
2. Stir in the flour and cook for 1–2 minutes. Gradually stir in the wine, mustard and salt and pepper. Cook for a further 5 minutes. Stir in the cream and gently reheat. Serve on a bed of boiled rice with a green vegetable.

TO MICROWAVE

 Melt the butter in a large bowl on HIGH for 45 seconds. Add the kidneys, mushrooms, celery and onion. Cook, covered, on HIGH for 10 minutes. Stir in the flour and cook on HIGH for 1 minute. Gradually stir in the wine, mustard and salt and pepper. Cook on HIGH for 3 minutes until boiling and thickened, stirring occasionally. Stir in the cream and cook on HIGH for 30 seconds. Complete the remainder of step 2.

FISH & SHELLFISH

COD IN A SPICY YOGURT CRUST

COUNTRYWIDE

Everyday cod takes on a touch of the Middle East in this recipe. A delicious mixture of herbs and spices is added to the yogurt marinade, which forms a crisp coating to the fish when grilled. Haddock could be used instead of cod, and either steaks or fillets would be equally suitable in this dish.

SERVES 4

30 ml (2 tbsp) chopped fresh mint
1 medium onion, or 2 large spring onions, skinned and roughly chopped
2 garlic cloves, skinned and crushed
5 ml (1 tsp) paprika
30 ml (2 tbsp) coriander seeds
10 ml (2 tsp) ground cumin
10 ml (2 tsp) dried dill
150 g (5 oz) natural yogurt
salt and pepper
4 thick cod or haddock steaks or fillets, each weighing about 225 g (8 oz)

1. First make the marinade mixture. Put the mint, onion, garlic, paprika, coriander, cumin, dill and yogurt in a blender or food processor and process until a thick paste is formed. Season the mixture to taste with salt and pepper.
2. Place the fish in a single layer in a shallow dish.
3. Spread the paste all over the top of the fish and leave in a cool place to marinate for 2–3 hours.
4. Cook under a hot grill, basting occasionally, until the fish is cooked and the yogurt mixture has formed a crust. Serve straight away with rice and chutney, accompanied by a green salad.

CREAMED FISH PIE

COUNTRYWIDE

Firm, juicy cod is used for the filling of this warming pie. Caraway seeds add interest and flavour to the sauce, and the dish has a creamy topping of mashed potato which is baked until well browned and appetising. Coley could be used for a more economical version.

SERVES 4

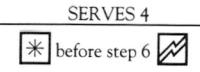 before step 6

450 g (1 lb) cod fillets, skinned
100 g (4 oz) button mushrooms
1 bay leaf
300 ml (½ pint) fresh milk, plus 60 ml (4 tbsp)
25 g (1 oz) butter
25 g (1 oz) plain flour
2.5 ml (½ tsp) caraway seeds
salt and pepper
700 g (1½ lb) potatoes, peeled and diced
1 egg

1. Place the cod, mushrooms and bay leaf in a saucepan. Pour over the 300 ml (½ pint) milk and bring to the boil. Cover lightly and simmer for 15–20 minutes or until the fish is just cooked. Drain, reserving the cooking liquor. Discard the bay leaf and flake the fish, discarding any bones. Set the fish aside while making the sauce.
2. Melt the butter in a saucepan. Add the flour and cook gently, stirring, for 1–2 minutes. Remove from the heat and gradually stir in the reserved milk. Bring to the boil, stirring continuously, until the sauce thickens, boils and is smooth. Stir in the caraway seeds. Simmer for 1–2 minutes.
3. Add the flaked fish and mushrooms to the sauce. Season to taste. Spoon into a shallow 1.4 litre (2½ pint) ovenproof serving dish. Set aside.
4. Cook the potatoes in boiling salted water for 20–30 minutes or until very tender. Drain the potatoes thoroughly.
5. Mash the potatoes and remaining milk with a potato masher. Beat in the egg and season to taste. Spoon evenly over the fish mixture.
6. Bake at 200°C (400°F) mark 6 for about 35 minutes, until golden brown.

TO MICROWAVE

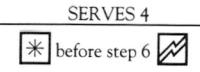 Put the cod, mushrooms and bay leaf in a shallow dish. Pour over the milk, cover and cook on HIGH for 3–4 minutes or until the fish is cooked. Complete the remainder of step 1. Put the butter, flour, reserved milk and caraway seeds in a medium bowl and cook on HIGH for 3–4 minutes, until the sauce has boiled and thickened, whisking frequently. Complete the remainder of step 3. Put the potatoes in a medium bowl with 30 ml (2 tbsp) water. Cover and cook on HIGH for 10–12 minutes or until very tender. Drain well. Complete step 5. Cook on HIGH for 4–5 minutes to heat through, then brown under a hot grill.

FISH CAKES WITH HERBS

THE NORTH

Fish cakes are an economical way of making fish go further. You can, if necessary, replace some of the fish with more breadcrumbs but check the seasoning carefully to make sure the finished cakes don't taste too bland. The addition of herbs gives flavour and also produces attractive green flecks.

SERVES 4

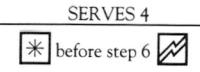

275 g (10 oz) haddock, skinned and boned
15 ml (1 tbsp) lemon juice
15 ml (1 tbsp) Worcestershire sauce
15 ml (1 tbsp) creamed horseradish
100 ml (4 fl oz) fresh milk
15 ml (1 tbsp) snipped fresh chives
15 ml (1 tbsp) chopped fresh parsley
350 g (12 oz) potatoes, cooked and mashed
50 g (2 oz) fresh wholemeal breadcrumbs

1. Purée the fish in a blender or food processor with the lemon juice, Worcestershire sauce and horseradish. Stir in the milk, chives, parsley and potatoes.
2. Shape the mixture into 4 fish cakes and coat with breadcrumbs.
3. Grill under a moderate heat for 5 minutes on each side, until browned. Serve with a tomato sauce and salad.

ABOVE
FISH CAKES WITH HERBS. Everyday favourites, that taste all the better for the clever use of flavouring. Horseradish, Worcestershire sauce, lemon juice and herbs each add their own distinctive note.

OPPOSITE
COD IN A SPICY YOGURT CRUST. A sensational way to add a little something extra to cod, by cooking it in a thick coating of beautifully spiced yogurt.

ROUND WHITE FISH

COD

Season June to February. Good baked, braised, poached, shallow-fried or grilled – especially in kebabs, as the firm flesh cubes well. Goes well with strong accompanying flavours like garlic and herbs (see recipe, page 184) and various sauces. Also available smoked, as is the roe (see Cod's Roe Ramekins, page 90).

HADDOCK

Season May to February. Good flavour and flakes well, so excellent in kedgeree (see recipe, page 198). Delicious fried in batter with chips or baked with egg sauce. Smoked haddock is sold in fillets (these make a lovely soufflé) or on the bone as Finnan haddies (see Cullen Skink, page 84) or the smaller Arbroath smokies.

HAKE

Season June to March. Very firm white flesh, shown to advantage in a fish salad, perhaps accompanied by a garlicky mayonnaise.

POLLACK

Season May to September. May be cooked like cod, to which it is related, though has less delicate flavour. Excellent in mixed fish chowder.

WHITING

Season June to February. Abundant and cheap most of the year. Sold whole or in fillets. Good shallow-fried or in mousses.

COLEY

Season August to February. Member of the cod family. Flesh darkish grey but turns white when cooked. Good choice for fish pie or casserole (see recipe, page 186).

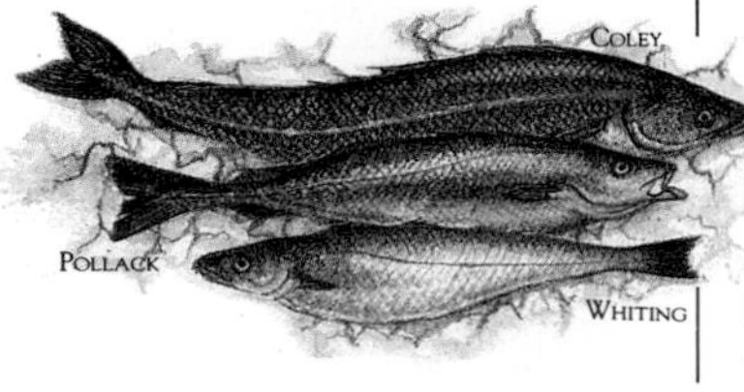

HOT FISH LOAF
COUNTRYWIDE

Hake, a cousin of cod, is available all year round. It has a good, flaky texture and is ideally suited to this recipe, where the flavour is sparked up with prawns, garlic and anchovy essence to make a tasty loaf, served with a cheese sauce.

SERVES 4–6

65 g (2½ oz) butter
1 garlic clove, skinned and crushed
75 ml (5 tbsp) plain flour
750 ml (1¼ pints) fresh milk
550 g (1¼ lb) hake fillets, skinned and chopped
150 ml (5 fl oz) fresh whipping cream
10 ml (2 tsp) anchovy essence
3 eggs
1 egg yolk
salt and pepper
30 ml (2 tbsp) chopped fresh parsley
100 g (4 oz) shelled prawns, chopped
50 g (2 oz) mature Cheddar cheese, grated
watercress sprigs and 6 whole prawns, to garnish

1. Lightly butter and base line a 1.6 litre (2¾ pint) loaf tin or terrine.
2. Melt 40 g (1½ oz) of the butter in a saucepan. Add the garlic. Stir in 45 ml (3 tbsp) of the flour and cook gently, stirring, for 2 minutes. Remove from the heat and gradually stir in 450 ml (¾ pint) of the milk. Bring to the boil, stirring constantly, then simmer for 2 minutes until thick and smooth.
3. In a blender or food processor, purée the sauce, raw chopped fish, cream, anchovy essence, eggs and yolk. Season lightly.
4. Spoon half the fish mixture into the tin. Sprinkle with parsley and half the prawns. Spoon in the rest of the fish mixture. Cover tightly with buttered greaseproof paper.
5. Place in a roasting tin with hot water to come halfway up the sides of the terrine. Cook in the oven at 150°C (300°F) mark 2 for about 1¾ hours.
6. Just before the terrine is cooked, make the sauce. Put the remaining 25 g (1 oz) butter, 30 ml (2 tbsp) flour and remaining milk in a saucepan. Heat, whisking continuously, until the sauce thickens, boils and is smooth. Simmer for 1–2 minutes. Stir in the grated cheese and remaining prawns. Season to taste.
7. Invert the loaf on to a warm serving dish and tilt slightly to drain off juice. Remove cooking container. Spoon a little sauce over terrine and garnish with watercress and prawns. Serve the rest separately.

TO MICROWAVE

Put 40 g (1½ oz) of the butter, garlic, flour and 450 ml (¾ pint) milk in a large bowl and cook on HIGH for 5–6 minutes, whisking frequently until boiling and thickened. Complete step 3. Complete step 4,

spooning the mixture into a 1.7 litre (3 pint) microwave loaf dish. Stand the loaf dish on a roasting rack and cook on MEDIUM for 20 minutes until firm to the touch. Complete the recipe.

SOMERSET FISH CASSEROLE
THE WEST

Cider is a flavoursome – and British – alternative to white wine when cooking fish. Its robust taste makes it a good partner for the stronger brill or coley suggested in the recipe. For a more pronounced cider flavour use slightly more than suggested and boil it down to the required quantity.

SERVES 4

900 g (2 lb) brill or coley fillets, skinned
50 g (2 oz) plain flour
salt and pepper
65 g (2½ oz) butter
1 medium onion, skinned and finely chopped
300 ml (½ pint) dry cider
10 ml (2 tsp) anchovy essence
15 ml (1 tbsp) lemon juice
1 eating apple
chopped fresh parsley, to garnish

1. Cut the fish into 5 cm (2 inch) chunks, then coat the chunks in 25 g (1 oz) of the flour, seasoned with salt and pepper.
2. Melt 25 g (1 oz) of the butter in a medium saucepan and cook the onion gently for 5 minutes, until softened. Add the fish and cook for a further 3 minutes or until lightly browned on all sides. Remove the fish and onion to a buttered ovenproof serving dish.
3. To make the sauce, add 25 g (1 oz) of the butter to that remaining in the pan, then add the remaining flour and cook, stirring, for 1 minute. Gradually stir in the cider, anchovy essence and lemon juice. Bring to the boil, stirring continuously, then simmer for 2–3 minutes, until thick and smooth.
4. Pour the sauce over the fish and cook in the oven at 180°C (350°F) mark 4 for 20 minutes.
5. Meanwhile, peel, core and slice the apple into rings, then fry the apple rings in the remaining butter for 1–2 minutes. Drain on kitchen paper and use to top the fish. Serve garnished with chopped parsley.

TO MICROWAVE

Put the onion and butter in a large bowl. Cover and cook on HIGH for 5–7 minutes, until softened. Sprinkle in the flour, then add the cider, anchovy essence and lemon juice and cook on HIGH for 4–5 minutes, until the sauce has boiled and thickened, whisking frequently. Stir in the fish, cover and cook on HIGH for 5–6 minutes, until the fish is tender, stirring occasionally. Meanwhile complete step 5.

SKATE WITH CAPERS

COUNTRYWIDE

Skate has a soft, pinkish tinge. The wings may look bony but in fact the bones are soft and gelatinous, and the flesh is easily picked off them when the fish is cooked. The delicacy of the flavour is perfectly complemented by the sharp piquancy of capers.

SERVES 4

2 skate wings, each weighing about 550 g (1¼ lb), halved

salt
50 g (2 oz) butter
45 ml (3 tbsp) drained capers
30 ml (2 tbsp) vinegar from the capers

1. Put the skate in a roasting tin and cover with salted water. Bring to the boil, then simmer for 10–15 minutes, until tender.
2. Meanwhile, melt the butter in a small saucepan and cook until it turns golden brown. Add the capers and vinegar and cook until bubbling.
3. Drain the fish and place on serving plates. Pour over the sauce and serve at once, accompanied with boiled new potatoes and peas.

SKATE WITH CAPERS. This buttery, pleasantly acidic sauce is an ideal complement to the flavour of skate.

MONKFISH AND MUSSEL SKEWERS

COUNTRYWIDE

The bright ochre of mussels adds a dash of colour to the barbecue, and monkfish has a firm texture and a delicious flavour that lend themselves well to a simple cooking method. Keep the skewers well brushed with butter while grilling to prevent them from drying out.

SERVES 6

MONKFISH AND MUSSEL SKEWERS. Bacon goes surprisingly well with the lovely fishy flavours of these tasty kebabs.

12 streaky bacon rashers, rinded and halved
900 g (2 lb) monkfish, skinned, boned and cut into 2.5 cm (1 inch) cubes
36 frozen cooked mussels, thawed
25 g (1 oz) butter
60 ml (4 tbsp) chopped fresh parsley
finely grated rind and juice of 1 large lemon
4 garlic cloves, skinned and crushed
salt and pepper
shredded lettuce and lemon slices, to garnish

1. Roll the bacon rashers up neatly. Thread the cubed fish, mussels and bacon alternately on to 12 oiled skewers.
2. Melt the butter in a saucepan, remove from the heat, then add the parsley, lemon rind and juice and garlic. Season to taste. (Take care when adding salt as both the mussels and the bacon are naturally salty.)
3. Place the skewers on an oiled grill. Brush with the

butter mixture, then grill under a moderate grill for 15 minutes. Turn the skewers frequently during cooking and brush with the butter mixture with each turn. Alternatively, cook over hot coals on a barbecue rack.

4. Arrange the hot skewers on a serving platter lined with shredded lettuce. Garnish with lemon slices and serve at once with any remaining flavoured butter and saffron rice, if liked.

HADDOCK IN BUTTER SAUCE
COUNTRYWIDE

You can usually find haddock on the fishmonger's slab all year round but it is at its best during the winter. If you want to use a slightly cheaper fish, cod, coley or pollack are all good substitutes, and to make a change you can use orange instead of lemon in the simple sauce.

SERVES 4

700 g (1½ lb) haddock fillets, skinned and cut into 4 portions

300 ml (½ pint) fresh milk plus 30 ml (2 tbsp) finely grated rind of 1 lemon

salt and pepper

15 ml (1 tbsp) cornflour

25 g (1 oz) butter

lemon slices and fresh parsley sprigs, to garnish

1. Place the haddock in a large frying pan with 300 ml (½ pint) milk and the lemon rind. Season to taste. Gently simmer for 8 minutes, until the fish is tender. Transfer to a serving dish with a fish slice and keep warm.
2. Blend the cornflour with the 30 ml (2 tbsp) milk, then stir into the poaching liquid with the butter. Heat, whisking continuously, until the sauce thickens, boils and is smooth.
3. Spoon the sauce over the fish. Serve at once, garnished with lemon slices and fresh parsley sprigs.

TO MICROWAVE

Place the haddock in a large shallow dish with half the milk, lemon rind and seasonings. Cook on HIGH for 7 minutes. Remove fish and keep warm. Blend the cornflour with the remaining milk, then stir into the poaching liquid with the butter. Cook on HIGH for 4–5 minutes, until boiling and thickened, whisking frequently. Complete step 3.

PLAICE IN CREAM
THE EASTERN COUNTIES

Top-quality fish abounds off the East Anglian coast and plaice often features in the catch. It is a flat white fish with a delicate flavour. The skin on one side is brownish, with orange spots, and on the other is pearly white. Plaice is best enjoyed in a simple recipe.

SERVES 4

15 g (½ oz) butter

1 small onion, skinned and finely chopped

150 ml (5 fl oz) fresh double cream

150 ml (¼ pint) fish or vegetable stock

blade of mace

salt and pepper

8 single plaice fillets, each weighing 75 g (3 oz), skinned

fresh parsley sprigs and lemon twists, to garnish

1. Melt the butter in a large frying pan, add the onion and cook for about 3 minutes, stirring occasionally, until softened.
2. Stir in the cream and stock and bring to the boil. Lower the heat, add the mace and season lightly to taste. Gently add the fish to the pan, loosely folded in half. Spoon the cream over the fish. Cover and poach gently for about 5 minutes, until the fish is tender and just flakes.
3. Carefully transfer the fish to a warmed plate, using a fish slice, cover and keep warm. Boil the cooking liquor until slightly thickened.
4. Spoon the sauce over 4 warmed plates, discarding the mace. Arrange the fish on top and garnish with parsley sprigs and lemon twists.

TO MICROWAVE

Put the butter and the onion in a large shallow dish. Cover and cook on HIGH for 4–5 minutes, until softened. Stir in the cream, stock and mace. Season to taste. Fold the fish loosely in half, then arrange around the edge of the dish. Re-cover and cook on HIGH for 4–5 minutes, until the fish is tender. Carefully transfer the fish to a warmed plate, then cover and keep warm. Cook the cooking juices, uncovered, on HIGH for 5 minutes or until slightly thickened. Complete step 4.

2. Seal the foil, weigh the fish and place on a baking sheet. Calculate the cooking time at 10 minutes per 450 g (1 lb). Bake at 180°C (350°F) mark 4 until tender.
3. Remove the fish from the foil, reserving the cooking liquor, then carefully remove the skin while still warm. Arrange the fish on a serving dish and leave to cool.
4. To make the sauce, put the cooking liquor and the remaining 25 g (1 oz) butter in a saucepan and heat gently. Add the watercress, spinach, parsley, chervil and dill, then cook for 2–3 minutes, until softened.
5. Put the sauce in a food processor or blender and work until smooth. Transfer to a bowl and add the remaining lemon juice and season to taste. Leave to cool, then fold in the mayonnaise. Turn into a small serving bowl and refrigerate until required.
6. When the fish is cold, garnish with fresh herbs and whole prawns, if liked. Serve with the herb sauce.

TO MICROWAVE

 Cut the head and tail off the fish and discard. Weigh the fish, wrap in a double sheet of greaseproof paper, then place in a large shallow dish or on the oven turntable. Cook on HIGH for 4 minutes per 450 g (1 lb) or until the fish is tender, turning the fish over once halfway through the cooking time. Complete the recipe from step 3.

SEA TROUT WITH HERB SAUCE. Stunning to look at, and easier than you might think to prepare. Go to town on the decoration to make the finished dish as pretty as a picture.

SEA TROUT WITH HERB SAUCE

WALES

The Welsh call sea trout sewin and they come mainly from the fast-flowing rivers of Wales. Their pink flesh and delicate flavour are admirably complemented by the pretty green sauce. If you can't get the herbs specified use other ones but beware of those like thyme with an overpowering flavour.

SERVES 4

900 g (2 lb) sea trout, cleaned

45 ml (3 tbsp) lemon juice

50 g (2 oz) butter

salt and pepper

1 bunch watercress, trimmed and roughly chopped

100 g (4 oz) fresh spinach leaves, roughly chopped

45 ml (3 tbsp) chopped fresh parsley

30 ml (2 tbsp) chopped fresh chervil

5 ml (1 tsp) chopped fresh dill

150 ml (¼ pint) mayonnaise

fresh herbs and whole unpeeled cooked prawns, to garnish

1. Place the fish in the centre of a large piece of foil. Add 30 ml (2 tbsp) of the lemon juice, then dot with 25 g (1 oz) of the butter. Season to taste.

BAKED TROUT WITH CUCUMBER SAUCE

COUNTRYWIDE

A cold dish that would be ideal for a summer gathering. Use freshwater trout, that is, river, lake or rainbow trout. These are now increasingly easy to find at supermarkets. Shiny, slippery skin and bright eyes are the hallmarks of freshness to look for in fresh fish, although frozen can also be used in this recipe.

SERVES 4

4 trout, each weighing about 275 g (10 oz), cleaned

salt and pepper

300 ml (½ pint) fish or vegetable stock

½ small cucumber

300 ml (10 fl oz) fresh soured cream

5 ml (1 tsp) tarragon vinegar

5 ml (1 tsp) chopped fresh tarragon

fresh tarragon, to garnish

1. Arrange the trout in a single layer in a shallow dish. Season to taste. Pour over the stock.
2. Cover and bake at 180°C (350°F) mark 4 for about 25 minutes, until the trout are tender.
3. Remove the fish from the cooking liquor and carefully peel off the skin, leaving the head and tail intact. Leave to cool.

4. Just before serving, make the sauce. Coarsely grate the cucumber, then add the cream, vinegar and tarragon. Season to taste.

5. Coat the trout in some of the sauce, leaving the head and tail exposed. Garnish with tarragon. Serve the remaining sauce separately in a bowl. Accompany with potatoes and a green vegetable.

TO MICROWAVE

 Cook 2 trout at a time. Arrange in a shallow dish. Cover and cook on HIGH for 5–7 minutes or until tender. Repeat with the remaining 2 trout. Complete the recipe.

STUFFED TROUT IN
A WINE SAUCE

COUNTRYWIDE

An old recipe which originally called for 'savoury herbs' in the stuffing. This term covered all the common garden herbs, so although thyme and rosemary are specified here, you could equally well substitute marjoram, dill, tarragon or chervil. Use wild trout if you are able to buy them.

SERVES 4

100 g (4 oz) fresh wholemeal breadcrumbs

15 ml (1 tbsp) chopped fresh mixed herbs, such as parsley, thyme, rosemary

finely grated rind and juice of ½ lemon

pinch of freshly grated nutmeg

salt and pepper

1 egg, beaten

4 trout, each weighing about 275 g (10 oz), cleaned

25 g (1 oz) butter

30 ml (2 tbsp) plain flour

150 ml (¼ pint) dry white wine

150 ml (¼ pint) vegetable stock

60 ml (4 tbsp) fresh double cream

1. Put the breadcrumbs, herbs, grated lemon rind and juice and nutmeg in a bowl. Season to taste. Add the egg and mix together well.

2. Fill the cavities of the trout with the stuffing. Wrap the fish in greased foil. Place the parcels on a baking sheet and bake at 180°C (350°F) mark 4 for 30–35 minutes, until tender.

3. Meanwhile, put the butter, flour, wine and stock in a saucepan and heat, whisking continuously, until the sauce thickens, boils and is smooth. Simmer for 1–2 minutes. Stir in the cream and season to taste.

4. Pour a little sauce over the trout and serve the remaining sauce in a warmed sauceboat or jug.

TO MICROWAVE

 Complete step 1. Slash the fish twice on each side. Fill the cavities of the trout with the stuffing. Place the fish side-by-side in a large shallow dish. Add the lemon juice. Cover and cook on HIGH for 10–12 minutes or until the fish is tender, rearranging once during cooking. Meanwhile, complete steps 3 and 4.

BAKED TROUT WITH CUCUMBER SAUCE. Soured cream makes a memorably piquant sauce, packed with texture and flavour, that sets off the simple baked fish superbly.

2. Meanwhile, melt the butter in a large frying pan and cook the garlic and mushrooms, stirring frequently, until just softened. Crumble in the Stilton cheese and cook for a couple of minutes, stirring continuously. Stir in the cream and season to taste.

3. Drain the pasta and season with lots of pepper. Mix into the mushroom sauce. Stir in the egg and mix together thoroughly.

4. Turn the mixture into a buttered ovenproof dish and grate the mozzarella on top. Cover with foil and bake at 180°C (350°F) mark 4 for 10 minutes, then remove the foil and bake at 220°C (425°F) mark 7 for a further 10–15 minutes, until brown and crusty on top. Serve with a green salad.

TO MICROWAVE

 Complete step 1. Meanwhile, put the butter, garlic and mushrooms in a large bowl, cover and cook on HIGH for 3–4 minutes, until the mushrooms are softened, stirring occasionally. Stir in the Stilton cheese and the cream and cook on HIGH for 2 minutes, stirring once. Complete step 3. Turn the mixture into a buttered flameproof dish and grate the mozzarella on top. Cook on HIGH for 3–4 minutes or until heated through. Brown the top under a hot grill.

PASTA AND MUSHROOMS BAKED WITH TWO CHEESES. Ribbon noodles are fun to fork up in this delicious supper dish. The creamy mushroom sauce is enriched with egg.

PASTA AND MUSHROOMS BAKED WITH TWO CHEESES

COUNTRYWIDE

Stilton cheese is marvellous for cooking, and gives a very distinctive flavour to the mushroom sauce in this pasta dish. Mozzarella, used here for the topping, is a famous Italian cheese, which is now also being made in Britain. It is deliciously creamy when melted.

SERVES 2–3

225 g (8 oz) ribbon noodles

25 g (1 oz) butter

1 garlic clove, skinned and crushed

225 g (8 oz) mushrooms, thinly sliced

50 g (2 oz) Stilton cheese

60 ml (4 tbsp) fresh double cream

salt and pepper

1 egg, lightly beaten

100 g (4 oz) mozzarella cheese

1. Cook the noodles in boiling salted water for about 7 minutes, until just tender.

PARSNIP AND LENTIL POTS

COUNTRYWIDE

Like all vegetables, parsnips should be used as fresh as possible. If you do need to keep them for a day or two, buy them unwashed and store in a cool, dry place. Always buy firm parsnips that have a good creamy colour, with no brown patches.

SERVES 4
before step 5

900 g (2 lb) parsnips, peeled and thinly sliced

75 g (3 oz) green lentils

75 g (3 oz) long-grain brown rice

salt and pepper

40 g (1½ oz) butter

1 small onion, skinned and finely chopped

30 ml (2 tbsp) plain flour

568 ml (1 pint) fresh milk

pinch of grated nutmeg

1. Place the parsnips in a large saucepan. Cover with cold water and bring to the boil for 2 minutes, then drain immediately.

2. Put the lentils and rice together in a large saucepan. Cover with cold water, bring to the boil and simmer for 35–40 minutes, until just cooked. Drain well and season to taste.

3. Melt 25 g (1 oz) of the butter in a medium saucepan. Add the onion and cook for 2–3 minutes, until

beginning to soften. Stir in the flour and cook for a further 1–2 minutes. Remove from the heat and gradually stir in the milk. Slowly bring to the boil and continue to cook, stirring all the time, until the sauce comes to the boil and thickens. Simmer for a further 2–3 minutes. Season with nutmeg and salt and pepper.

4. Lightly grease four 450 ml (¾ pint) deep ovenproof dishes or one 1.7 litre (3 pint) dish. Reserve some parsnip slices for garnish. Spoon alternate layers of parsnip, lentils and brown rice and onion sauce into each dish. Finish with a layer of onion sauce and the reserved parsnip slices. Melt the remaining butter and brush over the tops.

5. Place on a baking sheet and bake at 190°C (375°F) mark 5 for about 1–1¼ hours, until golden brown. Serve hot.

TO MICROWAVE

 The sauce, in step 3, can be prepared in the microwave. Put 25 g (1 oz) of the butter in a medium bowl and cook on HIGH for 45 seconds, until melted. Add the onion and cook on HIGH for 4–5 minutes, until softened, stirring occasionally. Stir in the flour and cook on HIGH for 30 seconds. Gradually stir in the milk and cook on HIGH for 5–6 minutes until the sauce has boiled and thickened, whisking frequently. Season with nutmeg and salt and pepper.

CHILLED SPINACH STUFFED SHELLS

COUNTRYWIDE

Don't buy tiny pasta shells for this recipe, as you'll need extra large ones to hold the cheesy spinach filling, which is well seasoned with garlic and nutmeg. As the shells are served cold, you can cook the pasta and prepare the stuffing ahead of time and assemble the dish when you are ready to serve.

SERVES 2

10 large pasta shells
450 g (1 lb) fresh spinach, trimmed, or 225 g (8 oz) frozen spinach
1–2 garlic cloves, skinned and crushed
100 g (4 oz) low-fat soft cheese
freshly grated nutmeg
salt and pepper
150 g (5 oz) natural yogurt
15 ml (1 tbsp) tomato purée
finely grated rind and juice of ½ lemon

1. Cook the pasta in a large saucepanful of boiling salted water for 8–10 minutes or until tender.
2. Meanwhile, wash the fresh spinach in several changes of water and roughly chop. Cook with just the water clinging to the leaves for 3–4 minutes or until just

wilted. If using frozen spinach, cook for about 10 minutes or until thawed. Drain the spinach and finely chop.
3. Mix the spinach with the garlic and cheese and season generously with nutmeg and salt and pepper. Leave to cool.
4. Drain the pasta and rinse with cold water, then drain again. When the spinach mixture is cold, use to stuff the shells. Arrange on two plates.
5. Mix the yogurt, tomato purée and lemon rind and juice together and season with salt and pepper to taste. Pour over the stuffed shells. Cover and chill until ready to serve.

TO MICROWAVE

 Complete step 1. Meanwhile, prepare the fresh spinach and put in a large bowl with just the water clinging to the leaves. Cover and cook on HIGH for 2–3 minutes or until just wilted. If using frozen spinach, cook on HIGH for 5–7 minutes or until thawed, stirring occasionally. Complete the recipe.

CHILLED SPINACH STUFFED SHELLS. An attractive and unusual way with pasta, that could be served as a starter or main course. The light yogurt sauce is coloured pale pink with tomato purée.

VEGETARIAN
MEDLEY
COUNTRYWIDE

Protein-rich pulses combine with fresh vegetables, fresh and dried fruit, nuts and dairy products to make an exceptionally well-balanced, nutritious vegetarian meal, perfect for a warming winter supper.

SERVES 4

25 g (1 oz) butter
2 carrots, sliced
1 large onion, skinned and chopped
1 green pepper, seeded and sliced
2 tomatoes, skinned and chopped
1 large cooking apple, peeled and chopped
1 clove garlic, skinned and crushed
15 ml (1 tbsp) chopped fresh sage or 5 ml (1 tsp) dried

VEGETARIAN MEDLEY. Colourful and tasty, a chunky mixture of pulses, fruit, nuts and vegetables is combined in a yogurt and cream cheese sauce. Fresh sage adds its distinctive bite.

100 g (4 oz) lentils, cooked
15 ml (1 tbsp) raisins
30 ml (2 tbsp) unsalted peanuts
salt and pepper
300 g (10 oz) natural yogurt
25 g (1 oz) cream cheese

1. Melt the butter in a large frying pan. Lightly fry the carrots, onion, green pepper, tomatoes, apple, garlic and sage for 15 minutes, until softened.
2. Add the lentils, raisins and peanuts. Season to taste. Stir the yogurt into the cream cheese and mix well to blend. Stir into the mixture. Reheat gently for 5 minutes. Serve at once.

TO MICROWAVE

 Melt the butter in a large bowl on HIGH for 45 seconds. Add the carrots, onion, green pepper, tomatoes, apple, garlic and sage and cook on HIGH for 7 minutes, stirring occasionally. Add the remaining ingredients as in step 2 and cook on HIGH for 2 minutes. Serve at once.

LYMESWOLD AND
WATERCRESS FLAN
THE MIDLANDS

Lymeswold is a full-fat soft blue cheese with a white rind, the texture of which varies as it ages. Watercress is available all year round now that it is specially cultivated, and its strong distinctive taste gives a nice zest to this flan.

SERVES 4

✳

100 g (4 oz) plain wholemeal flour
salt and pepper
50 g (2 oz) butter, diced
150 g (5 oz) Lymeswold cheese, rinded and sliced
2 eggs, beaten
150 ml (¼ pint) fresh milk
1 small onion, skinned and chopped
50 g (2 oz) watercress, trimmed and chopped

1. Put the flour and salt in a bowl. Rub in the butter until the mixture resembles fine breadcrumbs. Add 30–45 ml (2–3 tbsp) cold water and mix to form a dough.
2. Roll out on a lightly floured work surface and use to line an 18 cm (7 inch) flan dish. Bake blind at 200°C (400°F) mark 6 for 10–15 minutes, until set but not too brown.
3. Put the Lymeswold on the base of the flan case. Mix together the eggs and milk, and season to taste. Add the onion and watercress and pour into the flan case.
4. Bake at 190°C (375°F) mark 5 for 40–45 minutes. Serve warm.

BACK
LEEK AND PEA FLAN.
There's Cheddar in the
pastry, as well as on top, to
bring out the flavours of the
vegetables.

FRONT
BROCCOLI FLAN. Florets
of broccoli give the filling an
appetising finish.

LEEK AND PEA FLAN

WALES

This attractive green flan makes excellent use of traditional Welsh leek. Frozen peas taste just as good in it as fresh but don't use canned ones or the flavour will be altered.

SERVES 4–6

✳

450 g (1 lb) leeks, trimmed, sliced and washed

100 g (4 oz) fresh or frozen shelled peas

salt and pepper

150 ml (¼ pint) fresh milk

150 g (5 oz) natural yogurt

3 eggs

175 g (6 oz) plain wholemeal flour

100 g (4 oz) Cheddar cheese, grated

75 g (3 oz) butter

1. Cook the leeks and peas in a little salted water in a tightly covered medium saucepan until tender. Drain well.
2. Purée together the leeks, peas, milk and yogurt in a blender or food processor.
3. Beat 2 of the eggs into the purée and season to taste. Lightly beat the remaining egg in a small bowl.
4. Put the flour and half the cheese in a bowl. Rub in the butter until the mixture resembles fine breadcrumbs, then bind together with the remaining egg.
5. Roll out the pastry on a lightly floured surface and use to line a 23 cm (9 inch) flan dish. Pour in the leek mixture.
6. Sprinkle over the remaining cheese. Bake at 190°C (375°F) mark 5 for 50–55 minutes, until golden.

BROCCOLI FLAN

THE SOUTH-EAST

As well as heads of green broccoli, often sold prepacked, you will sometimes find purple sprouting broccoli in the shops. Whichever variety you choose, buy the freshest possible, with no yellowing leaves, and eat within a couple of days. The pastry in this recipe uses rolled oats for an unusual texture.

SERVES 4–6

✳

175 g (6 oz) plain wholemeal flour

50 g (2 oz) porridge oats

salt and pepper

100 g (4 oz) butter

350 g (12 oz) broccoli, trimmed

3 eggs

300 ml (½ pint) fresh milk

1. Put the flour, oats and 2.5 ml (½ tsp) salt into a bowl. Rub in the butter until the mixture resembles fine breadcrumbs. Add enough cold water to bind the mixture together and form a firm dough.
2. Roll out the pastry on a lightly floured surface and use to line a 23 cm (9 inch) flan dish. Bake blind at 200°C (400°F) mark 6 for 10–15 minutes, until set but not too brown.
3. Roughly chop the broccoli, then cook in boiling, salted water until just tender. Drain well. Arrange in the flan case.
4. Whisk together the eggs, milk and season to taste. Pour into the flan case, making sure the broccoli is covered.
5. Bake at 190°C (375°F) mark 5 for about 40 minutes, until lightly set. Serve warm.

GOAT'S CHEESE WITH PEAR AND WALNUT SALAD. The strong, salty flavour of goat's cheese is complemented by the sweet pears and sharp lemon dressing.

SPINACH ROLL
When rolling up Spinach Roll use a sheet of greaseproof to help you.

GOAT'S CHEESE WITH PEAR AND WALNUT SALAD

THE WEST

Goat's cheese has a distinctive taste which is, for some people, acquired. It is produced in much smaller quantities than cow's milk cheese, often on individual farms. The flavour will vary according to the time of year and the type of feed. If you prefer, use another white variety such as Caerphilly, Lancashire, Wensleydale or white Stilton.

SERVES 2

a few lettuce leaves, such as Webbs and radicchio, torn into pieces
100 g (4 oz) goat's cheese, halved into 2 discs
2 ripe pears, cored and chunked
50 g (2 oz) walnuts, chopped
½ bunch watercress, trimmed
30 ml (2 tbsp) lemon juice
45 ml (3 tbsp) vegetable oil

1. Arrange the lettuce on 2 plates and top with the goat's cheese. Mix together the pears, walnuts and watercress.
2. Blend the lemon juice and oil together, then toss into the salad ingredients. Serve on top of the cheese.

SPINACH ROLL

COUNTRYWIDE

Fromage frais is an unripened, soft fresh cheese. Many different types are stocked by supermarkets and delicatessens, and they all have one thing in common – their light, fresh taste. The fat content, however, varies widely, so check the labels before buying.

SERVES 3–4

900 g (2 lb) fresh spinach, trimmed, or 450 g (1 lb) packet frozen chopped spinach
4 eggs, separated
pinch of freshly grated nutmeg
salt and pepper
15 g (½ oz) butter
1 medium onion, skinned and finely chopped
100 g (4 oz) fromage frais
50 g (2 oz) Cheddar cheese, grated
30 ml (2 tbsp) fresh soured cream

1. Grease a 33×23 cm (13×9 inch) Swiss roll tin and line with non-stick baking parchment. Set aside.
2. Wash the fresh spinach in several changes of cold water. Place in a saucepan with only the water that clings to the leaves and cook gently, covered, for about 5 minutes, until wilted. If using frozen spinach cook for 7–10 minutes, until thawed.
3. Drain the spinach well and chop finely. Turn into a bowl and cool slightly for about 5 minutes, then beat in the egg yolks and nutmeg, and season with salt and pepper to taste.
4. Whisk the egg whites until stiff, then fold into the spinach mixture with a large metal spoon until they are evenly incorporated.
5. Spread the mixture in the prepared tin. Bake at 200°C (400°F) mark 6 for 15–20 minutes, until firm.
6. Meanwhile, prepare the filling. Melt the butter in a saucepan. Add the onion and fry gently for about 5 minutes, until soft and lightly coloured. Remove from the heat and stir in the fromage frais, cheese and soured cream. Season to taste.
7. Turn the roll out on to greaseproof paper, peel off the lining paper and spread immediately and quickly with the cheese mixture.
8. Roll up by gently lifting the greaseproof paper. Serve hot, cut into thick slices. Accompany with boiled new potatoes.

TO MICROWAVE

☑ Complete step 1. If using fresh spinach, place in a large bowl with only the water that clings to the leaves. Cover and cook on HIGH for 4–5 minutes, until just wilted. If using frozen spinach, cover and cook on HIGH for 7–10 minutes, until thawed. Complete steps 3, 4 and 5. Meanwhile, put the butter and onion in a medium bowl, cover and cook on HIGH for 5 minutes, until softened. Complete the remainder of step 6 and steps 7 and 8.

SAVOURY NUT BURGERS

COUNTRYWIDE

The nut mixture is quite sticky, so coat your hands with flour to make shaping the burgers easier. Buy a ready chopped mixture of nuts, or a selection of whole nuts to chop yourself.

SERVES 4

25 g (1 oz) butter
1 large onion, skinned and chopped
15 ml (1 tbsp) chopped fresh parsley
15 g (½ oz) plain wholemeal flour
150 ml (¼ pint) fresh milk
225 g (8 oz) chopped mixed nuts
15 ml (1 tbsp) soy sauce
15 ml (1 tbsp) tomato purée
175 g (6 oz) fresh wholemeal breadcrumbs
1 egg, beaten
pepper

1. Melt the butter in a medium saucepan and lightly fry the onion and parsley until soft. Stir in the flour and cook for 2 minutes.
2. Remove from heat, gradually add the milk, bring back to boil, stirring until the sauce thickens, boils and is smooth. Simmer for 1–2 minutes.
3. Add the nuts, soy sauce, tomato purée, breadcrumbs, eggs and pepper to taste. Mix well.
4. Divide into 8 and shape into rounds. Place under a grill for 4 minutes, then turn and grill for 4 minutes more. Serve with cheese sauce, tomatoes and parsley.

TO MICROWAVE

Melt the butter in a large bowl on HIGH for 45 seconds. Add the onion, cook on HIGH for 5 minutes. Add the flour, cook on HIGH for 1 minute. Gradually add the milk, cook on HIGH for 3 minutes until boiling and thickened, whisking frequently. Complete step 3. Divide mixture into 8 and shape into rounds. Preheat a browning dish on HIGH for 8–10 minutes or according to manufacturer's instructions. Quickly put the burgers in the browning dish and cook on HIGH for 2 minutes, turn over and cook for a further 2 minutes.

STUFFED MARROW

COUNTRYWIDE

This recipe makes the most of English root vegetables. Autumn is the time to make it, when supplies are plentiful. The skin should be shiny and pressing it with the thumb should leave an impression.

SERVES 4

550 g (1¼ lb) marrow, peeled and halved lengthways
25 g (1 oz) butter
175 g (6 oz) aubergine, cubed
2 parsnips, peeled and diced
2 carrots, diced
100 g (4 oz) swede, peeled and diced
100 g (4 oz) turnip, peeled and diced
15 ml (1 tbsp) chopped fresh parsley
15 ml (1 tbsp) tomato purée
150 ml (¼ pint) vegetable stock
salt and pepper
natural yogurt, to serve

1. Scoop the seeds out of the marrow.
2. Melt the butter in a large frying pan and lightly fry the vegetables for 10 minutes.
3. Add the parsley, tomato purée and stock. Season to taste. Simmer gently for 15 minutes.
4. Fill one half of the marrow with the mixture. Top with the other half of marrow and wrap in foil. Bake at 190°C (375°F) mark 5 for about 45 minutes, until tender. Serve at once, in slices, with natural yogurt.

TO MICROWAVE

Complete step 1. Melt the butter in a large bowl on HIGH for 45 seconds. Add the vegetables and cook on HIGH for 10 minutes. Add the parsley, tomato purée and stock and cook on HIGH for 20 minutes, stirring occasionally. Fill one half of the marrow, top with the other half and put into a large shallow dish. Cook on HIGH for 10–12 minutes, until tender. Serve at once, in slices, with natural yogurt.

SAVOURY NUT BURGERS. Moist and nutty inside, crispy and well browned outside, these tempting burgers will be just as popular with non-vegetarians.

VEGETABLE CURRY. A subtle blend of spices gives this curry its flavour. Adjust the amount of chilli powder according to how much heat you like, and vary the vegetables according to what's in season.

VEGETABLE CURRY
COUNTRYWIDE

Spices were very costly until the 16th century, because they had to be brought to Britain overland from the East. We have to thank great explorers like Drake and Raleigh for first making these vital ingredients of good cooking more readily available. Buy your spices freshly and in small amounts, as they lose their strength quickly when stored.

SERVES 4

30 ml (2 tbsp) vegetable oil

10 ml (2 tsp) ground coriander

5 ml (1 tsp) ground cumin

2.5–5 ml (½–1 tsp) chilli powder

2.5 ml (½ tsp) ground turmeric

2 garlic cloves, skinned and crushed

1 medium onion, skinned and chopped

1 small cauliflower, cut into small florets

2 potatoes, roughly chopped

2 carrots, sliced

1 green pepper, seeded and chopped

225 g (8 oz) tomatoes, roughly chopped

150 g (5 oz) natural yogurt

salt and pepper

1. Heat the oil in a large saucepan, then add the coriander, cumin, chilli, turmeric, garlic and onion and fry for 2–3 minutes, stirring continuously.

2. Add the cauliflower, potatoes, carrots and green pepper and stir to coat in the spices. Stir in the tomatoes and 150 ml (¼ pint) water. Bring to the boil, cover and gently simmer for 25–30 minutes or until the vegetables are tender.

3. Remove from the heat, stir in the yogurt and season to taste. Serve with rice and chutney.

TO MICROWAVE

Put the oil, coriander, cumin, chilli, turmeric, garlic and onion in a large bowl and cook on HIGH for 2 minutes, stirring once. Add the cauliflower, potatoes, carrots and green pepper and stir to coat in the spices. Stir in the tomatoes and 150 ml (¼ pint) water. Cover and cook on HIGH for 20 minutes or until the vegetables are tender, stirring occasionally. Complete step 3.

WHOLEMEAL VEGETABLE AND HERB PIE
COUNTRYWIDE

The herb used here is fresh parsley, which is often found in supermarkets. If you grow your own, sow some in spring and again in late summer to keep a supply going all year round. Wholemeal pastry needs gentle handling, as it tears easily, but the nutty-flavoured, crumbly result is worth the extra care.

SERVES 4

90 g (3½ oz) butter

3 carrots, sliced

40 g (1½ oz) plain flour

300 ml (½ pint) fresh milk

salt and pepper

1 small cauliflower, broken into florets

100 g (4 oz) broccoli

50 g (2 oz) pearl barley, cooked

30 ml (2 tbsp) chopped fresh parsley

100 g (4 oz) plain wholemeal flour

fresh milk, to glaze

1. Melt 40 g (1½ oz) of the butter in a medium saucepan. Lightly fry the carrots for 7 minutes. Stir in the plain flour and cook for 1 minute. Gradually add the milk, whisking continuously, until the sauce thickens, boils and is smooth. Simmer for 1–2 minutes. Season to taste.

2. Blanch the cauliflower and broccoli in boiling salted water for 5 minutes. Drain.

3. Mix the sauce with the cauliflower, broccoli, pearl barley and parsley. Spoon into a 1.1 litre (2 pint) pie dish.

4. Put the plain wholemeal flour and salt in a bowl. Rub in the remaining butter until the mixture resembles fine breadcrumbs. Add 75 ml (3 tbsp) cold water to mix to form a dough. Roll out on a lightly floured work surface to 5 cm (2 inch) wider than the pie dish. Cut a 2.5 cm (1 inch) wide strip from the outer edge and place on the dampened rim of the dish. Brush the strip with water. Cover with the pastry lid, press lightly to seal the edges. Trim off excess pastry. Knock the edges back to seal and crimp. Garnish with pastry leaves and brush with milk.

5. Bake at 200°C (400°F) mark 6 for 30 minutes, until golden.

TO MICROWAVE

 Dice 40 g (1½ oz) of the butter, place in a large bowl and cook on HIGH for 1 minute. Add the carrots and cook on HIGH for 2 minutes. Stir in the flour and cook on HIGH for 1 minute. Stir in the milk and cook on HIGH for 4–5 minutes, until boiling and thickened, stirring frequently. Blanch the cauliflower and broccoli in boiling water from the kettle on HIGH for 3 minutes. Complete steps 3, 4, 5 and 6.

MIXED VEGETABLE RING

COUNTRYWIDE

Cotswold cheese is a tangy blend of Double Gloucester with chopped chives and onions. Here it is used to make a light pastry ring, filled with a delicious mixture of colourful vegetables. Serve as a lunch or supper dish with salad.

SERVES 4

100 g (4 oz) butter
1 large onion, skinned and sliced
50 g (2 oz) mushrooms, wiped
2 courgettes, sliced
175 g (6 oz) aubergine, quartered and sliced
1 red pepper, seeded and sliced
3 tomatoes, skinned and chopped
salt and pepper
215 ml (7½ oz) fresh milk
100 g (4 oz) plain flour
3 eggs, beaten
40 g (1½ oz) walnut pieces, chopped
100 g (4 oz) Cotswold cheese, grated

1. Melt 25 g (1 oz) of the butter in a large saucepan. Lightly fry the onion and mushrooms for 5 minutes, until softened.

2. Add the courgettes, aubergines and red pepper and cook for 5 minutes, stirring occasionally. Add the tomatoes and season to taste.

3. Melt the remaining butter in a medium saucepan with the milk, then bring to the boil. Remove the pan from the heat, tip in all the flour and beat thoroughly with a wooden spoon. Allow to cool slightly, then beat in the eggs, a little at a time. Stir in the walnuts. Pipe or spoon around the edge of a well-greased 900 ml (1½ pint) ovenproof serving dish.

4. Fill the centre with vegetables. Bake at 200°C (400°F) mark 6 for 35–40 minutes, until the pastry is risen and golden. Sprinkle with the cheese, return to the oven until the cheese has melted. Serve at once.

TO MICROWAVE

Melt 25 g (1 oz) of the butter in a large shallow dish on HIGH for 45 seconds. Add the onions and mushrooms and cook on HIGH for 3 minutes. Add the courgettes, aubergine and red pepper and cook on HIGH for 5 minutes, stirring occasionally. Add the tomatoes and season to taste. Cook on HIGH for 1 minute. Complete steps 3 and 4.

MIXED VEGETABLE RING. Everyone gets a piece of the cheesy ring and a generous helping of the filling, made from juicy Mediterranean vegetables.

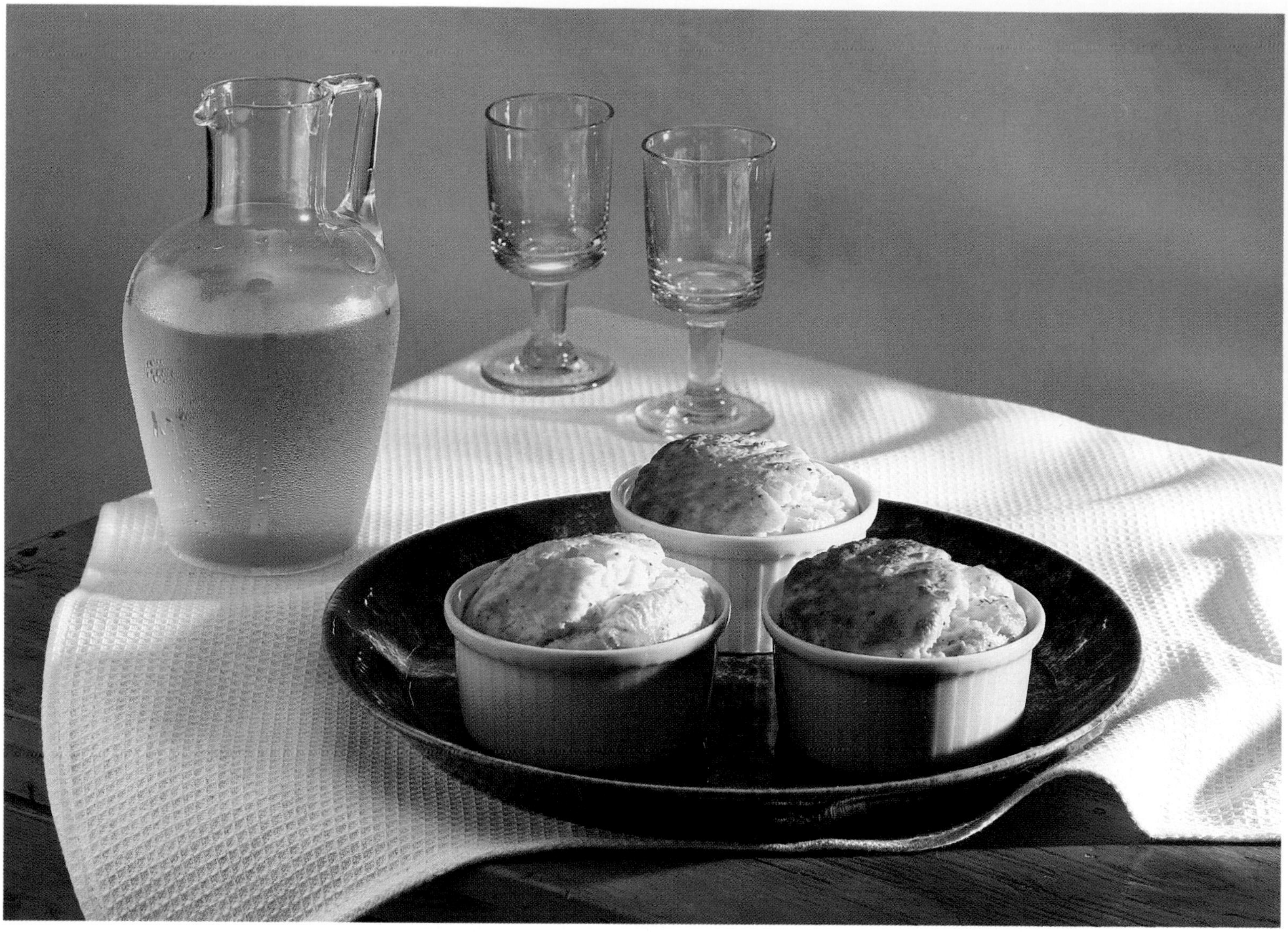

FARMHOUSE CAULIFLOWER SOUFFLES. The mellowness of Farmhouse Cheddar can be enjoyed at its best in these light and airy soufflés.

FARMHOUSE CAULIFLOWER SOUFFLES

THE WEST

The distinctive flavour of cauliflower lends itself to soufflé treatment. This dish, like all soufflés, can be started and left before finishing off. If the sauce base is allowed to cool, allow about 10 minutes extra cooking time. Ensure people are ready to eat the soufflé as soon as it is done.

SERVES 8

225 g (8 oz) small cauliflower florets
salt and pepper
40 g (1½ oz) butter
45 ml (3 tbsp) plain flour
200 ml (7 fl oz) fresh milk
15 ml (1 tbsp) wholegrain mustard
100 g (4 oz) mature Farmhouse Cheddar cheese, grated
4 eggs, separated

1. Grease eight individual ramekin dishes.
2. Put the cauliflower in a saucepan and just cover with boiling salted water. Cover and simmer until tender, then drain.
3. Meanwhile, prepare a white sauce. Put the butter, flour and milk in a saucepan. Heat, whisking continuously, until the sauce thickens, boils and is smooth. Simmer for 1–2 minutes. Add the mustard and season to taste.
4. Turn the sauce into a blender or food processor. Add the cauliflower and work to an almost smooth purée.
5. Turn into a large bowl and leave to cool slightly. Stir in the cheese with the egg yolks.
6. Whisk the egg whites until stiff but not dry and fold into the sauce mixture. Spoon into the dishes.
7. Bake at 180°C (350°F) mark 4 for 25 minutes or until browned and firm to the touch. Serve at once.

TO MICROWAVE

The sauce can be prepared in the microwave. Put the butter, flour and milk in a medium bowl. Cook on HIGH for 4–5 minutes, until boiling and thickened, whisking frequently. Add the mustard and season to taste.

RED KIDNEY BEAN HOT-POT
COUNTRYWIDE

Make this dish in the late summer or early autumn, when runner beans, courgettes and celery are all in season together. Ensure that the dried beans are simmered for the full time given in the recipe. Substitute a 397 g (14 oz) can kidney beans to speed things up, if you prefer.

SERVES 2

100 g (4 oz) dried red kidney beans, soaked overnight

25 g (1 oz) butter

1 medium onion, skinned and roughly chopped

100 g (4 oz) celery, sliced

100 g (4 oz) carrots, sliced

15 ml (1 tbsp) plain flour

300 ml (½ pint) vegetable stock

salt and pepper

100 g (4 oz) runner beans, topped and tailed

100 g (4 oz) courgettes, sliced

25 g (1 oz) fresh wholemeal breadcrumbs

75 g (3 oz) Cheddar cheese, grated

1. Drain the kidney beans and rinse well under running cold water. Put in a large saucepan, cover with plenty of fresh cold water and slowly bring to the boil.
2. Skim off the surface with a slotted spoon, then boil rapidly for 10 minutes. Half cover the pan and simmer for about 1½ hours, until tender.
3. Melt the butter in a large saucepan, add the onion and gently fry for about 5 minutes, until softened. Add the celery and carrots, cover and gently cook for 5 minutes.
4. Add the flour and gently cook, stirring, for 1–2 minutes. Remove from the heat and gradually blend in the stock. Bring to the boil, stirring constantly, then simmer for 5 minutes. Season to taste.
5. Add the runner beans and simmer for a further 5 minutes, then add the courgettes. Cook for a further 5–10 minutes, until the vegetables are tender but still with a bite to them.
6. Drain the kidney beans, add to the vegetables and heat through for about 5 minutes. Taste and adjust seasoning, then turn into a deep flameproof dish.
7. Mix the breadcrumbs and cheese together. Sprinkle on top of the bean mixture, then brown under a hot grill until crisp and crusty. Serve hot, accompanied with wholemeal bread and a green salad.

TO MICROWAVE

Complete steps 1 and 2. Put the butter, onion, celery and carrot in a large bowl. Cover and cook on HIGH for 10–12 minutes, until softened. Sprinkle in the flour and cook on HIGH for 30 seconds. Gradually add the stock, then cook on HIGH for 3–4 minutes, until boiling and thickened, stirring occasionally. Add the runner beans, cover and cook on HIGH for 2 minutes. Stir in the courgettes and drained kidney beans and season to taste. Re-cover and cook on HIGH for 4–5 minutes, until the courgettes are just tender. Complete step 7.

BAKED ONIONS WITH NUT STUFFING
COUNTRYWIDE

Choose onions that are hard, with no obvious soft spots, and avoid any that are showing signs of sprouting. Although raw onions are known for their pungent smell, when cooked they have a mild, sweet flavour which contrasts well with the cheesy stuffing.

SERVES 4

4 large onions, each weighing 225–275 g (8–10 oz)

150 g (5 oz) long-grain brown rice

salt and pepper

50 g (2 oz) hazelnuts

50 g (2 oz) salted peanuts

225 g (8 oz) tomatoes, roughly chopped

100 g (4 oz) Cheddar cheese, grated

2.5 ml (½ tsp) dried basil

1.25 ml (¼ tsp) dried oregano

5 ml (1 tsp) turmeric

1. Boil the onions in their skins for 45–50 minutes, until very tender. Drain and leave to cool.
2. Meanwhile, cook the rice in plenty of boiling salted water for about 30 minutes, until tender. Drain well.
3. Put the hazelnuts and peanuts on a sheet of foil and cook under a grill until brown, turning frequently. Leave the skins on the hazelnuts and finely chop with the peanuts.
4. Mix the tomatoes with the rice, cheese, nuts, herbs and turmeric and season to taste.
5. Slice off the tip and root of each onion, but leave on the coloured outer skin. Down one side of each onion cut through to the centre from tip to root. Ease the onions open.
6. Divide the stuffing between each onion, pressing it well into the centre.
7. Place in a roasting tin, cover and bake at 200°C (400°F) mark 6 for about 40 minutes. Serve hot.

TO MICROWAVE

Prick the onions with a fork (do not skin), then put the onions and 300 ml (½ pint) boiling water in a large bowl. Cover and cook on HIGH for 20–25 minutes, until tender. Meanwhile, complete steps 2, 3 and 4. Drain the onions and complete steps 5, 6 and 7.

ACCOMPANYING VEGETABLES & SALADS

The great variety and quality of fresh vegetables and salad ingredients now available from all over the country is wonderful. Vegetable accompaniments so often get forgotten, and yet they are a vital part of any main course. This chapter will fire your imagination and turn your vegetable accompaniments and salads into dishes to be savoured in their own right.

MUSHROOMS

Mushrooms enhance the flavour of any dish, blending deliciously with most types of foods. They are a source of vitamins and vegetable protein and are quick and easy to prepare. Keep them in a paper bag within a plastic bag in the salad drawer of the refrigerator. Wipe with a clean damp cloth just before use, never wash. Here are five common types of mushroom:

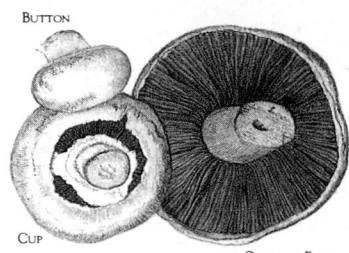

BUTTON

CUP

OPEN AND FLAT

BUTTON

The least mature, with firm, tightly-closed caps. Ideal for sauces, as in the Mushrooms in White Wine recipe featured opposite. Take care not to overcook.

CUPS

More mature with a fuller flavour. Use in casseroles, soups or pies, or as a stuffing (see recipe, page 128).

OPEN AND FLAT

Fully mature with a rich flavour. Best grilled, fried or stuffed.

OYSTER

Less widely known. They have a stronger flavour and are good fried, grilled or stewed lightly with butter, parsley and garlic.

CHESTNUT

Similar in shape to cup mushrooms, but firmer and with a stronger taste. Available in a few main supermarkets. Use as for cups.

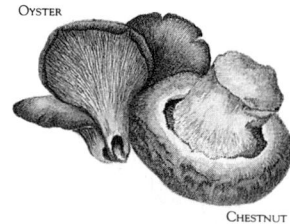

OYSTER

CHESTNUT

STUMP

THE NORTH

This tasty vegetable purée combines three of the best of Britain's traditional root vegetables. It is a particularly good method of using up older carrots and swede, which tend to be tough unless cooked well. You can vary the quantities if you prefer one vegetable to predominate but do include enough carrots to give an attractive colour.

SERVES 4

225 g (8 oz) carrots, peeled and sliced

225 g (8 oz) swede, peeled and sliced

225 g (8 oz) potatoes, peeled and sliced

15 g (½ oz) butter

150 ml (¼ pint) fresh milk

salt and pepper

1. Simmer the vegetables in lightly salted water in a medium saucepan for 30 minutes or until soft. Drain well.
2. Mash the vegetables with the butter and milk. Reheat gently and season to taste. Serve hot.

TO MICROWAVE

Cook the vegetables in 150 ml (¼ pint) water in a large bowl, covered, on HIGH for 15 minutes. Complete step 2.

CREAMED PARSNIPS

COUNTRYWIDE

This smooth purée is an excellent accompaniment to roast meats, poultry and game, and makes a pleasant change from roast parsnips. This was a popular dish in the 16th and 17th centuries, when food with a sweet flavour, such as parsnips, was often served as a complement to savoury dishes.

SERVES 4

900 g (2 lb) parsnips, peeled and roughly chopped

salt and pepper

150 ml (5 fl oz) fresh single cream

chopped fresh parsley, to garnish

1. Cook the parsnips in boiling salted water for 35–40 minutes, until very tender.
2. Drain thoroughly then return to the pan and mash, using a potato masher. Stir in the cream and season to taste. Heat gently, then serve hot, garnished with parsley.

TO MICROWAVE

Put the parsnips and 120 ml (8 tbsp) water in a large bowl. Cover and cook on HIGH for 25–30 minutes, until very tender. Drain thoroughly and mash with a

potato masher. Add the cream and season to taste. Cook on HIGH for 2–3 minutes or until hot. Serve hot, garnished with parsley.

MUSHROOMS IN WHITE WINE

THE WEST

Firm, whole button mushrooms are the best choice for this recipe as they keep their shape when cooked. The dish also makes a good starter or an appetising snack.

SERVES 4

225 g (8 oz) button mushrooms

300 ml (½ pint) dry white wine

1 garlic clove, skinned and crushed

1 medium onion, skinned and finely chopped

15 ml (1 tbsp) chopped fresh parsley

60 ml (4 tbsp) fresh soured cream

1. Put the mushrooms in a small saucepan with the wine, garlic, onion and parsley. Simmer gently for 20 minutes.
2. Remove the pan from the heat and stir in the soured cream. Serve at once.

TO MICROWAVE

Use only 200 ml (7 fl oz) white wine. Put the mushrooms, wine, garlic, onion and parsley in a large bowl. Cover and cook on HIGH for 15–20 minutes, until the onions and mushrooms are softened. Stir in the cream and serve.

BAKED BEETROOT

COUNTRYWIDE

Beetroot is usually served cold in salads, but it is also delicious served hot. Be careful when preparing the beetroots for cooking in a conventional oven – if the skin is damaged the colour will 'bleed' during baking. For the same reason, do not prod them with a fork to see if they are done, but instead test whether the skin slides off easily.

SERVES 4

4 raw beetroots, each weighing about 225 g (8 oz)

butter or fresh soured cream, to serve

salt and pepper

1. Wash the beetroots, but do not trim. Wrap them in greased foil or place in a greased ovenproof dish.
2. Cover tightly and bake at 180°C (350°F) mark 4 for 2–3 hours. When the beetroots are cooked the skin will slide off easily. Serve with a slice cut off the top, but not skinned, topped with the butter or soured cream and seasoned to taste.

TO MICROWAVE

 Prick the beetroot skins with a fork. Arrange in a circle in a shallow dish and pour over 45 ml (3 tbsp) water. Cover and cook on HIGH for 20–25 minutes or until tender. Drain, then serve with a slice cut off the top, but not skinned, topped with the butter and seasoned to taste.

CABBAGE WITH JUNIPER BERRIES

THE EASTERN COUNTIES

You can use any type of cabbage that happens to be in season for this delicious recipe. Juniper berries are wrinkled and black and, when crushed, release their delightful aroma. The flavour is reminiscent of gin, since juniper is a basic ingredient of the spirit. As a faint background hint, married with garlic, it adds a very special touch to cabbage.

SERVES 4

25 g (1 oz) butter
1 medium onion, skinned and chopped
1 garlic clove, skinned and crushed
6 juniper berries, crushed
450 g (1 lb) cabbage, shredded
salt and pepper

1. Melt the butter in a large saucepan. Add the onion, garlic and juniper berries and lightly cook for 5 minutes, until the onion is soft.
2. Add the cabbage and stir until well coated in butter. Season to taste. Cover and cook the cabbage in its own juice for 10 minutes, stirring occasionally. The cabbage should still be slightly crunchy and not soft. Serve hot.

TO MICROWAVE

 Melt the butter on HIGH for 45 seconds. Add the onion, garlic and juniper berries. Cook on HIGH for 5 minutes, until the onion is softened. Add the cabbage and season to taste. Cook, covered, on HIGH for 7–8 minutes, stirring occasionally.

LEFT
CABBAGE WITH JUNIPER BERRIES. A lovely, warming way to prepare cabbage, that gives it an extra special tang. Good with sausages or bacon.

RIGHT
BAKED BEETROOT. Soured cream and beetroot is a classic combination that works wonders in this unusual recipe.

2. Mix the allspice, garlic and cream together and season to taste. Pour over the celery. Sprinkle with the breadcrumbs.
3. Bake at 200°C (400°F) mark 6 for about 1¼ hours or until the celery is tender. Serve hot, garnished with the reserved celery leaves.

TO MICROWAVE

 Complete steps 1 and 2, omitting the breadcrumbs. Cover and cook on HIGH for about 20 minutes, until tender, stirring occasionally. Sprinkle with the breadcrumbs, then brown under a hot grill. Serve hot, garnished with the reserved celery leaves.

BRUSSELS SPROUTS WITH CHESTNUTS
COUNTRYWIDE

Brussels sprouts and chestnuts are a delicious combination, traditionally served at Christmas to accompany the turkey. Buy Brussels sprouts on the day they are needed if possible, as they will only keep for a day or two before starting to turn yellow even if in the refrigerator. If you have to store them, prepare them for cooking and keep in the fridge in a polythene bag. Peeling the chestnuts is a fiddly job, which can be done in advance. Take care when peeling the hot chestnuts not to burn the tips of your fingers.

SERVES 4–6

350 g (12 oz) fresh chestnuts
salt and pepper
700 g (1½ lb) Brussels sprouts, trimmed
25 g (1 oz) butter

1. With the point of a small sharp knife make a small cut on the flat side of each chestnut.
2. Bake the nuts in their skins in the oven at 200°C (400°F) mark 6 for 20 minutes, then peel off the outer shell and the inner skin. (They are easier to peel while hot.)
3. Meanwhile, cook the Brussels sprouts in boiling salted water for 8–10 minutes, until just tender. Drain.
4. Over a high heat, toss the chestnuts and Brussels sprouts with the butter and pepper to taste, until the butter is melted. Serve at once.

TO MICROWAVE

With the point of a small sharp knife cut a lengthways slash in each chestnut. Spread out half of the chestnuts on a large plate and cook on LOW for 3–4 minutes, until the shells can easily be removed. Repeat with the remaining chestnuts. Complete step 2. Put the Brussels sprouts and 45 ml (3 tbsp) water in a large bowl, cover and cook on HIGH for 10–12 minutes, until just tender. Drain. Add the cooked chestnuts, butter, salt and pepper to taste and cook on HIGH for 1–2 minutes or until hot and the butter is melted. Serve at once.

CELERY BAKED IN CREAM. A little cream is a delicious way of bringing out the full superb flavour of celery. Serve with plain grilled meat or fish.

CELERY BAKED IN CREAM
THE EASTERN COUNTIES

Celery grows well in the rich black soil of the fen country surrounding Ely in Cambridgeshire, where more than half the British outdoor crop comes from. Both white and green celery are available and either variety can be used for this recipe.

SERVES 4

1 large head of celery, trimmed
1.25 ml (¼ tsp) ground allspice
2 garlic cloves, skinned and crushed
300 ml (10 fl oz) fresh single cream
salt and pepper
25 g (1 oz) fresh wholemeal breadcrumbs

1. Reserve a few celery leaves to garnish, then cut the sticks lengthways into thin strips. Cut each strip into 5 cm (2 inch) lengths and put into an ovenproof serving dish.

MARROW WITH TOMATO AND ONION

COUNTRYWIDE

Use well-flavoured English tomatoes for this recipe. Marrows are excellent cooked in a tasty sauce, as they happily absorb all the delicious herby juices.

SERVES 4–6

25 g (1 oz) butter

2 medium onions, skinned and chopped

1 garlic clove, skinned and crushed

1 medium marrow, peeled, seeded and cubed

6 large tomatoes, skinned and chopped

30 ml (2 tbsp) tomato purée

30 ml (2 tbsp) chopped fresh mixed herbs or 10 ml (2 tsp) dried mixed herbs

salt and pepper

1. Melt the butter in a large saucepan and gently fry the onions and garlic for 5 minutes, until soft. Add the marrow and cook for a further 5 minutes.
2. Stir in remaining ingredients, cover and simmer for 30 minutes, until the vegetables are tender. Season to taste. Serve at once.

TO MICROWAVE

Melt the butter in a large bowl on HIGH for 45 seconds. Cook the onions and garlic on HIGH for 4 minutes, then add the marrow and continue cooking on HIGH for a further 4 minutes. Add remaining ingredients, cover and cook on HIGH for 30 minutes, until the vegetables are tender. Serve at once.

MARROW WITH TOMATO AND ONION. A lively way to make the most of marrows. The colourful mixture tastes as good as it looks.

CARROTS WITH MINT AND LEMON
THE EASTERN COUNTIES

Tender young carrots, in the shops during spring and early summer, have a lovely sweet flavour which is brought out to the full by the sugar and lemon juice in this recipe. Unwashed carrots, which sometimes still have their feathery foliage, keep better than those sold washed and prepacked.

SERVES 4

700 g (1½ lb) small new carrots, trimmed and scrubbed

salt and pepper

finely grated rind and juice of ½ lemon

5 ml (1 tsp) light soft brown sugar

15 g (½ oz) butter

30 ml (2 tbsp) chopped fresh mint

1. Cook the carrots in boiling salted water for about 10 minutes, until just tender. Drain.
2. Return the carrots to the pan with the remaining ingredients and toss together over a high heat until the butter melts. Serve at once.

TO MICROWAVE

 Put the carrots in a large bowl with the lemon rind and juice, sugar and the butter. Cover and cook on HIGH for about 10 minutes or until just tender. Stir in the mint and serve at once.

CARROTS WITH MINT AND LEMON. A mouthwatering mix of flavours in a simple and attractive dish which takes only a few minutes to prepare.

RED CABBAGE WITH PEARS
COUNTRYWIDE

This recipe rings the changes on the old favourite, cabbage with apples, using pears instead. All varieties of dessert pears can be used successfully in this dish, which has a gentle, mellow flavour after long, slow cooking. It's a perfect accompaniment for bacon.

SERVES 4–6

1 garlic clove, skinned and crushed

900 g (2 lb) red cabbage, finely shredded

2 large firm pears, peeled, cored and thickly sliced

salt and pepper

150 ml (¼ pint) vegetable or chicken stock

30 ml (2 tbsp) lemon juice

1. Rub the garlic round the sides of a 3.4 litre (6 pint) casserole. Spoon half of the cabbage into the dish, followed by a layer of pears. Season to taste and repeat the layers. Pour over the stock and lemon juice.
2. Cover tightly and bake at 170°C (325°F) mark 3 for about 2 hours or until the cabbage is just tender. Adjust the seasoning and stir gently to mix together before serving.

TO MICROWAVE

Complete step 1 (substituting a large bowl or microwave casserole). Cover and cook on HIGH for 20–25 minutes or until the cabbage is tender. Adjust the seasoning and stir gently to mix together before serving.

GLAZED SHALLOTS
COUNTRYWIDE

Shallots are smaller than onions and have a milder flavour. They keep well, so it's worth buying a supply when you see them. Store them in a cool, dry place and use them up as soon as they show any signs of sprouting.

SERVES 4

700 g (1½ lb) shallots, skinned

40 g (1½ oz) butter

salt and pepper

chopped fresh parsley, to garnish

1. Put the shallots in a medium saucepan, cover with water and bring to the boil and cook for 5 minutes. Drain.
2. Melt the butter in a medium frying pan, add the shallots and season to taste. Cover and cook for about 10 minutes, until the shallots are tender and well glazed. Turn into a warm serving dish and sprinkle with parsley.

TO MICROWAVE

☑ Put the shallots in a medium bowl, add 45 ml (3 tbsp) water and cook on HIGH for 4 minutes. Melt the butter in a medium bowl on HIGH for 1 minute. Add the shallots and cook on HIGH for 10 minutes. Turn into a warm serving dish and sprinkle with parsley.

RUNNER BEANS WITH ONIONS AND TOMATOES

COUNTRYWIDE

Runner beans used to be grown for their attractive red flowers and have only been produced for food since the last century. They are grown mainly in the south of England.

SERVES 4–6

☑

15 g (½ oz) butter

1 medium onion, skinned and chopped

1 garlic clove, skinned and crushed

397 g (14 oz) can chopped tomatoes

700 g (1½ lb) young runner beans, topped and tailed and cut into 1 cm (½ inch) lengths

15 ml (1 tbsp) chopped fresh basil or 5 ml (1 tsp) dried

salt and pepper

1. Melt the butter in a large saucepan and cook the onion and garlic gently for 3–5 minutes, until softened but not browned. Add the tomatoes with their juice, bring to the boil and simmer for 10–15 minutes, until reduced.
2. Stir the beans into the sauce with the dried basil, if using, cover tightly and cook for 10–15 minutes, until the beans are tender but still crisp. Stir in the fresh basil, if using, and season to taste. Serve hot or cold.

TO MICROWAVE

☑ Put the butter, onion and garlic in a large bowl, cover and cook on HIGH for 5–7 minutes, until softened. Add the tomatoes and their juice and cook, uncovered, on HIGH for 8–10 minutes, until reduced and thickened. Stir the beans into the sauce with the dried basil, if using, re-cover and cook on HIGH for 10–12 minutes or until the beans are tender but still crisp, stirring occasionally. Stir in the fresh basil, if using, and season to taste. Serve hot or cold.

LEFT
GLAZED SHALLOTS.
Their buttery sheen and sprinkling of parsley give these sweet-tasting little shallots plenty of eye-appeal.

RIGHT
RUNNER BEANS WITH ONIONS AND TOMATOES. An interesting way to serve one of the best summer vegetables. Garlic and basil make this a deliciously aromatic dish.

CABBAGE

Cabbage has always been one of Britain's most popular vegetables and is available all year round in seasonal varieties. The main growing areas are Lincolnshire, Lancashire and Kent.

ROUNDHEAD SPRING CABBAGE

RED CABBAGE   WHITE CABBAGE

ROUNDHEADED SPRING CABBAGE

Looser, with a smaller heart, than other types. Don't overcook – it's delicious steamed until tender but still crunchy, then tossed in butter. Strong flavours like caraway seeds or juniper berries (see recipe, page 225) go well with cabbage.

RED CABBAGE

Popular in autumn and winter, this is often cooked with apple and vinegar (see recipe, page 228 for an interesting variation with pears), and served with game or pork. Also good raw in salads.

WHITE CABBAGE

Very firm, with densely packed leaves, and stores well. Good raw, grated or shredded in winter salads and coleslaw (see recipe, page 231). An autumn and winter vegetable.

SAVOY CABBAGE

Distinctive for its crinkly, curly leaves. The whole head or individual leaves are good for stuffing. Available all year.

CHINESE LEAF

This cabbage originally from Asia is crunchy with a mild celery flavour. Good raw in salads and cooked in stir-fries. Available from spring to autumn.

SAVOY CABBAGE

CHINESE LEAF

NEW POTATO SALAD
THE WEST

The warm climate of Cornwall produces tender young vegetables earlier than other parts of the UK. Buy the smallest freshest potatoes you can find and cook them the same day. For a luxury touch use clotted instead of double cream. Dress the potatoes while still warm, even if you are serving them cold, as this allows the flavours to be absorbed.

SERVES 4–6

700 g (1½ lb) small new potatoes
2 hard-boiled egg yolks
large pinch of cayenne pepper
5 ml (1 tsp) caster sugar
1.25 ml (¼ tsp) anchovy essence
15 ml (1 tbsp) herb vinegar
150 ml (5 fl oz) fresh double cream
snipped fresh chives, to garnish

1. Cook the potatoes in their skins, in boiling salted water for 10–15 minutes, until tender.
2. Meanwhile, make the dressing. Mash the egg yolks, cayenne pepper and sugar to a paste with the anchovy essence, the vinegar and 5 ml (1 tsp) cold water. Stir in the cream.
3. When the potatoes are cooked, drain thoroughly and toss with the dressing. Serve warm or cold, garnished with snipped chives.

VARIATION
Replace the fresh cream with fresh soured cream or natural yogurt and substitute the anchovy essence for 15 ml (1 tbsp) chopped fresh herbs such as tarragon, chives, mint or parsley.

TO MICROWAVE

Put the potatoes and 90 ml (6 tbsp) water in a large bowl. Cover and cook on HIGH for 9–12 minutes, until tender, stirring occasionally. Complete the recipe.

ENDIVE, ORANGE AND HAZELNUT SALAD
COUNTRYWIDE

Endive is rather like a lettuce with very crinkly leaves, ranging through shades of green to yellow. It is sometimes sold as 'frisée'. Endive wilts quickly, so buy it fresh when needed and don't store for more than a day.

SERVES 4–6

4 large oranges
1 head of endive, torn into small pieces

1 bunch of watercress, trimmed, torn into sprigs and washed

1 small red pepper, seeded and cut into thin strips

150 g (5 oz) natural yogurt

salt and pepper

25 g (1 oz) hazelnuts

1. Remove all of the peel and the white pith from 3 of the oranges, then segment them. Mix the orange segments with the endive, watercress and pepper in a large salad bowl.
2. To make the dressing, finely grate the rind from the remaining orange into a small bowl, then squeeze in the juice. Whisk in the yogurt and season to taste with salt and pepper.
3. Spread the hazelnuts out on a baking sheet and toast lightly under a hot grill. Turn the nuts on to a clean tea-towel and rub off the loose skins. Roughly chop the nuts.
4. Just before serving, drizzle the dressing over the salad and sprinkle with the nuts. Serve at once while the nuts are still crunchy.

COLESLAW SALAD WITH BLUE CHEESE DRESSING

COUNTRYWIDE

Lymeswold was the first new English cheese to appear for 200 years, when it was launched on the market in 1982. It quickly became popular for its creamy texture and rich flavour, with an added tang from the blue veining. Somerset Blue is a similar style, full-fat, soft cheese. Use either to make the tasty dressing for this salad, which is ideal to serve in winter.

SERVES 4

50 g (2 oz) Lymeswold or Somerset Blue cheese, rinded

30 ml (2 tbsp) mayonnaise

15 ml (1 tbsp) lemon juice

150 g (5 oz) natural yogurt

salt and pepper

225 g (8 oz) white cabbage, very finely shredded

225 g (8 oz) red cabbage, very finely shredded

1 eating apple, unpeeled, cored and cut into matchstick strips

50 g (2 oz) sultanas

1. To make the dressing, put the cheese, mayonnaise and lemon juice in a food processor and work until smooth. Gradually beat in the yogurt and season to taste.
2. Put the cabbages, apple and sultanas in a salad bowl. Pour over the dressing and toss together until well coated in the dressing. Cover and chill until ready to serve.

WINTER SALAD

COUNTRYWIDE

A crunchy combination of colourful fresh vegetables. British chicory is available from mid-April to mid-November. It has a distinctive, bitter flavour and comes as tightly packed heads of white leaves, with yellow tips. Store it in the salad drawer of the fridge, where it will keep well for up to one week.

SERVES 4–6

1 eating apple, cored and chopped

1 head of celery, sliced

1 cooked beetroot, peeled and sliced

2 heads of chicory, sliced

1 punnet of mustard and cress, trimmed

2.5 ml (½ tsp) prepared English mustard

2.5 ml (½ tsp) sugar

60 ml (4 tbsp) fresh single cream

10 ml (2 tsp) white wine vinegar

salt and pepper

3 eggs, hard-boiled and cut into wedges

1. Lightly mix the apple, celery, beetroot and chicory together with the cress in a large salad bowl.
2. To make the dressing, whisk the mustard, sugar, cream and vinegar together. Season to taste. Pour over the salad and toss together so that everything is coated in the dressing. Add the eggs, then serve at once.

WINTER SALAD. An attractively arranged dish, that can be served either alone, for a light lunch or supper, or as a main course accompaniment.

OPPOSITE
LEFT
ENDIVE, ORANGE AND HAZELNUT SALAD. A glorious mixture of flavours and textures, combined to make a bright and colourful salad.

RIGHT
NEW POTATO SALAD. Tiny potatoes, coated in a rich, piquant dressing, for a tempting early summer salad.

PUDDINGS & DESSERTS

For over three centuries puddings from Britain have had a great and well deserved reputation. Substantial, or light and delicate, there's much to be said for rounding off a meal with one of these fabulous dishes. They range from traditional puddings to dinner party desserts. Choose from fresh fruit puddings, pies, milk, custard and cream puddings, cheesecakes and ice creams.

OSBORNE PUDDING
COUNTRYWIDE

*A delicious variation on that much-loved nursery favourite,
bread and butter pudding, which uses brown bread, spread
with marmalade. The recipe has been round for centuries
and has always been popular, partly because it is such a good
way to use up day-old bread. But, of course, there's nothing
to stop you cutting a few slices specially to make it.*

SERVES 4

4 thin slices day-old wholemeal bread
butter for spreading
orange marmalade for spreading
50 g (2 oz) currants or sultanas
450 ml (¾ pint) fresh milk
2 eggs
15 ml (1 tbsp) brandy or rum (optional)
finely grated rind of 1 orange
15 ml (1 tbsp) light soft brown sugar
grated nutmeg

1. Spread the bread with butter and marmalade, then
cut into triangles. Arrange, buttered side up, in a
buttered ovenproof serving dish, sprinkling the layers
with the fruit.
2. Heat the milk, but do not boil. Beat the eggs with
the brandy, if using, and the orange rind, then gradually
pour on the warm milk, stirring continuously. Pour over
the bread and leave to stand for at least 15 minutes to
allow the bread to absorb the milk.
3. Sprinkle the sugar and nutmeg on top of the pudding
and bake at 180°C (350°F) mark 4 for 30–40 minutes,
until set and lightly browned. Serve hot with custard or
fresh cream.

TO MICROWAVE

Complete step 1. Put the milk in a heatproof jug
and cook on HIGH for 2 minutes or until hot but
not boiling. Complete the remainder of step 2. Cook the
pudding on LOW for 15–20 minutes or until just set.
Sprinkle with the sugar and nutmeg, then brown under
a hot grill. Serve hot with custard or fresh cream.

MILK PUDDING
COUNTRYWIDE

*There's nothing nicer than a lovingly made milk pudding – do
use creamy, fresh milk though, and don't omit the butter or
spice. Opt for rice, tapioca, sago or semolina, whichever you
have. The method's easy for them all.*

SERVES 4

50 g (2 oz) short-grain white or brown pudding rice, flaked rice or tapioca, or 40 g (1½ oz) semolina or sago
568–900 ml (1–1½ pints) fresh milk
30 ml (2 tbsp) sugar
15 g (½ oz) butter
1.25 ml (¼ tsp) ground cinnamon, ground mixed spice or grated nutmeg

1. If using rice, flaked rice or tapioca, put it in a
buttered 1.1 litre (2 pint) ovenproof serving dish. Pour
in 568 ml (1 pint) milk. If using brown rice, add an
extra 300 ml (½ pint) milk. Add the sugar and butter.
Sprinkle top with cinnamon, mixed spice or nutmeg.
2. If using semolina or sago, heat the milk in a
saucepan until lukewarm, then gradually sprinkle in the
semolina or sago, stirring continuously. Add the sugar
and butter and continue to cook for 10 minutes, until
thickened, stirring frequently. Pour into a buttered
1.1 litre (2 pint) ovenproof serving dish and sprinkle
the top with the cinnamon, mixed spice or nutmeg.
3. Bake the rice, flaked rice or tapioca pudding in the
oven at 170°C (325°F) mark 3 for 2–2½ hours (brown
rice for an extra 30 minutes). Stir the pudding 2 or 3
times during the first hour, but leave for the remaining
time to form a crust.
4. Bake the semolina or sago pudding at 180°C (350°F)
mark 4 for 30 minutes, without stirring.
5. Serve milk puddings hot or cold, plain or topped with
fresh fruit, chopped nuts, or thick natural yogurt.

MILK

Milk is a highly nutritious food and a major source of protein and calcium. A cool refreshing drink in summer, or a warming one in winter, milk is one of the most versatile ingredients in the kitchen. It is vital for making a wide range of dishes – sauces, soups, batters, pancakes and many delicious desserts.

Five different types of pasteurised milk are available, each classified according to fat content. Use the foil caps on milk bottles as a guide to each type.

CHANNEL ISLAND
(gold top)

This is the richest, creamiest milk, with 4.8% fat content.

WHOLE MILK
(silver top)

Most of the cream rises to the surface to give a visible cream line. It contains 3.8% fat.

HOMOGENISED
(red top)

Whole milk (3.8% fat) in which cream has been evenly distributed throughout.

SEMI-SKIMMED
(silver and red striped top)

A little over half the cream has been removed to give between 1.5 and 1.8% fat.

SKIMMED
(silver and blue checked top)

Almost all the cream has been removed to give 0.1% fat.

Other types of whole, semi-skimmed and skimmed milk widely available are:

STERILIZED

This has been heated to boiling point or above to ensure a sterile product and will keep for several weeks without refrigeration, provided it is not opened. Refrigerate after opening.

ULTRA-HEAT
TREATED

Known as UHT or long-life milk, this has been ultra-heated and aseptically packaged in foil-lined containers. It keeps unopened without refrigeration until expiry of date-stamp. Refrigerate after opening.

CHRISTMAS PUDDING

COUNTRYWIDE

Plum pudding only took on its connections with Christmas when it was introduced to the Victorians by Prince Albert. Burying a silver coin in the pudding mixture is said to bring good fortune to whoever finds it in their portion and all the family should make a wish while stirring the mixture on Stir Up Sunday, the Sunday before Advent. Keep an eye on the pudding during the long steaming, and be sure to keep the pan topped up with boiling water.

SERVES 6–8

---

50 g (2 oz) plain flour

2.5 ml (½ tsp) ground mixed spice

2.5 ml (½ tsp) grated nutmeg

2.5 ml (½ tsp) ground cinnamon

50 g (2 oz) shredded beef suet

50 g (2 oz) fresh breadcrumbs

50 g (2 oz) soft light brown sugar

175 g (6 oz) raisins

175 g (6 oz) sultanas

25 g (1 oz) mixed peel, chopped

1 eating apple, grated

1 carrot, peeled and grated

25 g (1 oz) blanched almonds, chopped

grated rind and juice of ½ lemon

grated rind ½ orange

10 ml (2 tsp) treacle

65 ml (2½ fl oz) barley wine

15 ml (1 tbsp) brandy

1. Grease a 1.1 litre (2 pint) ovenproof pudding basin. Mix all the ingredients together, cover and leave overnight in the refrigerator.
2. Spoon the mixture into the prepared basin, cover with pleated greaseproof paper and foil and secure with string. Steam for 6 hours. Cool, then remove the covers.
3. Turn out of the basin and cover the pudding tightly with greaseproof paper. Store for at least 1 month in a cool place.
4. To serve, uncover, place in a basin, re-cover and steam for 2 hours. Or, reheat in a pressure cooker, following the manufacturer's instructions. Serve with brandy butter, fresh cream or custard.

pudding. Spoon the flavouring of your choice into the bottom (see below).

2. Mix together the flour, salt, suet or softened butter and sugar. Make a well in the centre and add the egg and enough milk to give a soft dropping consistency. Pour into the prepared dish.

3. If steaming the pudding, cover with pleated greaseproof paper or foil and secure with string. Steam for 1½–2 hours.

4. If baking, cook, uncovered, at 180°C (350°F) mark 4 for about 1 hour, until well risen. Serve hot with custard.

VARIATIONS

CHOCOLATE PUDDING
Add 45 ml (3 tbsp) cocoa, sifted with the flour, or stir 25 g (1 oz) chocolate dots or chips into the basic mixture.

COCONUT PUDDING
Replace 25 g (1 oz) of the flour with 25 g (1 oz) desiccated coconut.

BLACK CAP PUDDING
Spoon 45 ml (3 tbsp) blackcurrant jam into the bottom of the basin.

MARMALADE PUDDING
Spoon 45 ml (3 tbsp) marmalade into the bottom of the basin.

TREACLE OR SYRUP PUDDING
Spoon 30 ml (2 tbsp) treacle or golden syrup into the bottom of the basin.

LEMON OR ORANGE PUDDING
Add the finely grated rind of 1 lemon or orange to the basic mixture.

CASTLE PUDDING
Divide lemon pudding mixture between 8 dariole moulds, then cover and steam for 30–40 minutes.

FRUIT PUDDING
Add 75 g (3 oz) no-soak mixed dried fruit to the basic mixture.

CANTERBURY PUDDING
Replace half of the flour with fresh breadcrumbs. Add the finely grated rind and juice of 1 lemon and replace half the milk with brandy.

GINGER PUDDING
Add 5 ml (1 tsp) ground ginger and 25 g (1 oz) chopped stem ginger to the basic mixture. Spoon 30 ml (2 tbsp) golden syrup into the bottom of the basin, if liked.

CANARY PUDDING
Replace half of the flour with fresh breadcrumbs. Add the finely grated rind of 1 lemon and 30 ml (2 tbsp) Madeira or sweet sherry instead of some of the milk.

COLLEGE PUDDING
Replace the flour with 100 g (4 oz) fresh breadcrumbs. Add 100 g (4 oz) mixed sultanas and raisins, 2.5 ml (½ tsp) baking powder and a large pinch each of ground cinnamon, ground cloves and grated nutmeg. Spoon into 6 greased dariole moulds, cover with foil and bake at 180°C (350°F) mark 4 for 45 minutes.

EVE'S PUDDING
Put 450 g (1 lb) peeled, cored and thickly sliced eating apples in the bottom of a deep pie dish. Make the mixture using butter and bake as above.

STEAMED SYRUP PUDDING. Ideal food for chilly days, steamed puddings are a childhood favourite which deserve to be made more often. This variation is served in a sticky pool of warm golden syrup, which also soaks into the top during cooking.

STEAMED AND BAKED PUDDINGS
COUNTRYWIDE

There are dozens of variations on the basic steamed pudding, and by adding ingredients to the mixture, or using different preserves for the topping, you can ring the changes almost indefinitely. But whichever version you go for, remember that no pudding is complete without a jug of creamy custard.

SERVES 4

175 g (6 oz) self-raising flour
pinch of salt
75 g (3 oz) shredded beef suet or softened butter
50 g (2 oz) caster sugar
1 egg
about 90 ml (6 tbsp) fresh milk

1. Grease a 1.1 litre (2 pint) pudding basin if making a steamed pudding, or a deep pie dish if baking the

TO MICROWAVE

 Complete steps 1, 2 and 3, covering with greaseproof paper. Cook on HIGH for 5–7 minutes, until well risen and firm to the touch. Serve hot with custard.

HASTY PUDDING
COUNTRYWIDE

All you need for this surprisingly good stand-by pudding are milk, flour, butter, sugar and a little spice. It takes just a few minutes to make, hence its name, and can be eaten hot or cold. It is particularly good served with poached fruit.

SERVES 2–4

50 g (2 oz) butter
30 ml (2 tbsp) plain flour
450 ml (¾ pint) fresh milk
1 egg
Freshly grated nutmeg or ground cinnamon
40 g (1½ oz) light soft brown sugar

1. Put 25 g (1 oz) of the butter, the flour and milk in a saucepan. Heat, whisking continuously, until the sauce thickens, boils and is smooth. Simmer for 1–2 minutes. Stir in the egg, then pour into a flameproof serving dish.
2. Dot with the remaining butter and sprinkle generously with nutmeg or cinnamon and the sugar. Brown quickly under a hot grill. Serve hot on its own or with poached fruit such as apples, pears or rhubarb.

ROLY-POLY PUDDINGS
COUNTRYWIDE

The same basic suet pastry is used for jam roly-poly and all its variations. It is fast and easy to make and, if mixed quickly and deftly, has a light, spongy texture – a far cry from the hefty steamed puds of schooldays. Steam or boil the puddings or, if less time is available, bake them instead.

SERVES 4

175 g (6 oz) self-raising flour
pinch of salt
75 g (3 oz) shredded beef suet

1. Mix the flour, salt and suet together in a bowl.
2. Using a round-bladed knife, stir in enough water to give a light, elastic dough. Knead very lightly until smooth.
3. Roll out to an oblong about 23×25 cm (9×11 inches) and use as required. (See variations below.)
4. Make a 5 cm (2 inch) pleat across a clean tea-towel or pudding cloth. Or pleat together sheets of greased greaseproof paper and strong foil. Wrap the roll loosely, to allow for expansion, in the cloth or foil, pleating the open edges tightly together. Tie the ends securely with string to form a cracker shape. Make a string handle across the top. Lower the suet roll into a roasting tin or large pan of boiling water, cover and boil for 1½ hours depending on filling and size. Lift the pudding out of the water using the string handle. Place on a wire rack standing over a plate and allow excess moisture to drain off. Snip the string and gently roll the pudding out of the cloth or foil on to a warmed serving plate. Roly-poly puddings can also be baked, uncovered at 200°C (400°F) mark 6 for about 40 minutes. Serve sliced with custard.

VARIATIONS

JAM ROLY-POLY
Spread the pastry with 60–90 ml (4–6 tbsp) jam. Brush the edges with milk and roll up, starting from the short end. Steam or bake as above.

SYRUP ROLY-POLY
Spread the pastry with 60 ml (4 tbsp) golden syrup mixed with 30–45 ml (2–3 tbsp) fresh white breadcrumbs. Steam or bake as above.

LEMON ROLY-POLY
Add the finely grated rind of 1 lemon to the pastry. Roll out and spread with 60–90 ml (4–6 tbsp) lemon curd. Steam or bake as above.

MINCEMEAT ROLY-POLY
Add the finely grated rind of 1 orange to the dough. Roll out and spread with 60–90 ml (4–6 tbsp) mincemeat. Steam or bake as above.

SPOTTED DICK OR DOG
Replace half of the flour with 100 g (4 oz) fresh breadcrumbs. Add 50 g (2 oz) caster sugar, 175 g (6 oz) currants, finely grated rind of 1 lemon and 75 ml (5 tbsp) milk. Mix everything together. Shape into a neat roll about 15 cm (6 inches) long. Boil as above.

TO MICROWAVE

 Complete steps 1, 2 and 3. Wrap the pudding in pleated greaseproof paper and cook on HIGH for 4–5 minutes.

BAKED APPLE AND COCONUT PUDDING

THE SOUTH-EAST

Eating apples are sweeter than cookers and many varieties – especially Cox's – hold their shape well when cooked. Juicy slices are baked on top of a light and airy pudding mixture, and a topping of toasted coconut completes the dish.

SERVES 6

finely grated rind and juice of 1 lemon

100 g (4 oz) soft light brown sugar, plus 30 ml (2 tbsp)

6 medium eating apples, each weighing about 100 g (4 oz), peeled, cored and sliced

100 g (4 oz) butter

2 eggs, separated

100 g (4 oz) plain wholemeal flour

7.5 ml (1½ tsp) baking powder

25 g (1 oz) desiccated coconut

about 60 ml (4 tbsp) apricot jam, warmed

shredded coconut, toasted, to decorate

1. Pour the lemon juice into a large bowl; stir in the 30 ml (2 tbsp) sugar and add the apples, making sure they are well coated.

2. Gradually beat the 100 g (4 oz) sugar into the butter until well blended. Add the lemon rind, then beat in

BAKED APPLE AND COCONUT PUDDING. Thin slices of apple sunk into the meltingly light base and arranged in patterns make for a very attractive dish that tastes wonderful too.

the egg yolks one at a time. Stir in the flour, baking powder and desiccated coconut.

3. Whisk the egg whites until stiff but not dry, then fold into the creamed ingredients. Spoon into a lightly greased 24–25.5 cm (9½–10 inch) fluted flan dish. Press the apples into the mixture, spooning any juices over them.

4. Stand the dish on a baking sheet and bake at 170°C (325°F) mark 3 for 1–1¼ hours or until well browned and firm to the touch, covering lightly with greaseproof paper if necessary.

5. Cool for about 15 minutes, then brush with the apricot jam and scatter over the toasted shredded coconut. Serve while still warm with custard.

APPLE CHARLOTTE
COUNTRYWIDE

There is much doubt surrounding the origin of the name 'charlotte'. Meat dishes called 'charlets' were around in the 15th century, but some say that the sweet dish took its name much later, from Queen Charlotte, wife of George III. Whatever the truth of the matter, this is a delicious dessert, with a crisp golden crust and a filling of apples.

SERVES 6

900 g (2 lb) cooking apples, peeled, cored and sliced

2.5 ml (½ tsp) ground cinnamon

finely grated rind and juice of 1 lemon

light soft brown sugar, to taste

75 g (3 oz) butter, melted

8 thin slices brown bread, crusts removed

1. Put the apples, cinnamon, lemon rind and juice and sugar in a heavy-based saucepan. Cover and simmer gently until pulpy, stirring occasionally.

2. Beat thoroughly with a wooden spoon, then cook, uncovered, over a high heat, stirring continuously, until any excess liquid has evaporated and the purée is very thick.

3. Brush the butter all over the slices of bread. Line the base and sides of a greased 15 cm (6 inch) Charlotte mould or deep cake tin with the slices of bread, making sure that they overlap.

4. Spoon in the apple purée and cover with more overlapping slices of bread. Bake at 190°C (375°F) mark 5 for about 30 minutes, until the top is golden brown. Serve at once, turned out and accompanied with custard or fresh cream.

TO MICROWAVE

To melt the butter, cut into small pieces, put in a small bowl and cook on HIGH for 1 minute. Put the apples, cinnamon, lemon rind and juice and sugar in a large bowl. Cover and cook on HIGH for 6–8 minutes, until the apple is soft, stirring occasionally. Uncover and cook on HIGH for 5 minutes, until any excess liquid has evaporated and the purée is very thick, stirring occasionally. Complete the recipe.

APPLE AND ORANGE CRUMBLE
COUNTRYWIDE

The beauty of crumbles is that they are very easy to make, and good-tempered enough to have their cooking time and temperature adjusted a little to fit in with the rest of the menu. The only thing to make sure of is that the top is nicely golden, but not too brown. The recipe here uses apple and orange but any type of fruit can be used.

SERVES 4–6

700 g (1½ lb) cooking apples, peeled, cored and sliced

grated rind and juice of 1 orange

25 g (1 oz) light soft brown sugar

100 g (4 oz) plain flour

50 g (2 oz) plain wholemeal flour

75 g (3 oz) butter

40 g (1½ oz) icing sugar, sieved

1.25 ml (¼ tsp) ground cinnamon

1. Put the apples, orange rind and juice and sugar into a 1.4 litre (2½ pint) ovenproof serving dish.

2. Put the flours into a mixing bowl and rub in the butter until the mixture resembles fine breadcrumbs. Stir in the icing sugar and cinnamon, making sure all the ingredients are thoroughly combined.

3. Sprinkle the crumble topping over the apple. Bake at 200°C (400°F) mark 6 for 30–40 minutes, until the topping is crisp and golden. Serve hot with fresh cream or custard.

VARIATIONS

1. Use any type of fresh fruit such as pears, rhubarb, plums, apricots, damsons or gooseberries.

2. Add the grated rind of an orange or lemon to the crumb mixture before sprinkling it over the fruit.

3. Replace 75 g (3 oz) of the flour with rolled oats, bran flakes or oatmeal.

4. Add 25 g (1 oz) chopped nuts such as almonds, walnuts or brazils to the crumble topping mixture.

5. Replace the cinnamon with mixed spice or ginger and add to the flour before rubbing in the butter.

BANBURY APPLE PIE. A spicy fruit filling, light, short pastry and a thick dredging of sugar on top make this apple pie extra special.

DAIRY ICE CREAM

Ice cream made with dairy cream can now bear a special logo that is a mark of high-quality. It will contain at least 10% butterfat, half of which must come from Welsh or English Double Cream. Choose from a wide variety of flavours, including vanilla, butter pecan, creamy toffee, almond, and many more.

BANBURY APPLE PIE

THE SOUTH-EAST

A traditional recipe which uses a pie dish with pastry on the top and bottom. Use wholemeal flour instead of white if you prefer a nuttier taste. Cooking apples have been used here, but if you like, you can substitute eating apples – they will not need extra sugar.

SERVES 6

✳

350 g (12 oz) plain flour
pinch of salt
150 g (6 oz) butter
15 ml (1 tbsp) caster sugar
1 egg, lightly beaten
700 g (1½ lb) cooking apples
juice of ½ lemon
100 g (4 oz) sultanas
75 g (3 oz) soft light brown sugar
pinch of ground cinnamon
pinch of freshly grated nutmeg
grated rind and juice of 1 orange
fresh milk, to glaze
caster sugar for sprinkling

1. To make the pastry, put the flour and salt in a bowl and rub in the butter until the mixture resembles fine breadcrumbs. Stir in the caster sugar, then stir in the egg and enough water to bind the mixture together.
2. Knead lightly on a lightly floured surface, then roll out two-thirds of the pastry and use to line a shallow 900 ml (1½ pint) pie dish.
3. Peel, core and thinly slice the apples. Put in a bowl and sprinkle with lemon juice.
4. Layer the apples, sultanas, brown sugar, spices and orange rind in the pie dish. Sprinkle with the orange juice.
5. Roll out the remaining pastry to form a lid, pressing the edges together. Scallop the edges, then make a slit in the centre of the pie.
6. Brush the top with milk to glaze, then bake at 200°C (400°F) mark 6 for 30 minutes, until golden brown. Sprinkle the top with caster sugar and serve hot or cold. Accompany with dairy ice cream.

CUMBERLAND RUM NICKY

THE NORTH

This rich and sticky tart is a northern speciality incorporating several of the exotic imports which came from Cumberland's trade with the West Indies. Dates, ginger and rum feature widely in many local dishes. This version also includes dried apricots and is made with wholemeal flour, making it a dish high in fibre.

SERVES 6

✳

225 g (8 oz) stoned dates, chopped
100 g (4 oz) no-soak dried apricots
50 g (2 oz) stem ginger, chopped
45 ml (3 tbsp) light rum
30 ml (2 tbsp) soft light brown sugar
225 g (8 oz) plain wholemeal flour
pinch of salt
115 g (4½ oz) butter
1 egg yolk, lightly beaten
demerara sugar, to decorate (optional)

1. Mix together the dates, apricots, ginger, rum and half of the sugar. Leave to soak while making the pastry.
2. Put the flour and salt in a bowl and rub in 100 g (4 oz) of the butter until the mixture resembles fine breadcrumbs. Add the remaining sugar, then the egg yolk and enough water to bind. Knead lightly on a floured surface.
3. Roll out half of the pastry and use to line a greased 25.5 cm (10 inch) flat pie plate.
4. Spread the pastry with the soaked dried fruit. Dot with the remaining butter.
5. Roll out the remaining pastry and use to cover the pie. Cut any pastry trimmings into leaves and use to decorate the pie. Brush with milk and bake at 200°C (400°F) mark 6 for 30–35 minutes until golden brown. Sprinkle with demerara sugar, if liked. Serve hot with natural yogurt.

BAKEWELL PUDDING
THE MIDLANDS

A buttery mixture, flavoured with ground almonds and baked in a light, flaky pastry case, is the basis of this traditional Derbyshire recipe, sometimes known as Bakewell tart, the origin of which is still secret.

SERVES 6

✳

212 g (7½ oz) frozen packet puff pastry, thawed

60 ml (4 tbsp) red jam

100 g (4 oz) ground almonds

100 g (4 oz) caster sugar

50 g (2 oz) butter

3 eggs, beaten

1.25 ml (¼ tsp) almond essence

1. Roll out the pastry on a floured surface and use to line a 900 ml (1½ pint) shallow pie dish.
2. Knock up the edge of the pastry in the pie dish with the back of a knife.
3. Mark the rim with the prongs of a fork. Brush the jam over the base. Chill in the refrigerator while making the filling.
4. Make the filling. Beat the almonds with the sugar, butter, eggs and almond essence.
5. Pour the filling over the jam and spread it evenly. Bake in the oven at 200°C (400°F) mark 6 for 30 minutes or until the filling is set. Serve warm or cold, with fresh cream or custard.

RIPE TART
THE SOUTH-EAST

The name comes from the village of Ripe in the Sussex South Downs, where a pie feast celebrated the cherry harvest.

SERVES 8

225 g (8 oz) plain flour

pinch of salt

25 g (1 oz) cornflour

100 g (4 oz), plus 10 ml (2 tsp) icing sugar

100 g (4 oz) butter

1 egg yolk

450 g (1 lb) cherries, stoned

2 eggs

75 g (3 oz) ground almonds

few drops of almond essence

1. Sift the flour, salt, cornflour and 10 ml (2 tsp) icing sugar into a bowl, then rub in the butter until the mixture resembles fine breadcrumbs. Add the egg yolk and 30 ml (2 tbsp) cold water and stir to bind together.
2. Knead lightly on a lightly floured surface, roll out. Use to line a 23 cm (9 inch) fluted flan tin. Bake blind at 200°C (400°F) mark 6 for 10–15 minutes, until set.
3. Arrange cherries in flan case. Mix 100 g (4 oz) icing sugar, eggs, almonds and essence, pour over cherries.
4. Bake at 170°C (325°F) mark 3 for 50–60 minutes, until the top is firm and golden. Serve hot or cold.

RIPE TART. Cherries and almonds are a great combination, and both are used in the mouthwateringly moist filling.

WALNUT AND HONEY TART
THE WEST

Walnuts were formerly grown far more widely in Britain than they are today and used in both sweet and savoury dishes. This West Country speciality combines them with local honey in a very rich tart which should be served in small portions only.

SERVES 6

175 g (6 oz) plain wholemeal flour
pinch of salt
75 g (3 oz) butter
finely grated rind and juice of 1 orange
60 ml (4 tbsp) clear honey
75 g (3 oz) fresh wholemeal breadcrumbs
45 ml (3 tbsp) dark soft brown sugar
3 eggs
100 g (4 oz) walnut pieces, roughly chopped

WALNUT AND HONEY TART. Chopped walnuts add crunch to the gooey honey and orange mixture inside this irresistible tart.

1. To make the pastry, put the flour and salt in a bowl and rub in the butter until the mixture resembles fine breadcrumbs. Stir in the orange rind and enough orange juice to bind the mixture together.
2. Roll out the pastry on a lightly floured surface and use to line a 20.5 cm (8 inch) fluted flan dish or tin. Bake blind at 200°C (400°F) mark 6 for 10–15 minutes, until set.
3. Mix the honey, breadcrumbs and the sugar together. Gradually beat in the eggs, one at a time, and any remaining orange juice.
4. Sprinkle the walnuts in the bottom of the pastry case and pour over the filling. Bake at 200°C (400°F) mark 6 for 20–25 minutes, until set. Cover the tart with greaseproof paper if it browns too quickly. Serve warm or cold with clotted or fresh double cream.

KENT LENT PIE
THE SOUTH-EAST

In the days when Lent was strictly observed, many cooks became very ingenious at thinking up new dishes to break the monotony of their abstemious diet. This recipe, sometimes called Kentish Pudding Pie, is rather like a baked cheesecake and made a pleasant change; it was particularly popular in the area round Folkestone.

SERVES 4–6

175 g (6 oz) plain wholemeal flour
pinch of salt
150 g (5 oz) butter
300 ml (½ pint) fresh milk
25 g (1 oz) ground rice
50 g (2 oz) sugar
2 eggs
finely grated rind of 1 lemon
1.25 ml (¼ tsp) grated nutmeg
25 g (1 oz) currants

1. To make the pastry, put the flour and salt in a bowl and rub in 75 g (3 oz) of the butter until the mixture resembles fine breadcrumbs. Stir in 45–60 ml (3–4 tbsp) cold water to bind the mixture together into a dough.
2. Roll out the pastry on a lightly floured surface and use to line a greased 20.5 cm (8 inch) fluted flan dish or tin. Bake blind at 200°C (400°F) mark 6 for 10–15 minutes, until set.
3. Meanwhile, put the milk and rice in a pan and bring to the boil, stirring continuously, until the mixture thickens. Remove the pan from the heat and leave to cool.
4. When the mixture is cold, cream the remaining butter and sugar together until pale and fluffy. Beat in the eggs, one at a time, then add the lemon rind, salt, nutmeg and the rice mixture. Mix thoroughly together and pour into the flan case. Sprinkle the currants on top.
5. Bake at 190°C (375°F) mark 5 for 40–45 minutes, until firm to the touch and golden brown. Serve the pie warm.

SQUIDGY CHOCOLATE ROLL

COUNTRYWIDE

Chocoholics will love this rich recipe, which uses cocoa powder to flavour a moist sponge, rolled and filled with fresh cream. It is an ideal dinner party dessert.

SERVES 6–8

60 ml (4 tbsp) cocoa powder
150 ml (¼ pint) fresh milk
4 eggs, separated
100 g (4 oz) caster sugar
225 ml (8 fl oz) fresh double cream
fresh strawberries and grated chocolate, to decorate

1. Grease and line a 20.5 × 30.5 cm (8 × 12 inch) Swiss roll tin. Mix the cocoa powder and milk in a small saucepan and heat gently until the cocoa powder has dissolved. Remove the pan from the heat and set aside to cool.
2. Whisk the egg yolks and sugar together until pale and fluffy. Whisk the cooled milk mixture into the egg yolk mixture.
3. Whisk the egg whites until stiff, then fold into the cocoa mixture. Spread the mixture evenly into the prepared tin and bake at 180°C (350°F) mark 4 for about 20 minutes until the sponge has risen and is just firm to the touch.
4. Turn out on to a sheet of greaseproof paper and cover with a warm, damp tea-towel to prevent the sponge from drying out. Leave the sponge to cool for 20 minutes.
5. Meanwhile, whip the cream until stiff. Spread over the sponge, reserving half for decorating and then roll it up carefully. Do not roll it up too tightly and do not worry if it cracks slightly. Pipe the reserved cream on top and decorate with strawberries and grated chocolate. Serve chilled.

GREENGAGE TART

THE EASTERN COUNTIES

Back in the 18th century, Sir William Gage planted some French plum trees at Hengrave Hall, near Bury St Edmunds, without knowing exactly what type of fruit to expect. The plums turned out to be green and became known as the green Gage's plum, which eventually became shortened to greengage. They are sweet, oval and yellowy-green with a good flavour and are in season late August and early September.

SERVES 4–6

175 g (6 oz) plain wholemeal flour
pinch of salt
75 g (3 oz) butter
25 g (1 oz) toasted hazelnuts, very finely chopped
15 ml (1 tbsp) soft light brown sugar
450 g (1 lb) greengages or plums, halved and stoned
2 eggs
300 ml (10 fl oz) fresh single cream
caster sugar (optional)

1. To make the pastry, put the flour and salt in a bowl and rub in the butter until the mixture resembles fine breadcrumbs. Stir in the hazelnuts and sugar and enough water to bind the mixture together.
2. Knead lightly on a lightly greased floured surface, then roll out and use to line a greased 20.5 cm (8 inch) fluted flan dish or tin. Bake blind at 200°C (400°F) mark 6 for 10–15 minutes, until set.
3. Arrange the fruit, cut side down, in the pastry case. Beat the eggs with the cream and a little sugar, if liked, and pour over the fruit. Bake at 200°C (400°F) mark 6 for 30–40 minutes, until golden and puffy. Serve warm.

SQUIDGY CHOCOLATE ROLL. Here's a dish that really lives up to its name. Topped with fresh strawberries and cream, it has everything you could want from a special occasion dessert.

RICH PANCAKES

COUNTRYWIDE

An outrageously extravagant version of an everyday dish, this recipe produces wickedly rich pancakes which melt in the mouth.

SERVES 4

⊞

3 eggs
30 ml (2 tbsp) plain flour
15 ml (1 tbsp) brandy or sherry
5 ml (1 tsp) orange flower water
300 ml (10 fl oz) fresh single cream
50 g (2 oz) butter, melted and cooled
extra butter for frying
caster sugar and lemon or orange wedges, to serve

1. Put the eggs, flour, brandy or sherry, orange flower water and cream in a bowl and whisk together. Whisk in the melted butter.
2. Heat a little butter in a small frying pan. When hot, pour in 45 ml (3 tbsp) batter, tilting the pan to cover the base. Cook until the pancake moves freely, then turn over and cook the underside until golden.
3. Transfer the pancake to an ovenproof plate, cover and keep hot in a warm oven. Repeat with the remaining batter to make 8 pancakes. Pile the cooked pancakes on top of each other with a piece of greaseproof paper in between each one. Serve as soon as they are all cooked with sugar and orange or lemon wedges.

OATEN HONEYCOMB

NORTHERN IRELAND

An unusual steamed pudding, which uses porridge oats instead of flour. Honey, both in the mixture and poured over the finished pudding, adds its own distinctive sweetness, which is very pleasant without being cloying.

SERVES 4–6

450 ml (¾ pint) fresh milk
175 g (6 oz) porridge oats
50 g (2 oz) caster sugar
30 ml (2 tbsp) clear honey
25 g (1 oz) butter
finely grated rind of 1 orange
2.5 ml (½ tsp) ground cinnamon
3 eggs, separated

1. Put the milk into a heavy-based saucepan and bring to the boil. Sprinkle in the oats and cook gently, stirring constantly, for 5 minutes.
2. Beat in the sugar, honey, butter, orange rind and cinnamon and mix well. Remove from the heat and beat in the egg yolks.

3. Whisk the egg whites until stiff and carefully fold into the mixture. Turn into a greased 1.2 litre (2 pint) pudding basin, cover with pleated greased greaseproof paper or foil and secure with string.
4. Steam for about 2 hours. Turn out on to a dish and serve with warm honey and single cream.

DAMSON AND APPLE TANSY

THE NORTH

Tansies originally always included the bitter-sweet herb called tansy, which still lends its name to many custard and omelette-type puddings. This sweet/tart combination with Cox's apples traditionally used the Witherslack damsons which grow south of Lake Windermere.

SERVES 4

2 large Cox's apples, peeled, cored and thinly sliced
225 g (8 oz) damsons, halved, stoned and quartered
15 g (½ oz) butter
40 g (1½ oz) sugar
pinch of ground cloves
pinch of ground cinnamon
4 eggs, separated
45 ml (3 tbsp) fresh soured cream or natural yogurt

1. Put the apples, damsons, butter and half of the sugar in a large frying pan.
2. Cook over a gentle heat, until the fruit is softened, stirring continuously. Stir in the cloves and cinnamon, then remove from the heat.
3. Beat the egg yolks with the cream and stir into the fruit. Whisk the egg whites until stiff, then carefully fold in.
4. Cook over a low heat until the mixture has set. Sprinkle the top with the remaining sugar, then brown under a hot grill. Serve immediately, straight from the pan, with soured cream or natural yogurt.

RHUBARB AND ORANGE FLAN

THE NORTH

The use of orange juice in this flan offsets the natural tartness of the rhubarb, while the ginger adds a touch of spice. Rhubarb flourishes in the north of England and 81 per cent of the forced early crop is from there, though rhubarb is grown outdoors throughout other parts of the country.

SERVES 4

75 g (3 oz) butter
150 g (6 oz) digestive biscuits, crushed

450 g (1 lb) fresh rhubarb, trimmed and cut into 2.5 cm (1 inch) lengths

finely grated rind and juice of 1 large orange

2 eggs, separated

50 g (2 oz) caster sugar

30 ml (2 tbsp) cornflour

2.5 ml (½ tsp) ground ginger

orange slices, to decorate

1. Melt the butter in a saucepan, then mix in the biscuit crumbs.
2. Press the mixture over the base and sides of a 20.5 cm (8 inch) fluted flan dish or tin. Chill in the refrigerator while preparing the filling.
3. Put the rhubarb in a saucepan with 45 ml (3 tbsp) water. Cover and simmer gently until the fruit is soft and pulpy. Stir occasionally to prevent the rhubarb sticking to the pan. Work the rhubarb to a purée in a blender or food processor.
4. Put the orange rind and juice into a heavy-based saucepan. Add the egg yolks, caster sugar, cornflour and ginger. Heat gently, stirring constantly, until thick. Stir into the rhubarb purée.
5. Whisk the egg whites until stiff. Fold into the rhubarb custard, then spoon the mixture into the biscuit crust. Refrigerate for at least 4 hours or overnight. Decorate with orange slices just before serving.

TO MICROWAVE

☑ Complete steps 1 and 2. Put the rhubarb and the water in a bowl. Cover and cook on HIGH for 5–6 minutes until tender, stirring occasionally. Complete the recipe.

DAMSON AND APPLE TANSY. Spices and fruit sunk in a deep, rich custard make a deliciously filling supper dish for winter evenings.

RED BERRY FOOL

THE MIDLANDS

The word 'fool' was used to describe a light and airy blend of cream and fresh fruit purée. Depending on the season, choose from any of the soft, juicy fruits that flourish in the Vale of Evesham. Raspberries, strawberries, red- or blackcurrants are all excellent.

SERVES 4

15–30 ml (1–2 tbsp) caster sugar
225 g (8 oz) raspberries
225 g (8 oz) redcurrants
225 g (8 oz) blackcurrants
15 ml (1 tbsp) custard powder
15 ml (1 tbsp) sugar
300 ml (½ pint) fresh milk
150 ml (5 fl oz) fresh whipping cream

1. Put the sugar to taste and 90 ml (6 tbsp) water in a saucepan large enough to hold the fruit and heat gently until the sugar dissolves. Reserve a little of each fruit to decorate and poach the remaining fruit for about 10 minutes, until soft.
2. Remove the pan from the heat and sieve the fruit into a large bowl, then set aside to cool.

3. Blend the custard powder and sugar with 30 ml (2 tbsp) milk. Bring the remaining milk to the boil and pour on to the mixture, stirring well. Return to a clean saucepan, bring to the boil, stirring continuously. Leave to cool completely.
4. Whip the cream until stiff. Fold the custard and most of the cream into the sieved fruit.
5. Spoon the fool into individual glasses. Pipe each dessert with a rosette of remaining cream and top with the reserved fruit to decorate. Serve with crisp biscuits.

TO MICROWAVE

Put most of the fruit and sugar to taste in a medium bowl with 45 ml (3 tbsp) of water. Cook on HIGH for 4–5 minutes. Complete step 2. Blend the custard powder, sugar and milk together in a medium bowl. Cook on HIGH for 4–5 minutes, until boiling and thickened, whisking frequently. Complete the recipe.

OLDE ENGLISH TRIFLE

COUNTRYWIDE

A perfect trifle should be a rich confection of fruit, light sponge, alcohol, real egg custard and whipped cream. The recipe has altered little over the centuries – at one time the custard was topped with syllabub, and fruit has not always been included.

SERVES 6–8

4 trifle sponges
60 ml (4 tbsp) cherry jam
15 ratafia biscuits
60 ml (4 tbsp) sherry
2 bananas, peeled and sliced
grated rind and juice of ½ lemon
225 g (8 oz) cherries, stoned
450 ml (¾ pint) fresh milk
3 eggs
50 g (2 oz) caster sugar
150 ml (5 fl oz) fresh double cream
glacé cherries, to decorate
25 g (1 oz) chopped nuts, toasted, to decorate

1. Cut the trifle sponges in half and spread with jam, then sandwich together. Arrange in the base of a glass serving dish.
2. Cover with ratafias and sprinkle with sherry. Coat the bananas in lemon juice. Arrange the bananas and cherries on top of the ratafias.
3. Heat the milk in a medium saucepan until almost boiling. In a large bowl, whisk together the eggs, lemon rind and sugar until pale, then pour on the hot milk, stirring continuously.
4. Return to the saucepan and heat gently, stirring continuously, until the custard thickens enough to coat

OLDE ENGLISH TRIFLE. Use a clear glass dish to show off this moreish dessert. Nuts and cherries are used to decorate the thick topping of whipped cream.

AUTUMN PUDDING. Always a pleasure to eat, at any time of year. The bread soaks up the ruby red juices beautifully.

the back of a wooden spoon. Do not allow to boil. This takes about 20 minutes. Set aside to cool.

5. Pour the custard over the trifle and leave until cold.

6. Whip the cream until stiff and pipe on the top of the trifle and decorate with glacé cherries and nuts.

TO MICROWAVE

 Complete steps 1 and 2. Put the milk into a medium bowl, cook on HIGH for 5 minutes. Complete remaining part of step 3. Cook the custard on MEDIUM for 7–8 minutes, whisking frequently. Complete the recipe

AUTUMN PUDDING

COUNTRYWIDE

Exactly the same as summer pudding, but this time the bread-lined basin is filled with a juicy mixture of the finest fruits of autumn. Keep any left-over juice to 'top up' any dry patches of bread.

SERVES 4–6

❄ ◪

700 g (1½ lb) mixed autumn fruit, such as apples, blackberries, plums, prepared

about 25 g (1 oz) light soft brown sugar

8–10 thin slices of day-old bread, crusts removed

fresh fruit and mint sprigs, to decorate

1. Stew the fruit gently with 60–90 ml (4–6 tbsp) water and the sugar until soft but still retaining their shape. The exact amounts of water and sugar depend on the ripeness and sweetness of the fruit.

2. Meanwhile, cut a round from one slice of bread to neatly fit the bottom of a 1.1 litre (2 pint) pudding basin and cut 6–8 slices of the bread into fingers about 5 cm (2 inches) wide. Put the round at the bottom of the basin and arrange the fingers around the sides, overlapping them so there are no spaces.

3. When the fruit is cooked, and still hot, pour it gently into the basin, being careful not to disturb the bread framework. Reserve about 45 ml (3 tbsp) of the juice. When the basin is full, cut the remaining bread and use to cover the fruit so a lid is formed.

4. Cover with foil, then a plate or saucer which fits just inside the bowl and put a weight on top. Leave the pudding until cold, then put into the refrigerator and chill overnight.

5. To serve, run a knife carefully round the edge to loosen, then invert the pudding on to a serving dish. Pour the reserved juice over the top. Serve cold with cream. Decorate with fruit and mint sprigs.

TO MICROWAVE

 Put the fruit, water and sugar in a large bowl, cover and cook on HIGH for 4–8 minutes, stirring occasionally. The time will depend on the type of fruit used. Complete the recipe.

LEFT
BARNSTAPLE FAIR
PEARS. Whole pears turn a
tempting deep red, after
simmering gently in clove-
flavoured wine until tender.

RIGHT
RASPBERRY AND
WALNUT SHORTBREAD.
Layer upon layer of good
things for a rich dessert that
simply oozes with fresh cream.

BARNSTAPLE FAIR PEARS

THE WEST

The pear orchards of Devon used to supply stalls at the annual Barnstaple Fair and these pears would originally have been simmered in local cider or scrumpy. This dessert makes the perfect end to a meal with its spicy flavour and rich syrupy liquid complemented by clotted cream.

SERVES 4

4 large firm Comice pears

25 g (1 oz) blanched almonds, split in half

50 g (2 oz) caster sugar

300 ml (½ pint) red wine

2 cloves

1. Peel the pears, leaving the stalks on. Spike the pears with the almond halves.

2. Put the sugar, wine and the cloves in a saucepan just large enough to hold the pears and heat gently until the sugar has dissolved. Add the pears, standing them upright in the pan, cover and simmer gently for about 15 minutes, until the pears are just tender, basting from time to time with the liquid.

3. Using a slotted spoon transfer the pears to a serving dish. Remove the lid from the pan of syrup, increase the heat and boil fast until the liquid is reduced by half. Pour over the pears and serve hot or cold with thick natural yogurt or clotted cream.

TO MICROWAVE

Complete step 1. Put the sugar, wine and the cloves in a large bowl and cook on HIGH for 3–4 minutes, until boiling, stirring occasionally. Add the pears, cover and cook on HIGH for 8–10 minutes, until the pears are tender. Using a slotted spoon transfer the pears to a serving dish. Uncover the syrup and cook on HIGH for about 10 minutes, until reduced by half. Pour over the pears and serve hot or cold with thick natural yogurt or clotted cream.

RASPBERRY AND WALNUT SHORTBREAD

SCOTLAND

Two of Scotland's most celebrated foods – shortbread and raspberries – come together in this recipe to make a truly mouth-watering dessert that tastes even better than it looks. The walnuts are ground and added to the shortbread mixture for a subtle nutty flavour. The shortbread could also be made with strawberries.

SERVES 8

100 g (4 oz) walnut pieces
100 g (4 oz) butter
75 g (3 oz) caster sugar
175 g (6 oz) plain flour
450 g (1 lb) fresh raspberries
50 g (2 oz) icing sugar
30 ml (2 tbsp) raspberry-flavoured liqueur or kirsch (optional)
300 ml (10 fl oz) fresh whipping cream

1. Draw three 20.5 (8 inch) circles on non-stick baking parchment. Place the parchment circles on baking sheets.
2. Grind the walnuts finely in a blender or food processor.
3. Cream the butter and sugar together in a mixing bowl until pale and fluffy, then beat in the walnuts and flour. Divide the dough into 3 shortbread portions.
4. Put a portion of shortbread dough in the centre of each parchment circle and press out with the heel of your hand until the dough is the same size as the circle.
5. Cut one of the circles into eight triangles with a sharp knife and ease them slightly apart. Refrigerate the circles and triangles for 30 minutes. Bake at 190°C (375°F) mark 5 for15–20 minutes, swapping over the sheets to ensure the pastries brown evenly. Leave to cool and harden for 10 minutes on the paper, then transfer to wire racks to cool completely.
6. Meanwhile, reserve one-third of the raspberries for decoration. Put the rest in a bowl with the icing sugar and liqueur, if using. Crush the raspberries with a fork, then leave them to macerate while the pastry rounds are cooling.
7. Assemble the shortbread just before serving, to ensure that the pastry remains crisp. Whip the cream until thick, then fold in the crushed raspberries and juice. Stand one round of pastry on a flat serving plate and spread with half of the cream mixture. Top with the remaining round of pastry, then the remaining cream mixture.
8. Arrange the triangles of pastry on top of the cream, wedging them in at an angle. Scatter the reserved whole raspberries in between. Serve the shortbread as soon as possible.

ETON MESS

THE SOUTH-EAST

When the annual prize-giving is held at Eton College, one of Britain's most famous public schools, parents and pupils have a picnic on the playing fields. Among the dishes then served is this marvellously boozy mixture of strawberries, cream and crushed meringues, to which the school has lent its name.

SERVES 4–6

450 g (1 lb) strawberries, hulled
75 ml (3 fl oz) kirsch
375 ml (12 fl oz) fresh double or whipping cream
6 small meringues, crushed

1. Reserve a few small strawberries for the decoration. Chop the remainder and place in a bowl. Sprinkle with the kirsch, cover and chill for 2–3 hours.
2. Whip the cream until it just holds its shape, then gently fold in the strawberries and their juices and the crushed meringues. Spoon into a glass serving dish, decorate with the reserved strawberries and serve immediately.

WHIM WHAM

SCOTLAND

This is a very simple recipe for a delicious and swiftly made trifle. It originates from the 18th century, when the word whim-wham was used to describe something light and fanciful.

SERVES 6

25 g (1 oz) butter
50 g (2 oz) blanched almonds
25 g (1 oz) sugar
30 trifle sponge fingers
150 ml (¼ pint) sweet sherry
60 ml (4 tbsp) brandy
finely grated rind and juice of 1 large orange
300 ml (10 fl oz) fresh double cream
300 g (10 oz) natural yogurt

1. Melt the butter in a heavy-based frying pan and fry the almonds until golden brown. Stir in the sugar and cook for 1 minute, stirring continuously, until the sugar dissolves and the almonds are well coated. Tip on to a greased baking sheet and leave to cool.
2. About 30 minutes before ready to serve, break the sponge fingers in half and put into a serving bowl. Pour the sherry, brandy and orange rind and juice over and leave to soak for 30 minutes.
3. Whip the cream until it just holds its shape, then carefully fold in the yogurt. Spoon it on top of the sponge. Roughly chop the almonds, sprinkle on top and serve immediately.

CREAM

Cream lends a special touch to all kinds of dishes. Different types are most easily distinguished by butterfat content.

HALF CREAM

For pouring only, like top of milk. Good in coffee or on porridge and cereal. 12% butterfat.

SINGLE CREAM

Will not whip. Ideal for soups and sauces; in casseroles, omelettes and batter; or poured over desserts. 18% butterfat.

SOURED CREAM

Single cream treated with bacterial culture, with a rich tangy taste and thicker texture. Use in dressings, goulash or cheese cakes (see recipe, page 253). 18% butterfat.

WHIPPING CREAM

Doubles in volume when whipped. Ideal for cake fillings and light-textured fools, mousses and syllabubs. 35% butterfat.

WHIPPED CREAM

Whipping cream sold ready-whipped and sweetened.

CREME FRAICHE

May be whipped. Treated with bacterial culture. Has a distinctive, slight sharp taste. 35% butterfat.

DOUBLE CREAM

May be whipped stiffly, almost doubling in volume. Ideal all-purpose cream. Excellent for piping as holds shape well. 48% butterfat.

EXTRA THICK DOUBLE CREAM

For spooning only; will not whip.

CLOTTED CREAM

Thick, straw-coloured with a strong flavour. Spreads well; serve with scones for Devon tea. 55% butterfat.

EVERLASTING SYLLABUB

COUNTRYWIDE

The first syllabubs were made centuries ago by dairy maids, who would direct the warm milk straight from the cow into a pail containing sherry or cider. The froth was then skimmed off and served for breakfast. These days, syllabub is thicker and richer, and so called "everlasting" because it can be kept in the glass for several hours before serving.

SERVES 4

finely grated rind and juice of 1 lemon

75 g (3 oz) caster sugar

15–30 ml (1–2 tbsp) brandy

30 ml (2 tbsp) sweet sherry

300 ml (10 fl oz) fresh double cream

lemon twists, to decorate

1. Soak the lemon rind in the juice for 2–3 hours, then mix with sugar, brandy and sherry. Stir until dissolved.
2. Whip the cream lightly until it is just beginning to hold its shape, then gradually add the liquid, whipping continuously. Take care not to over-beat. Chill before serving in glasses, decorated with lemon twists.

BOODLES ORANGE FOOL. Plan this recipe in advance, so that the sponge cakes in the base have time to soak up all the citrus flavour.

LONGER LIFE CREAMS

UHT CREAM

Long life cream treated at high temperature. Unlike pasteurised cream, UHT (available in half, single, double and whipping varieties) may be stored unopened without refrigeration.

AEROSOL CREAM

UHT cream in aerosol cans. Collapses quickly after use.

FROZEN CREAM

Single, double, whipping and clotted creams are commercially available ready-frozen.

CANNED CREAM

Sterilised, with a slight caramel taste. Good for spooning on desserts; will not whip. 23% butterfat.

BOODLES ORANGE FOOL

THE SOUTH-EAST

Boodle's Club, in London's St. James's Street, was founded in 1764 and this luscious fool has been a speciality on the menu for many years. It's a bit like a trifle, with a sponge-cake base which sops up the creamy, fruit-flavoured mixture on top.

SERVES 6

4–6 trifle sponges, cut into 1 cm (½ inch) thick slices

grated rind and juice of 2 oranges

grated rind and juice of 1 lemon

25–50 g (1–2 oz) sugar

300 ml (10 fl oz) fresh double cream

orange slices or segments, to decorate

1. Use the sponge slices to line the bottom and halfway up the sides of a deep serving dish or bowl.
2. Mix the orange and lemon rinds and juice with the sugar and stir until the sugar has completely dissolved.
3. In another bowl, whip the cream until it just starts to thicken, then slowly add the sweetened fruit juice, whipping the cream as you do so. Whip until the cream is light and thickened and all the juice absorbed.
4. Pour the mixture over the sponge and refrigerate for at least 2 hours, longer if possible, so that the juice can soak into the sponge and the cream thicken. Serve decorated with segments or slices of fresh orange.

COMPOTE OF FRUIT WITH ELDERFLOWER CREAM

COUNTRYWIDE

The mixture of fruit, which can include any varieties in season, is here poached in fruit juice rather than the sugary syrup preferred by the Victorians. Elderflowers are beautifully aromatic and grow abundantly in the hedgerows. You can find dried elderflowers in health food shops.

SERVES 4

25 g (1 oz) sugar

6 large heads of fresh elderflowers or 25 g (1 oz) dried elderflowers

150 ml (5 fl oz) fresh double cream

900 g (2 lb) mixed fresh fruit, such as gooseberries, rhubarb, pears, strawberries, cherries, prepared

300 ml (½ pint) unsweetened orange or apple juice

1 cinnamon stick

2 strips of lemon rind

clear honey, to taste (optional)

1. To make the elderflower cream, put the sugar and 150 ml (¼ pint) water in a saucepan and heat gently until the sugar has dissolved, then boil rapidly until the liquid is reduced by half. Take off the heat and submerge the fresh or dried flowers in the syrup.

2. Leave to infuse for at least 2 hours, then press the syrup through a sieve, discarding the elderflowers. Whip the cream until it just holds its shape, then fold in the elderflower syrup. Chill until ready to serve.

3. Put the fruit, fruit juice, cinnamon and lemon rind in a large saucepan and simmer gently for 3–5 minutes until the fruits are softened, but still retain their shape. Serve the compote warm or cold with the elderflower cream.

TO MICROWAVE

Put the sugar and 150 ml (¼ pint) water in a medium bowl. Cook on HIGH for 5–6 minutes until the liquid is reduced by half, stirring occasionally. Complete steps 1 and 2. Put the fruit, fruit juice, cinnamon and lemon rind in a large bowl. Cover and cook on HIGH for about 5 minutes, until the fruit is tender, but still retains its shape. The time will depend on the type of fruit used. Serve warm or cold with the elderflower cream.

WINE JELLY CREAM
COUNTRYWIDE

A pretty pudding with a lovely flavour. The wine jelly glows enticingly from beneath the topping of rich and creamy custard. Propping the glasses at an angle as the jelly sets is a simple trick that gives an unusual effect.

SERVES 4

300 ml (½ pint) white wine
45 ml (3 tbsp) sugar
15 g (½ oz) gelatine
450 ml (¾ pint) fresh milk
2 egg yolks
15 ml (1 tbsp) cornflour
2.5 ml (½ tsp) vanilla flavouring
150 ml (5 fl oz) fresh whipping cream
fresh strawberries, to decorate

1. Heat half the wine, 30 ml (2 tbsp) of the sugar and the gelatine in a small saucepan. Dissolve over a gentle heat, then mix with remaining wine and set aside to cool.

2. Pour into 4 wine glasses. Place in the refrigerator to set at a 45° angle.

3. Pour the milk into a medium saucepan and heat almost to the boiling point. In a medium bowl, blend together the egg yolks, cornflour, remaining sugar and vanilla flavouring until pale, then pour on the hot milk, stirring continuously.

4. Strain the mixture into a medium heavy-based or double saucepan and stir over a gentle heat until the custard thickens enough to coat the back of a wooden spoon. This takes about 20 minutes. Cool, then whip the cream until stiff, then fold into the custard.

5. When the wine jelly is set, stand the glasses upright and pour in the custard. Return to the refrigerator to chill. Decorate with strawberries and serve with finger biscuits.

WINE JELLY CREAM. The jelly is clear and golden and the smooth topping flavoured with a touch of vanilla.

STRAWBERRY YOGURT MOULD

THE MIDLANDS

A light mousse made in a ring mould always looks pretty filled with fresh fruit, and strawberries are probably the most decorative of all the soft summer berries. The delicately flavoured mould has a very light set, just firm enough to turn it out. Substitute buttermilk for the yogurt if you prefer.

SERVES 6

3 eggs
50 g (2 oz) caster sugar
finely grated rind and juice of 1 lemon
450 g (1 lb) strawberries
20 ml (4 tsp) gelatine
150 g (5 oz) natural yogurt
150 g (5 oz) strawberry yogurt

STRAWBERRY YOGURT MOULD. A hint of lemon brings out the flavour of strawberries to the full, in this prettily fluted ring.

1. Put the eggs, sugar and lemon rind in a large bowl. Using an electric mixer, whisk together until the mixture is pale, thick and creamy and leaves a trail when the whisk is lifted from the bowl.

2. Hull half of the strawberries and place in a blender or food processor with half of the lemon juice. Purée until smooth.

3. Gradually whisk the purée into the mousse mixture, whisking well to keep the bulk.

4. Sprinkle the gelatine over the remaining lemon juice in a small bowl and leave to soak for 5 minutes. Place the bowl over a saucepan of simmering water and stir until dissolved. Leave until lukewarm, then gradually add to the mousse mixture with the natural and strawberry yogurts. Stir carefully but thoroughly to mix. Pour into a greased 1.7 litre (3 pint) ring mould and chill for 4–5 hours or until set.

5. To serve, dip the mould briefly in hot water, then invert on to a serving plate. Hull most of the remaining strawberries, but leave a few of the green hulls on for decoration. Fill the centre of the ring with the fruit. Serve with extra natural yogurt, if liked.

TO MICROWAVE

Complete steps 1, 2 and 3. Sprinkle the gelatine over the remaining lemon juice and leave to soak for 5 minutes. Cook on HIGH for 30–45 seconds. Do not boil. Stir until dissolved. Complete the recipe.

CHOCOLATE ORANGE SOUFFLE

COUNTRYWIDE

Dark plain chocolate is the best kind to use for mouth-watering desserts like this one, which call for a good depth of flavour. Cold soufflés and mousses, concocted from whipped cream and egg whites, have been popular puddings since the 17th century.

SERVES 6–8

450 ml (¾ pint) fresh milk
175 g (6 oz) plain chocolate
3 eggs, separated, plus 1 egg white
75 g (3 oz) sugar
15 ml (1 tbsp) gelatine
grated rind and juice of 1 orange
300 ml (10 fl oz) fresh whipping cream
15 ml (1 tbsp) chocolate liqueur

1. Line a 900 ml (1½ pint) soufflé dish with greaseproof paper to make a collar.
2. Put the milk in a saucepan and break 150 g (5 oz) chocolate into it. Heat gently until the chocolate melts, then cook over a high heat until almost boiling.
3. Whisk the egg yolks and sugar together until pale and thick. Gradually pour on the chocolate milk, stirring. Return to the saucepan and cook, stirring continuously, until it coats the back of a wooden spoon. This takes about 20 minutes. Do not boil.
4. Sprinkle the gelatine in 45 ml (3 tbsp) water in a small bowl and leave to soak. Place the bowl over a saucepan of simmering water and stir until dissolved. Stir into the custard with the orange rind and juice. Cool.
5. Whip the cream until it just holds its shape, then fold most of the cream into the cold mixture. Whisk the egg whites until stiff and fold into the mixture.
6. Pour the mixture into the prepared dish and leave to set. Remove paper collar.
7. Stir the liqueur into the remaining cream and use to decorate the soufflé. Grate the remaining chocolate and sprinkle on top.

DOUBLE CHOCOLATE ICE CREAM

COUNTRYWIDE

This recipe uses bitter plain chocolate to flavour the smooth ice cream base and is then given added bite with chocolate chips. Home-made ice cream is in a class of its own, and well worth taking a little time and trouble over.

SERVES 4–6

300 ml (½ pint) fresh milk
100 g (4 oz) plain chocolate

3 egg yolks
50 g (2 oz) sugar
300 ml (10 fl oz) fresh whipping cream
50 g (2 oz) chocolate chips

1. Put the milk in a saucepan and break the plain chocolate into it. Heat gently over a low heat until the chocolate melts, then cook over a high heat until almost boiling.
2. Whisk the egg yolks and sugar together until pale and thick. Gradually pour on the chocolate milk, stirring. Return to the saucepan and cook over a gentle heat, stirring continuously, until it coats the back of a spoon. Do not boil. This takes about 20 minutes.
3. Pour into a shallow freezer container and leave to cool. When the mixture is cool, cover and freeze for 2 hours, until mushy.
4. Turn into a large bowl and beat with a fork or whisk to break down any large ice crystals. Whip the cream until it just holds its shape, then fold into the frozen custard with the chocolate chips. Return the mixture to the freezer container and freeze for 2 hours.
5. Beat the mixture again, to break down any large ice crystals, then freeze until firm.
6. Transfer to the refrigerator to soften for 30 minutes before serving.

TO MICROWAVE

Put the milk and chocolate in a large bowl and cook on HIGH for 2–3 minutes, until the chocolate melts, stirring occasionally, then cook on HIGH for 1 minute, until almost boiling. Beat the egg yolks and sugar together, stir in the milk, then pour back into the bowl. Cook on MEDIUM for 3–4 minutes, stirring frequently, until the custard coats the back of a spoon. Do not boil. Complete the recipe.

CHOCOLATE ORANGE SOUFFLE. Grated chocolate curls and liqueur-flavoured cream whirls are used to decorate this handsome dessert.

APPLE AND HAZELNUT LAYER. To make serving easy, the meltingly short pastry is cut into portions before being placed on the fruity centre.

APPLE AND HAZELNUT LAYER

THE SOUTH-EAST

If you make this pudding during the autumn, look out for Kentish hazelnuts to add a nutty crunch to the layers.

SERVES 8

75 g (3 oz) hazelnuts, shelled
75 g (3 oz) butter
45 ml (3 tbsp) caster sugar
115 g (4½ oz) plain flour
pinch of salt
450 g (1 lb) Cox's apples, peeled, cored and sliced
15 ml (1 tbsp) apricot jam or marmalade
grated rind of 1 lemon
15 ml (1 tbsp) candied peel, chopped
30 ml (2 tbsp) currants
30 ml (2 tbsp) sultanas
icing sugar, whipped fresh cream and hazelnuts, to decorate

1. Cut out two 20.5 cm (8 inch) circles of greaseproof paper.

2. Reserve 8 nuts and finely chop the remainder. Cream the butter and sugar until pale and fluffy. Stir in the flour, salt and chopped nuts, then form into a ball and chill for 30 minutes.

3. Put the apple in a saucepan with the jam and lemon rind and cook over a low heat for 5 minutes, until soft. Add the candied peel and dried fruit and simmer for 5 minutes.

4. Divide the pastry in half, place on the sheets of greaseproof paper and roll out into two circles. Transfer to greased baking sheets.

5. Bake at 190°C (375°F) mark 5 for 7–10 minutes, until light brown. Cut one circle into 8 triangles while warm. Leave to cool.

6. Just before serving, place the complete circle on a serving plate and cover with the apple mixture. Arrange the triangles on top. Dust with icing sugar, pipe cream on top and decorate the apple layer with hazelnuts.

YOGURT AND BANANA DESSERT

COUNTRYWIDE

Any type of yogurt can be used for this very quick and easy recipe, and there are many varieties to choose from.

SERVES 4

300 g (10 oz) natural yogurt
150 ml (5 fl oz) fresh double cream
3 ripe bananas, mashed
grated rind and juice of 1 lemon
15–30 ml (1–2 tbsp) caster sugar
1 egg white
grated lemon rind and fresh mint leaves, to decorate

1. In a large bowl, whisk the yogurt and cream together until lightly stiff, then stir in the bananas, lemon rind and juice and sugar to taste.
2. In a medium bowl, whisk the egg white until stiff, then fold gently into the mixture. Chill until ready to serve.
3. Pour into 4 glass dishes, and serve, decorated with lemon rind and fresh mint leaves.

VARIATION

Replace the bananas with 450 g (1 lb) raspberries, 2 medium mangoes or 4 ripe, skinned nectarines or peaches.

CHERRIES IN BRANDY

THE SOUTH-EAST

A simple way to serve cherries, which shows them off at their best, steeped in a spicy alcoholic syrup and accompanied by a light orange cream. For easy eating, stone the cherries first, using a special cherry stoner or a skewer.

SERVES 6

900 g (2 lb) cherries, stoned
15 g (½ oz) sugar
1 cinnamon stick
finely grated rind and juice of 2 oranges
30 ml (2 tbsp) redcurrant jelly
60 ml (4 tbsp) cherry brandy or brandy
150 ml (5 fl oz) fresh double cream
150 g (5 oz) natural yogurt

1. Place the cherries in a saucepan with the sugar, cinnamon, half of the orange rind and the juice of both oranges. Cover and cook over a low heat for about 10 minutes or until the cherries are soft and the juice runs.
2. Stir in the redcurrant jelly and the brandy and cook gently until the jelly melts. Cool, then chill.
3. Mix the remaining orange rind and the cream together in a bowl. Whip until the cream just holds its shape, then fold in the yogurt. Serve the cherries in brandy, with the orange cream handed separately.

TO MICROWAVE

Put the stoned cherries, sugar, cinnamon, half of the orange rind and the juice of both oranges in a large bowl. Cover and cook on HIGH for 4–6 minutes or until the cherries are soft and the juice runs. Stir in the redcurrant jelly and the brandy and cook on HIGH for 1 minute. Complete the recipe.

CHILLED BLACKBERRY SNOW

THE SOUTH-EAST

The swirled layers of iced fruit purée and creamy egg white are very effective in this recipe but do finish it off just before it is needed and serve immediately. If really necessary, it can be kept refrigerated for a couple of hours, but it will start to lose some volume.

SERVES 6

450 g (1 lb) blackberries, fresh or frozen, thawed
2 egg whites
50 g (2 oz) caster sugar
300 ml (10 fl oz) fresh double cream

1. Rub the blackberries through a nylon sieve. Pour the purée into a rigid container and freeze for about 2 hours or until mushy.
2. Whisk the egg whites until stiff, then add the sugar gradually, whisking until the mixture stands in soft peaks. Whip the cream until it just holds its shape.
3. Remove the frozen blackberry purée from the freezer and mash to break down the large ice crystals, being careful not to break it down completely.
4. Fold the cream and whites together, then quickly fold in the semi-frozen blackberry purée to form a 'swirled' effect. Spoon into tall glasses and serve immediately.

CHILLED BLACKBERRY SNOW. A lovely, marbled dessert to serve in individual tall glasses. Place one fresh berry on top of each one to finish.

CAKES, PASTRIES, BISCUITS & SWEETS

Few can resist a freshly baked home-made cake or a batch of biscuits for tea. In this chapter you'll find lots to inspire you. There are cakes and bakes for every taste and occasion. Fruit, chocolate and cream cakes, flaky pastries, melt-in-the-mouth biscuits and sweets too – they're all here for you to make for your family or friends.

PASTRIES

LEFT
ECCLES CAKES. Each crisp
round, glazed with egg white
and sugar, is crammed with
fruity filling.

RIGHT
APPLE CREAM BUNS.
Pack the creamy mixture in
generously, to make each bun
a finger-licking, squishy treat.

ECCLES CAKES

THE NORTH

*Baked originally at Eccles in Lancashire, but now available
countrywide, these cakes are pastries with a sweet spicy
mixture enclosed in a puff pastry case. They should have a
shiny coating and are best eaten warm.*

MAKES 8

25 g (1 oz) butter

100 g (4 oz) currants

25 g (1 oz) chopped mixed peel

50 g (2 oz) demerara sugar

2.5 ml (½ tsp) ground mixed spice

212 g (7½ oz) packet frozen puff pastry, thawed

1 egg white

caster sugar for sprinkling

1. Melt the butter in a saucepan, then stir in the
currants, peel, sugar and spice and mix thoroughly
together.
2. On a lightly floured surface, roll out the pastry very
thinly and cut out eight 12.5 cm (5 inch) circles using a
saucer as a guide. Divide the fruit mixture between the
circles, damp the edges of the pastry and draw them to
the centre, sealing well together.
3. Turn the cakes over and roll gently into circles with
a rolling pin. Brush with egg white and sprinkle with
caster sugar. Make 3 diagonal cuts across the top of
each.
4. Place on dampened baking sheets and bake at 220°C
(425°F) mark 7 for about 15 minutes, until light golden
brown. Eccles cakes are best eaten while still slightly
warm.

APPLE CREAM BUNS

THE WEST

*These delicious choux pastry buns conceal a traditional
mixture of apples and cream, and make a soft and surprising
tea-time treat. Make sure the apples are completely cool
before folding them into the cream or it will separate.*

MAKES 16 BUNS

50 g (2 oz) butter

65 g (2½ oz) plain flour, sifted

pinch of salt

2 eggs, beaten

450 g (1 lb) Bramley apples, peeled, cored and sliced

25 g (1 oz) sugar

150 ml (5 fl oz) fresh double cream

icing sugar

1. Put 150 ml (¼ pint) water and the butter into a medium saucepan. Heat slowly until the butter melts, then bring to a brisk boil. Lower the heat and tip in all the flour and salt at once.
2. Stir briskly until the mixture forms a soft ball and leaves the side of the pan.
3. Remove from the heat and cool slightly. Gradually add the eggs, a little at a time, beating until the mixture is smooth and shiny.
4. Pipe or spoon 16 buns of the mixture on to a buttered baking sheet. Bake the buns at 200°C (400°F) mark 6 for 10 minutes.
5. Remove from the oven and make a slit in the side of each. Return to the oven for a further 5 minutes. Cool on a wire rack.
6. Poach the apple slices in 150 ml (¼ pint) water with the sugar for 15 minutes, until soft. Cool.
7. Whip the cream until stiff peaks form. Remove the apple slices from the syrup with a slotted spoon, then fold them into the whipped cream. Split the buns, fill with the apple mixture and dust with sifted icing sugar.

TO MICROWAVE

 Put 150 ml (¼ pint) water and butter into a large bowl and cook on HIGH for 3 minutes. Complete steps 2 through 5. Put the apples and 65 ml (2½ fl oz) water and sugar in a large bowl and cook on HIGH for 6–7 minutes. Cool and complete step 7.

HAZELNUT CARTWHEEL

THE SOUTH-EAST

Hazelnuts are found in many parts of the world and are also called cob nuts or filberts. In Britain, the crop comes from Kent and is famous for the sweetness of the nuts. As well as being useful for lending crunch and flavour to recipes like this, hazelnuts are good on their own, as a healthy snack, or as an accompaniment to wine and cheese.

SERVES 8

❋

212 g (7½ oz) packet frozen puff pastry, thawed

25 g (1 oz) butter

25 g (1 oz) soft light brown sugar

1 egg, beaten

75 g (3 oz) plain cake crumbs

75 g (3 oz) hazelnuts, chopped

50 g (2 oz) raisins

finely grated rind of 1 lemon

1 egg, beaten, to glaze

caster sugar, to dredge

1. Roll out the pastry to a rectangle about 40.5×25.5 cm (16×10 inches). Cream the butter and sugar together until pale and fluffy, then beat in the egg and stir in the cake crumbs, hazelnuts, raisins and lemon rind. Spread the mixture over the pastry to within 0.5 cm (¼ inch) of the edges.
2. Roll up like a Swiss roll starting from the narrow end. Trim the ends, if necessary.
3. Place on a dampened baking sheet and curl round into a circle. Seal the ends together.
4. Snip all round the ring at 4 cm (1½ inch) intervals so the cuts come to within about 2 cm (¾ inch) of the ring's inner edge. Brush with beaten egg to glaze. Bake at 220°C (425°F) mark 7 for 25–30 minutes, until golden brown. Dredge with caster sugar and serve warm.

HAZELNUT CARTWHEEL. Puff pastry is spread with a nutty, lemon mixture before being rolled up to bake. Best eaten warm.

BREADS &
TEABREADS

There's nothing quite like the aroma of baked bread to whet the appetite. Loaves come in all shapes and sizes, are plain or fancy and are surprisingly easy to make at home. There is a vast selection from which to choose, from Barm Brack and the traditional British cottage loaf to marmalade teabread and potato scones.

SAGE AND ONION BREAD
COUNTRYWIDE

This is a mouth-watering savoury bread that fills the kitchen with an aroma of herbs as it bakes. Serve it warm with soup, or well buttered with cheese or pâté and salad, for a simple lunch. Using dried sage will still give good results.

MAKES 2 SMALL LOAVES

SAGE AND ONION BREAD. The cracked wheat topping gives an appetising crunch to this deliciously flavoured, close-textured loaf.

15 g (½ oz) fresh yeast or 7.5 ml (1½ tsp) dried

300 ml (½ pint) warm fresh milk

1 large onion, skinned and finely chopped

25 g (1 oz) butter

225 g (8 oz) strong white flour

225 g (8 oz) strong wholemeal flour

5 ml (1 tsp) salt

pepper

30 ml (2 tbsp) chopped fresh sage or 5 ml (1 tsp) dried

cracked wheat for sprinkling

1. Blend the fresh yeast with the milk. If using dried yeast, sprinkle it into the milk and leave in a warm place for 15 minutes, until frothy.
2. Meanwhile, put the onion and the butter in a small saucepan, cover and cook gently for about 5 minutes, until the onion is soft and transparent but not browned.
3. Put the flours, salt, pepper and sage in a large bowl and mix together. Make a well in the centre, then pour in the softened onion and the butter and the yeast liquid. Beat well together until the dough leaves the sides of the bowl clean.
4. Turn on to a lightly floured surface and knead well for about 10 minutes, until smooth and elastic. Place in a clean bowl. Cover with a clean tea-towel and leave in a warm place for about 1 hour, until doubled in size.
5. Turn the dough on to a floured surface and knead lightly. Divide into two, shape into rounds and place on a large greased baking sheet.
6. Brush with a little milk and sprinkle with cracked wheat. Cover and leave in a warm place for about 30 minutes, until doubled in size. Bake at 230°C (450°F) mark 8 for 15 minutes, then reduce the oven temperature to 200°C (400°F) mark 6 and bake for a further 15 minutes. When cooked the loaves will be well risen and golden brown, and sound hollow if tapped on the bottom. Cool slightly and serve warm, or turn on to a wire rack and leave to cool completely.

SODA BREAD
NORTHERN IRELAND

Round loaves of soda bread were traditionally baked on a hot griddle over the fire and had a lovely crisp crust. The bread is moist, close-textured and delicious, with a distinctive flavour which comes from the soda and buttermilk.

MAKES 1 LARGE LOAF

450 g (1 lb) plain wholemeal flour

100 g (4 oz) plain flour

50 g (2 oz) rolled oats

5 ml (1 tsp) bicarbonate of soda

5 ml (1 tsp) salt

about 450 ml (¾ pint) buttermilk

1. Put the flours, oats, bicarbonate of soda and salt in a large bowl and mix together. Add enough buttermilk to mix to a soft dough.
2. Knead very lightly, then shape into a large round and place on a greased baking sheet. Cut a deep cross in the top. Bake at 230°C (450°F) mark 8 for 15 minutes, then reduce the oven temperature to 200°C (400°F)

mark 6 and bake for a further 20–25 minutes or until the loaf sounds hollow when tapped on the bottom. Eat while still warm.

TO MICROWAVE

 Complete step 1. Knead very lightly, then shape into a large round. Place on a greased microwave baking tray or large flat plate and cut a deep cross in the top. Stand on a microwave roasting rack and cook on HIGH for 9–10 minutes or until the bread is well risen and the surface looks dry, turning 2 or 3 times during cooking. Turn the bread over and cook on HIGH for a further 1–1½ minutes or until the bottom looks dry. Eat while still warm.

HERBED GRANARY BREAD STICK

COUNTRYWIDE

This is one recipe where dried herbs are no substitute for fresh, as they just cannot provide the herby flavour that makes these bread sticks so delicious, especially if they are served warm.

MAKES 1 BREAD STICK

❄

15 g (½ oz) fresh yeast or 7.5 ml (1½ tsp) dried and a pinch of sugar

450 g (1 lb) Granary flour

5 ml (1 tsp) salt

30 ml (2 tbsp) chopped fresh parsley

30 ml (2 tbsp) chopped fresh mixed herbs, such as mint, thyme, marjoram, rosemary, chives

1 garlic clove, skinned and crushed (optional)

10 ml (2 tsp) clear honey

fine oatmeal for sprinkling

1. Blend the fresh yeast with 300 ml (½ pint) warm water. If using dried yeast, sprinkle it into 300 ml (½ pint) warm water with the sugar and leave in a warm place for 15 minutes, until frothy.
2. Put the flour, salt and herbs in a bowl and mix together. Make a well in the centre. Stir the garlic, if using, and the honey into the yeast liquid, then pour into the centre of the dry ingredients. Beat together until the dough leaves the sides of the bowl clean.
3. Turn on to a lightly floured surface and knead well for about 10 minutes, until smooth and elastic. Place in a clean bowl. Cover with a clean tea-towel and leave in a warm place for about 1 hour, until doubled in size.
4. Turn the dough on to a floured surface and knead lightly. Shape into a sausage shape about 40 cm (16 inches) long. Place on a greased baking sheet. Cut several slashes on the top of the loaf. Cover and leave in a warm place for about 30 minutes, until doubled in size.
5. Brush with a little milk and sprinkle with oatmeal. Bake at 230°C (450°F) mark 8 for 10 minutes, then reduce the oven temperature to 200°C (400°F) mark 6 and bake for a further 15–20 minutes. Leave to cool on a wire rack.

HERBED GRANARY BREAD STICK. Perfect for bread-and-cheese lunches, or as a partner for home-made soups, this crusty loaf with its fragrance of herbs is very moreish.

MARMALADE TEABREAD

COUNTRYWIDE

A moist, spicy cake with a fruity flavour. The tradition of making good, plain cakes grew up in the country, where a cake was part of an early supper, eaten at the end of the day in winter or before a last bout of work in summer.

MAKES 8–10 SLICES

200 g (7 oz) plain flour
5 ml (1 tsp) ground ginger
5 ml (1 tsp) baking powder
50 g (2 oz) butter, diced
50 g (2 oz) light soft brown sugar
60 ml (4 tbsp) orange marmalade
1 egg, beaten
75 ml (3 tbsp) fresh milk
25 g (1 oz) candied orange peel, chopped

1. Grease a 750 ml (1½ pint) loaf tin, then line the base with greaseproof paper and grease the paper.
2. Put the flour, ginger and baking powder in a bowl and rub in the butter until the mixture resembles fine breadcrumbs. Stir in the sugar.
3. Mix together the marmalade, egg and most of the milk. Stir into the dry ingredients and mix to a soft dough. Add the rest of the milk, if necessary.
4. Turn the mixture into the prepared tin, level the surface and press the candied orange peel on top. Bake at 170°C (325°F) mark 3 for about 1¼ hours or until golden brown. Turn out on to a wire rack to cool.

TO MICROWAVE

 Grease a 1.7 litre (3 pint) loaf dish and line the base with greaseproof paper. Complete steps 2 and 3, adding an extra 30 ml (2 tbsp) fresh milk. Turn the mixture into the prepared dish, level the surface and press the candied peel on top. Cover with kitchen paper, stand on a roasting rack and cook on HIGH for 6 minutes until well risen and firm to the touch. Complete step 4.

CHEESE AND WALNUT LOAF

THE WEST

This tasty teabread combines two West Country specialities which are now readily available throughout the country: walnuts, which were originally grown in the Vale of Pewsey in Wiltshire, and Cheddar cheese. Use a mature version for a stronger taste.

MAKES 1 LARGE LOAF

15 g (½ oz) fresh yeast or 7.5 ml (1½ tsp) dried and a pinch of sugar

450 g (1 lb) strong wholemeal flour
5 ml (1 tsp) salt
2.5 ml (½ tsp) paprika
7.5 ml (1½ tsp) mustard powder
175 g (6 oz) Cheddar cheese, grated
100 g (4 oz) walnut pieces, finely chopped
45 ml (3 tbsp) chopped fresh mixed herbs or 5 ml (1 tsp) dried

1. Grease a 900 g (2 lb) loaf tin.
2. Blend the fresh yeast with 300 ml (½ pint) warm water. If using dried yeast, sprinkle it into 300 ml (½ pint) warm water with the sugar and leave in a warm place for 15 minutes, until frothy.
3. Put the flour, salt, paprika, mustard powder, 100 g (4 oz) of the cheese, the walnuts and the herbs in a large bowl and mix together. Make a well in the centre, then pour in the yeast liquid. Mix together to make a smooth dough that leaves the sides of the bowl clean.
4. Turn the dough on to a lightly floured surface and knead well for about 10 minutes, until smooth and elastic. Place in a clean bowl. Cover with a clean tea-towel and leave in a warm place for about 1 hour, until doubled in size.
5. Turn the dough on to a floured surface and knead lightly. Shape the dough to fit the prepared tin. Cover and leave in a warm place for 30 minutes, until the dough rises almost to the top of the tin.
6. Sprinkle with the remaining cheese and bake at 190°C (375°F) mark 5 for 45 minutes, until well risen and the loaf sounds hollow when tapped on the bottom. Turn out on to a wire rack to cool.

MARBLED CHOCOLATE TEABREAD

COUNTRYWIDE

The Victorians were very fond of marbled cakes. The recipe is so called because the feathery swirls of chocolate that are revealed when it is sliced make a pattern similar to that of Italian marble.

MAKES ABOUT 10 SLICES

225 g (8 oz) butter
225 g (8 oz) caster sugar
4 eggs, beaten
225 g (8 oz) self-raising flour
finely grated rind of 1 large orange
15 ml (1 tbsp) orange juice
few drops orange flower water (optional)
75 g (3 oz) plain chocolate
15 ml (1 tbsp) cocoa powder

1. Grease a 900 ml (2 pint) loaf tin and line the base and sides with greaseproof paper.
2. Cream the butter and sugar together until pale and

fluffy, then gradually beat in the eggs, beating well after each addition. Fold in the flour.

3. Transfer half of the mixture to another bowl and beat in the orange rind, juice and orange flower water, if using.

4. Break the chocolate into pieces, put into a small bowl and place over a pan of simmering water. Stir until the chocolate melts. Stir into the remaining cake mixture with the cocoa powder.

5. Put alternate spoonfuls of the two mixtures into the prepared tin. Use a knife to swirl through the mixture to make a marbled effect, then level the surface.

6. Bake at 180°C (350°F) mark 4 for 1¼–1½ hours,

until well risen and firm to the touch. Turn out on to a wire rack to cool. Serve cut in slices.

TO MICROWAVE

Grease a 1.7 litre (3 pint) loaf dish and line the base with greaseproof paper. Complete steps 2 and 3, adding an extra 30 ml (2 tbsp) fresh milk. Break the chocolate into a small bowl and cook on LOW for 2–3 minutes until melted. Complete the remainder of step 4, adding 15 ml (1 tbsp) milk, and step 5. Cover with kitchen paper, stand on a roasting rack and cook on HIGH for 10 minutes, until well risen and firm to the touch.

LEFT
MARMALADE
TEABREAD. Serve this plain but well-flavoured bread thickly sliced and generously buttered.

RIGHT
MARBLED CHOCOLATE
TEABREAD. Seen at its best sliced, and arranged on a plate, to show off the intriguing pattern.

FLOUR

*Flour is
the basic ingredient in baking and
bread making. A wide range of
flours is available, each suitable
for specific uses. All contain
fibre and are a valuable source of
B vitamins.*

*Store flour in a cool, dry place in
a container with a tight-fitting
lid. Plain white flour keeps for up
to six months, self-raising for up
to three months. Wholemeal and
brown flour are best eaten within
two months.*

*There are three main types of
wheat flour:*

WHITE

*Most of the bran and wheatgerm
of the grain is removed. It is
available plain, for shortcrust
pastry, biscuits and thickening;
self-raising, with an added
raising agent, for cakes,
puddings and suet crust pastry;
and strong, with a high protein
content, for bread making, all
yeast cookery and puff and flaky
pastry. It can also be used with
wholemeal or brown flours
(below) for variety of colour,
flavour and texture.*

BROWN (also known as WHEATMEAL)

*Some of the bran and wheatgerm
is removed. Bread, pastries and
puddings using brown flour will
have a slightly darker colour and
heavier texture than those using
white. Available plain, self-
raising and strong.*

WHOLEMEAL or WHOLEWHEAT

*This is made from the entire
wheat grain. Bread made
entirely from this has a close
texture and slightly nutty taste.
Available plain, self-raising and
strong.*

*Both brown and wholemeal
flours are available
STONEGROUND. The
wheat is ground between two
stones which heats the flour and
gives it a nutty flavour and
coarser texture. Use as for
brown and wholemeal flours.*

POTATO SCONES
THE NORTH AND SCOTLAND

*These scones need to be made from floury potatoes such as
Pentland Squire or Maris Piper which will mash well without
lumps. You can use leftover cold cooked potatoes, but for the
best and lightest flavour boil them freshly. If using leftovers,
warm them in a conventional or microwave oven before
working in the flour and proceeding with the recipe.*

<u>MAKES ABOUT 12</u>

450 g (1 lb) floury potatoes, peeled
5 ml (1 tsp) salt
25 g (1 oz) butter
about 100 g (4 oz) plain flour

1. Cook the potatoes in boiling salted water for about
20 minutes or until tender. Drain and mash until
smooth. Add the salt and butter while the potatoes are
still hot, then work in enough flour to make a stiff
dough.
2. Turn on to a floured surface, knead lightly and roll
out until 0.5 cm (¼ inch) thick. Cut into 6.5 cm
(2½ inch) rounds.
3. Cook on a greased griddle or heavy-based frying pan
for 4–5 minutes on each side or until golden brown.
Serve hot with butter.

LARDY CAKE
THE WEST

*Warm or cold, this recipe is sweet, filling and delicious.
Lardy cake originates from Wiltshire, and in the West
Country local bakers still make it to their own recipes,
cramming in as much lard, sugar and fruit as they or their
customers choose.*

<u>MAKES ABOUT 12 SLICES</u>

15 g (½ oz) fresh yeast, or 7.5 ml (1½ tsp) dried and a pinch of sugar
450 g (1 lb) strong white flour
5 ml (1 tsp) salt
75 g (3 oz) lard, diced
75 g (3 oz) butter, diced
175 g (6 oz) mixed sultanas and currants
50 g (2 oz) chopped mixed peel
50 g (2 oz) sugar

1. Grease a 20.5 × 25 cm (8 × 10 inch) roasting tin.
2. Blend the fresh yeast with 300 ml (½ pint) warm
water. If using dried yeast, sprinkle it into 300 ml
(½ pint) warm water with the sugar and leave for
15 minutes, until frothy.
3. Put the flour and salt in a bowl and rub in 15 g
(½ oz) of the lard. Make a well in the centre and pour in
the yeast liquid. Beat together to make a dough that
leaves the sides of the bowl clean, adding more water if
necessary.

4. Turn on to a lightly floured surface and knead well
for about 10 minutes, until smooth and elastic. Place in
a clean bowl. Cover with a clean tea-towel and leave in
a warm place for about 1 hour, until doubled in size.
5. Turn the dough on to a floured surface and roll out to
a rectangle about 0.5 cm (¼ inch) thick. Dot one-third
of the remaining lard and the butter over the surface of
the dough. Sprinkle over one-third of the fruit, peel and
sugar. Fold the dough in three, folding the bottom third
up and the top third down. Give a quarter-turn, then
repeat the process twice more.
6. Roll the dough out to fit the prepared tin. Put in the
tin, cover and leave in a warm place for 30 minutes,
until puffy. Score the top in a criss-cross pattern with a
knife, then bake at 220°C (425°F) mark 7 for about
30 minutes, until well risen and golden brown. Turn
out and serve immediately or leave to cool on a wire
rack. Serve plain or with butter.

MALTED FRUIT TEABREAD
COUNTRYWIDE

*Fruit loaves keep well and the flavour actually improves if
they are kept for a day or two before eating. Malt is the raw
material from which beer and malt whisky are made and it's
this that makes this sticky cake particularly moreish. Serve
thinly sliced and spread with butter.*

<u>MAKES 10 SLICES</u>

225 g (8 oz) self-raising flour
pinch of salt
30 ml (2 tbsp) dark soft brown sugar
175 g (6 oz) mixed dried fruit
30 ml (2 tbsp) golden syrup
30 ml (2 tbsp) malt extract
150 ml (¼ pint) fresh milk

1. Grease a 900 ml (2 pint) loaf tin and line the base
and sides with greaseproof paper.
2. Put the flour, salt, sugar and fruit in a bowl and mix
together. Make a well in the centre.
3. Put the syrup, malt extract and milk in a saucepan
and heat gently until melted. Pour into the well in the
centre of the dry ingredients, then beat thoroughly
together. Add a little extra milk, if necessary, to make a
fairly sticky consistency.
4. Turn the mixture into the prepared tin and bake at
170°C (325°F) mark 3 for about 1¼ hours. Turn out and
leave to cool on a wire rack. When completely cold,
wrap in greaseproof paper and foil and store for 1 day
before eating. Serve sliced, spread with butter.

OAST CAKES

THE SOUTH-EAST

Named after the distinctive hop-drying houses that dot the Kent countryside, these cakes were originally eaten after the crop had been gathered. They are like thin, fried scones, and are good served lightly dredged with sugar or with cherry jam.

MAKES 12

✳

225 g (8 oz) plain flour

2.5 ml (½ tsp) salt

2.5 ml (½ tsp) baking powder

50 g (2 oz) lard, diced

40 g (1½ oz) caster sugar

75 g (3 oz) currants

45 ml (3 tbsp) vegetable oil

25 g (1 oz) butter

1. Put the flour, salt and baking powder into a bowl, then rub in the lard until the mixture resembles fine breadcrumbs.
2. Stir in the sugar and currants, then mix with 45–60 ml (3–4 tbsp) water to make a soft dough.
3. Turn out on to a lightly floured surface and roll out until 1 cm (½ inch) thick. Using a 5 cm (2 inch) plain cutter, cut out 12 rounds.
4. Heat the oil and the butter in a heavy-based frying pan and fry the cakes for 2–3 minutes on each side, until golden brown. Drain on kitchen paper. Eat warm or very fresh.

CHEESE AND CHIVE SCONES

THE NORTH

Crumbly Lancashire cheese is ideal in cooking. Combined with the onion flavour of freshly snipped chives, these scones are deliciously savoury. To increase flavour try spreading them with Welsh butter, which has a distinctive flavour.

MAKES 10

✳

225 g (8 oz) self-raising flour

pinch of salt

50 g (2 oz) butter, diced

100 g (4 oz) Lancashire cheese, grated

15 ml (1 tbsp) snipped fresh chives

150 ml (¼ pint) fresh milk and extra for brushing

1. Put the flour and salt into a bowl and rub in the butter until the mixture resembles fine breadcrumbs. Stir in 50 g (2 oz) of the cheese and the chives.
2. Add the milk and mix to form a soft dough, then knead quickly until smooth.
3. Roll out on a floured work surface until 1 cm (½ inch) thick. Cut into 10 rounds with a 5 cm (2 inch) plain cutter and brush the tops with milk. Transfer to baking sheets.
4. Bake at 230°C (450°F) mark 8 for 7–10 minutes, until well risen and golden brown.
5. Immediately put the remaining cheese on top of the scones and allow to melt before serving hot or cold.

CHEESE AND CHIVE SCONES. So simple to make, and so mouthwateringly good, these cheesy scones are the ideal teatime treat.

BOXTY BREAD
NORTHERN IRELAND

A traditional potato bread from Ireland, where potatoes were used to make cakes, dumplings and pancakes as well. Boxty would be served with milk and salt, and children sometimes called it 'dippity'.

MAKES 4 SMALL LOAVES

700 g (1½ lb) old potatoes, peeled
salt and pepper
25 g (1 oz) butter
150 ml (¼ pint) fresh milk
350 g (12 oz) self-raising flour
5 ml (1 tsp) baking powder

BOXTY BREAD. You'd never guess to look at it, that the main ingredient of this enticing loaf is potatoes. The texture and flavour are excellent; it's well worth trying for a change.

1. Roughly chop half the potatoes and cook in boiling salted water until tender, then drain and mash with the butter.

2. Grate the remaining potatoes into a bowl and mix with the milk. Beat in the cooked potato and salt and pepper to taste.
3. Sieve the flour and baking powder on to the potato mixture and beat together to make a dough. If the mixture is too soft, add a little extra flour.
4. Turn out on to a floured surface and knead lightly, then shape into four 10 cm (4 inch) flat round cakes. Put on to a greased baking sheet and mark each with a cross. Bake at 200°C (400°F) mark 6 for about 30 minutes, until well risen and golden brown. Break each loaf into quarters and serve warm spread with butter.

HOT CROSS BUNS
COUNTRYWIDE

A much-loved recipe, hot cross buns were traditionally eaten for breakfast on Good Friday and are still sold widely at Easter time. They were first made in the 18th century, when they were extra rich and spicy, and marked with a cross as a reminder of the festival.

MAKES 12

15 g (½ oz) fresh yeast or 7.5 ml (1½ tsp) dried
300 ml (½ pint) warm milk
450 g (1 lb) strong white flour
5 ml (1 tsp) salt
5 ml (1 tsp) ground mixed spice
5 ml (1 tsp) ground cinnamon
2.5 ml (½ tsp) grated nutmeg
50 g (2 oz) caster sugar
75 g (3 oz) butter
75 g (3 oz) currants
25 g (1 oz) chopped mixed peel
1 egg, beaten
50 g (2 oz) plain flour
For the glaze
60 ml (4 tbsp) fresh milk and water, mixed
45 ml (3 tbsp) caster sugar

1. Dissolve the fresh yeast in the milk. If using dried yeast, sprinkle it into the milk and leave in a warm place for about 15 minutes, until frothy.
2. Put the strong flour, salt, spices and sugar in a bowl. Rub in 50 g (2 oz) of the butter, then stir in the currants and peel. Make a well in the centre and stir in the egg and yeast liquid and beat together to a soft dough.
3. Turn on to a lightly floured surface and knead for about 10 minutes, until smooth and elastic and no longer sticky. Put into a clean bowl, cover with a clean tea-towel and leave to rise in a warm place for about 1 hour, until doubled in size.
4. Turn the dough out on to a floured surface and knead for 2–3 minutes. Divide the dough into 12 pieces and shape into round buns.
5. Place on greased baking sheets, cover and leave in a warm place for about 30 minutes, until doubled in size.

6. Meanwhile, make the pastry for the crosses. Put the plain flour in a bowl and rub in the remaining butter until the mixture resembles fine breadcrumbs. Stir in enough water to bind the mixture together. Knead lightly.

7. Roll out the pastry thinly on a floured surface and cut into thin strips about 9 cm (3½ inches) long. Dampen the pastry strips and lay two on each bun to make a cross.

8. Bake at 190°C (375°F) mark 5 for 15–20 minutes, until golden brown. For the glaze, heat the milk and water with the sugar. Brush the hot buns twice with glaze, then transfer to a wire rack to cool.

CHELSEA BUNS

THE SOUTH-EAST

The shop from which these buns originated would, in its heyday, sell as many as 250,000 buns in one day. The owner, Richard Hand, was known as 'Captain Bun'. The buns are easily recognised, as the dough is baked in a flat coil and given a shiny sugar glaze.

MAKES 12

15 g (½ oz) fresh yeast or 7.5 ml (1½ tsp) dried
100 ml (4 fl oz) warm fresh milk
225 g (8 oz) strong white flour
2.5 ml (½ tsp) salt
40 g (1½ oz) butter, diced
1 egg, beaten
100 g (4 oz) mixed dried fruit
50 g (2 oz) light soft brown sugar
clear honey, to glaze

1. Grease a 17.5 cm (7 inch) square tin.

2. Blend the fresh yeast with the milk. If using dried yeast, sprinkle it into the milk and leave in a warm place for 15 minutes, until frothy.

3. Put the flour and salt in a bowl, then rub in 25 g (1 oz) of the butter until the mixture resembles fine breadcrumbs. Make a well in the centre, pour in the yeast liquid and the egg, then beat together until the mixture forms a dough that leaves sides of bowl clean.

4. Turn on to a lightly floured surface and knead well for 10 minutes, until smooth and elastic. Cover with a clean tea-towel and leave in a warm place for about 1 hour, until doubled in size.

5. Knead the dough lightly on a floured surface, then roll it out to a large rectangle, measuring about 30×23 cm (12×9 inches). Mix the dried fruit and sugar together. Melt the remaining butter, then brush over the dough. Scatter with the fruit mixture, leaving a 2.5 cm (1 inch) border around the edges.

6. Roll the dough up tightly like a Swiss roll, starting at a long edge. Press the edges together to seal them, then cut the roll into 12 slices. Place the rolls cut side uppermost in a greased 17.5 cm (7 inch) square tin. Cover and leave in a warm place for 30 minutes, until doubled in size.

7. Bake the rolls at 190°C (375°F) mark 5 for 30 minutes, until they are well risen and golden brown. Brush them with the honey while still hot. Leave them to cool slightly in the tin before turning out. Serve the Chelsea Buns warm.

TO MICROWAVE

Complete steps 2, 3, 4, 5 and 6, placing the rolls in a greased 20.5 cm (8 inch) round dish. Complete the remainder of step 6. Stand on a roasting rack and cook on HIGH for 6–8 minutes, until well risen and firm to the touch. Leave to stand for 10 minutes, then turn out, brush all over with honey and brown under a hot grill. Serve warm.

CHELSEA BUNS. Wonderfuly sticky and packed with juicy dried fruit, these buns will disappear as fast as you can bake them.

Cut the rolled Chelsea bun dough into slices.

GRIDDLE PANCAKES.
What could be nicer than
these little pancakes, cooked
while you wait and eaten fresh
and hot, the minute they're
ready.

GRIDDLE PANCAKES

THE NORTH

*Today's cookers make cooking on a griddle much less of a hit
and miss business than when the griddle or bakestone was
perched over the coals of the fire. These pancakes or drop
scones should be eaten as soon as they are cooked. They are
quick and easy to make but don't reheat well.*

MAKES 15–18

100 g (4 oz) self-raising flour	
30 ml (2 tbsp) caster sugar	

1 egg, beaten	
150 ml (¼ pint) fresh milk	

1. Mix the flour and sugar. Make a well in the centre
and stir in the egg, with enough of the milk to make a
batter the consistency of thick cream. The mixing
should be done as quickly and lightly as possible.
2. Drop the mixture in spoonfuls on to a greased hot
griddle or heavy-based frying pan. For round pancakes,
drop it from the point of the spoon, for oval ones, drop
from the side.
3. Keep the griddle at a steady heat and when bubbles
rise to the surface of the pancakes and burst, after
2–3 minutes, turn the pancakes over with a palette
knife. Continue cooking for a further 2–3 minutes,

until golden brown on the other side.

4. Wrap the cooked pancakes in a clean tea-towel to keep them warm. Repeat with the remaining mixture to make 15–18 pancakes. Eat while still warm with butter or with golden syrup or honey.

CINNAMON TOAST
COUNTRYWIDE

Sugar and spice are extremely nice in this old-fashioned nursery tea-time recipe, which still tastes just as good today. You can substitute 2.5 ml (½ tsp) ground mixed spice, ground ginger or coriander, or a little grated nutmeg for the cinnamon.

SERVES 2

4 slices of bread
5 ml (1 tsp) ground cinnamon
30 ml (2 tbsp) caster sugar
butter for spreading

1. Toast the bread on one side only. Meanwhile, mix the cinnamon and sugar together.
2. Generously butter the untoasted side of the bread and sprinkle with the cinnamon sugar.
3. Grill until the mixture begins to melt. Cut into fingers and serve immediately.

MUFFINS
THE SOUTH-EAST

The muffin man hasn't been seen in the streets for many years, but this is an authentic recipe to make yourself. The correct way to toast muffins is not to split them and toast the two halves separately, as this makes them tough. Instead, cut them open, then close together again and toast slowly until warm right through, before opening out and buttering generously.

MAKES ABOUT 12

15 g (½ oz) fresh yeast or 7.5 ml (1½ tsp) dried
300 ml (½ pint) warm fresh milk
450 g (1 lb) strong white flour
5 ml (1 tsp) salt
5 ml (1 tsp) plain flour, for dusting
5 ml (1 tsp) semolina

1. Dissolve the yeast in the milk. If using dried yeast, sprinkle over the milk and leave in a warm place for about 15 minutes, until frothy.
2. Sift the flour and salt together, then make a well in the centre. Pour the yeast liquid into the well, draw in the flour and mix to a smooth dough.
3. Knead the dough on a lightly floured surface for about 10 minutes, until smooth and elastic. Place in a

clean bowl, cover with a tea-towel and leave in a warm place for about 1 hour, until doubled in size.

4. Roll out the dough on a lightly floured surface using a lightly floured rolling pin to about 0.5–1 cm (¼–½ inch) thick. Leave to rest, covered with a tea-towel, for 5 minutes, then cut into rounds with a 7.5 cm (3 inch) plain cutter.
5. Place the muffins on a well-floured baking sheet. Mix together the flour and semolina and use to dust the tops. Cover with a tea-towel and leave in a warm place until doubled in size.
6. Grease a griddle, electric griddle plate or heavy frying pan and heat over a moderate heat, until a cube of bread turns brown in 20 seconds.
7. Cook the muffins on the griddle or frying pan for about 7 minutes each side, until golden brown.

CINNAMON TOAST. The simplest things are often the best, and these buttery fingers, with their melting, sugary topping, are quite irresistible.

PRESERVES

Whether you have bought a quantity of fresh fruit and vegetables cheaply or have an abundance of produce from your garden, if you try the recipes in this chapter you can enjoy them all the year round. There are jams to go with scones, jellies, chutneys and pickles to accompany cooked meat and delicious vinegars to use in your favourite recipes.

HERBS

Used from earliest times as natural flavourings as well as aids to health and beauty, herbs have recently enjoyed a tremendous revival in Britain. Many specialist herb farms now offer mail order facilities, and fresh as well as frozen and dried herbs are increasingly available from supermarkets. It's a delight to experiment with herbs in cooking, to discover their nuances of flavour, from the robust to the delicate.

BAY

Often used as a flavouring with parsley and thyme sprigs; used to flavour slow-cooked dishes – soups, stocks, pâtés, casseroles, even baked custard in days gone by.

ROSEMARY

Pungent flavour, special affinity with lamb. Can give subtle aroma to scones and breads (see recipe, page 289). The sharp needles must be finely chopped or dried and crumbled.

PARSLEY

Curly and flat-leaved continental types available. Britain's most popular herb, used in stuffings (see recipe, page 166), sauces for fish, ham and eggs (see recipes, pages 151, 104), and as a garnish, both fresh and deep-fried. Loses flavour when dried; freezes well.

CHERVIL

Closely resembles parsley, more delicate flavour. With tarragon, parsley and chives it's a classic flavouring for sauces, herb butters and omelettes.

DILL

The feathery leaves are specially good with fish; seeds are used in pickling mixtures, potato salad, coleslaw.

GREEN TOMATO CHUTNEY

COUNTRYWIDE

The answer to the problem of what to do with tomatoes that refuse to ripen is to make this lightly spiced, smooth chutney, which goes well with cheese and all cold meats.

MAKES ABOUT 1.4 kg (3 lb)

450 g (1 lb) cooking apples, peeled, cored and finely chopped

225 g (8 oz) onions, skinned and finely chopped

1.4 kg (3 lb) green tomatoes, thinly sliced

225 g (8 oz) sultanas

225 g (8 oz) demerara sugar

10 ml (2 tsp) salt

450 ml (¾ pint) malt vinegar

4 small pieces of dried root ginger

2.5 ml (½ tsp) cayenne pepper

5 ml (1 tsp) mustard powder

1. Put all the ingredients in a preserving pan. Bring to the boil, reduce the heat and simmer gently for about 2 hours, stirring occasionally, until the ingredients are tender, reduced to a thick consistency and no excess liquid remains.
2. Remove the ginger, spoon the chutney into preheated jars and cover at once with airtight, vinegar-proof tops.

TO MICROWAVE

Reduce the vinegar to 300 ml (½ pint) and put in a large bowl with all the remaining ingredients. Cook on HIGH for 1 hour until thick and reduced, stirring frequently. Complete the recipe.

MINT JELLY

COUNTRYWIDE

A delicious herb jelly, made in the traditional way, and a pleasant change from mint sauce to go with roast lamb.
The yield will depend on the ripeness of the fruit and the time allowed for dripping.

2.3 kg (5 lb) cooking apples, such as Bramleys

a few large sprigs fresh mint

1.1 litres (2 pints) distilled white vinegar

sugar

90–120 ml (6–8 tbsp) chopped fresh mint

a few drops of green food colouring

1. Remove any bruised or damaged portions from the apples and roughly chop them into thick chunks without peeling or coring. Put them in a preserving pan

with 1.1 litres (2 pints) water and the mint sprigs. Bring to the boil, then simmer gently for about 45 minutes, until soft and pulpy. Stir from time to time to prevent sticking. Add the vinegar and boil for a further 5 minutes.
2. Spoon the apple pulp into a jelly bag or cloth attached to the legs of an upturned stool, and leave to strain into a large bowl for at least 12 hours. Do not squeeze.
3. Discard the pulp remaining in the jelly bag. Measure the extract and return it to the preserving pan with 450 g (1 lb) sugar for each 568 ml (1 pint) extract.
4. Heat gently, stirring, until the sugar has dissolved, then boil rapidly for about 10 minutes. Test for a set and, when setting point is reached, take the pan off the heat and skim the surface with a slotted spoon.
5. Stir in the chopped mint and add a few drops of green food colouring. Allow to cool slightly, then stir well to distribute the mint and pot and cover the jelly.

VARIATION

Herb jellies
Other fresh herbs, such as rosemary, parsley, sage and thyme, can be used equally as well as mint. Serve these herb jellies with roast meats – rosemary jelly with lamb; parsley jelly with gammon; sage jelly with pork; and thyme jelly with poultry.

SPICED CRAB-APPLES

COUNTRYWIDE

Crab-apples were used in medieval times to make verjuice, a kind of vinegar. Their pleasantly tangy acidity makes them well worth using in this recipe for spicy pickled fruits. Serve as an accompaniment to cold meat.
The yield will depend on how tightly the apples are packed and the capacity of the jars.

2.7 g (6 lb) crab-apples, trimmed

2–3 strips lemon rind

450 g (1 lb) sugar

450 ml (¾ pint) red wine vinegar

1 cinnamon stick

1–2 whole cloves

3 peppercorns

1. Put the crab-apples in a preserving pan with 900 ml (1½ pints) water and the strips of lemon rind and simmer gently until just tender.
2. Remove the pan from the heat and strain, reserving the liquid. Put the sugar and vinegar in a pan and add 900 ml (1½ pints) of the liquid from the fruit.
3. Tie the spices in a piece of muslin and add to the liquid. Heat gently, stirring, until the sugar has dissolved, then bring to the boil and boil for 1 minute.
4. Add the crab-apples and simmer gently for 30–40 minutes, until the syrup has reduced to a coating consistency. Remove the muslin bag after 30 minutes.
5. Pack the fruit in small jars, pour over the syrup and cover with airtight and vinegar-proof tops.

TARRAGON

Subtle flavour goes well with fish, chicken, eggs and veal. Makes fine vinegar.

BASIL

Sweet aroma goes superbly with tomatoes – cooked, in pasta sauces, raw in salads. Crushed leaves infused in oil give superb flavour to salads.

THYME

Can be used very successfully dried, to flavour hearty soups and stews.

MARJORAM

Good in meat loaf, shepherd's pie, pasta sauces, pizza toppings and stuffing mixtures.

CHIVES

Best added at end of cooking or as garnish: mild onion flavour lost when cooked. Snip over creamy soups, into salads, mix with cream cheese, use in potato (see recipe, page 230) and egg dishes.

BEET RELISH

THE NORTH

There are two types of beetroot: long and globe shaped. Use either for this spicy pickle, which makes an excellent accompaniment to cold meats. This is a good recipe for using up large, maincrop beetroots, available all year, which are tougher than the younger, small beetroots which are available in early summer and are so good in salads.

MAKES ABOUT 700 g (1½ lb)

900 g (2 lb) cooked beetroot, skinned and diced	
450 g (1 lb) white cabbage, finely shredded	
75 g (3 oz) fresh horseradish, grated	
15 ml (1 tbsp) mustard powder	
568 ml (1 pint) malt vinegar	

225 g (8 oz) sugar

pinch of cayenne pepper

salt and pepper

1. Combine all the ingredients in a large saucepan. Bring slowly to the boil, then simmer for 30 minutes, stirring occasionally.
2. Spoon into pre-heated jars and cover at once with airtight, vinegar-proof tops.
3. Store in a cool, dry, dark place and leave to mature for 2–3 months before eating.

TO MICROWAVE

Halve the ingredients. Put all the ingredients in a large bowl and cook on HIGH for about 40 minutes, stirring frequently. Complete the recipe. Makes about 350 g (12 oz).

LEFT
BEET RELISH. Fresh horseradish gives a spark of heat to this spicy relish which is particularly good with cold roast beef.

RIGHT
SPICED CRAB-APPLES. Spices, sugar and red wine vinegar are used to infuse the apples with flavour.

PLUM BUTTER
COUNTRYWIDE

It takes a lot of fruit to make a small amount of butter, so save this recipe for the end of the season, when there is a glut. Fruit butter does not keep very well, so eat it up fairly quickly. It is soft, and can be spread easily.

MAKES ABOUT 1.1 kg (2½ lb)

1.4 kg (3 lb) plums, skinned and stoned

grated rind and juice of 1 lemon

sugar

1. Put the plums, lemon rind and juice in a large saucepan and add about 450 ml (¾ pint) water to cover. Simmer gently for 15–20 minutes, until the fruit is soft and pulpy.
2. Using a wooden spoon, press the fruit pulp through a nylon sieve and measure the purée.
3. Return the purée to the pan and add 350 g (12 oz) sugar for each 568 ml (1 pint) purée.
4. Heat gently, stirring, until the sugar has dissolved, then bring to the boil and boil for 20–25 minutes, stirring frequently, until the mixture thickens and is like jam in consistency.
5. Pot and cover the butter.

TO MICROWAVE

 Put the plums, lemon rind and juice in a large bowl with 300 ml (½ pint) water. Cover and cook on HIGH for 10–15 minutes, until tender, stirring occasionally. Complete the recipe.

DAMSON CHEESE
COUNTRYWIDE

Fruit cheeses are traditional country preserves, with a very thick texture, and are usually served sliced, to accompany meat, poultry or game. They can be potted in small moulds and simply turned out whole when needed.

MAKES ABOUT 1.4 kg (3 lb)

1.4 kg (3 lb) damsons

sugar

1. Put the fruit and 150–300 ml (¼–½ pint) water, to just cover, in a saucepan. Cover and simmer gently for 15–20 minutes, until the fruit is really soft. Scoop out the stones with a slotted spoon as they come to the surface.
2. Using a wooden spoon, press the fruit pulp through a nylon sieve and measure the purée.
3. Return the purée to the pan and add 350 g (12 oz) sugar for each 568 ml (1 pint) purée.
4. Heat gently, stirring, until the sugar has dissolved, then bring to the boil and boil gently, stirring frequently, for 30–40 minutes, until so thick that the

wooden spoon leaves a clean line through the mixture when drawn across the bottom of the pan.
5. Pot and cover the cheese or, if preferred, prepare and fill a bowl or several small moulds from which the cheese can be turned out and served whole. Leave to set and cover as for jam. Store in a cool, dry place for 2 months to mature.

TO MICROWAVE

 Put the fruit and 150 ml (¼ pint) water in a large bowl. Cover and cook on HIGH for 10–15 minutes, until tender, stirring occasionally. Discard the stones. Complete the recipe.

BREAD AND BUTTER PICKLE
COUNTRYWIDE

Home-produced cucumbers, grown under glass, are available almost all year round, with just a brief gap from November to February. Choose firm, straight cucumbers that have an even colour to make this sharp-flavoured pickle, which is good with simple dishes such as sandwiches or bread and butter – hence its name.

The yield will depend on how tightly the vegetables are packed and the capacity of the jars.

3 large ridge or smooth-skinned cucumbers

4 large onions, skinned and sliced

45 ml (3 tbsp) salt

450 ml (¾ pint) distilled white vinegar

150 g (5 oz) sugar

5 ml (1 tsp) celery seeds

5 ml (1 tsp) black mustard seeds

1. Thinly slice the cucumbers, then layer the cucumber and onion slices in a large bowl, sprinkling each layer with salt. Leave for 1 hour, then drain and rinse well.
2. Put vinegar, sugar and celery and mustard seeds in a saucepan and heat gently, stirring, until sugar has dissolved. Bring to boil and boil for 3 minutes.
3. Pack the vegetable slices into pre-heated jars and add enough hot vinegar mixture to cover. Cover immediately with airtight, vinegar-proof tops.
4. This pickle must be stored in a dark place or the cucumber will lose its colour. Store for 2 months to mature before eating.

TO MICROWAVE

 Complete step 1. Put the vinegar, sugar and celery and mustard seeds in a large jug and cook on HIGH for 4–5 minutes, until boiling. Stir until the sugar has dissolved. Cook on HIGH for 2 minutes. Complete the recipe.

FRUIT VINEGARS

COUNTRYWIDE

Flavoured vinegars can be used wherever you would use ordinary vinegar, and add a subtle flavour all of their own. You can use one favourite herb by itself, or a mixture of several. The fruit-flavoured versions are unusual and make very successful salad dressings.

---

raspberries, blackberries or blackcurrants

red or white wine vinegar

sugar

---

1. Put the fruit in a bowl and break it up slightly with the back of a wooden spoon. For each 450 g (1 lb) fruit, pour in 568 ml (1 pint) red or white wine vinegar. Cover with a cloth and leave to stand for 3–4 days, stirring occasionally.
2. Strain through muslin and add 450 g (1 lb) sugar to each 568 ml (1 pint). Boil for 10 minutes, then cool, strain again, pour into bottles and seal with airtight and vinegar-proof tops. Add a few whole pieces of fruit to each bottle, if liked. Use when making salad dressings.

HERB VINEGARS

COUNTRYWIDE

---

sprigs of fresh herbs, such as rosemary, tarragon, mint, thyme, marjoram, basil, dill, sage, parsley

red or white wine vinegar

---

1. Fill bottles with sprigs of fresh herbs. Use either a mixture of herbs or one variety. Fill with red or white wine vinegar.
2. Seal with vinegar-proof tops and leave in a cool, dry place for about 6 weeks. Use when making salad dressings.

FRUIT AND HERB VINEGARS. Raid the garden to make a stunning array of vinegars in jewel colours to liven up the larder shelf. And they taste every bit as good as they look.

FROM THE SHOP TO THE KITCHEN

BUYING FRESH FOOD

Knowing what to look for and how to select wisely are important factors when buying foods. The following notes will help you in your choice.

CHOOSING MEAT

When choosing meat, it helps to bear in mind the cooking method that you intend using. If you want something to cook quickly by a dry heat method such as grilling or roasting, it must be a lean, tender cut from a prime-quality animal and will inevitably be more expensive. Slower cooking with added moisture is suitable for one of the tougher, probably fattier cuts, which will be cheaper. If in doubt, ask your butcher for advice. Many prepackaged meat cuts carry labels suggesting suitable methods of cooking, and these should be considered. The nutritional quality of the cheaper cuts is the same as that of the dearer cuts and the flavour of both is just as good if cooked properly.

Generally speaking, choose meat which has no undue amount of fat surrounding it; what fat there is should be firm and free from dark marks or discoloration. The colour of fat may vary for a number of reasons, none of which will affect the taste. Lean meat should be finely grained, firm and slightly elastic; a fine marbling, or flecks of fat in the meat, will help to keep the meat moist during cooking and often gives a better flavour. Coarse-grained meat is usually an indication that the meat is suitable only for stewing or

braising. Do not worry about the colour of meat. The redness of meat will vary after cutting and exposure to air, but this need not affect your choice.

Whether you choose fresh or frozen meat is a matter mainly of personal preference, but frozen meat that has been thawed should not be refrozen unless cooked first.

CHOOSING POULTRY AND GAME

If buying *fresh poultry*, choose a bird that looks plump and well rounded. The skin should be free from blemishes and bruising. In a young chicken the tip of the breast bone will be soft and flexible; if it is hard and rigid the bird is probably too old to roast satisfactorily although it will be suitable for steaming or boiling.

Modern poultry production methods ensure a moist, tender-fleshed bird. Prompt freezing also guarantees freshness, so you can expect high quality from any of the well-known brands of frozen poultry. Traditionally reared farmyard birds are inclined to have more flavour.

Larger birds generally give the best value as the proportion of meat to bone is higher and the extra meat, particularly chicken and turkey, left over from the first meal is excellent cold or made up in another dish. Remember that packaged poultry, frozen or fresh, is sold by oven-ready weight, but a fresh bird bought from a traditional poulterer or butcher will probably be sold at 'plucked weight' – plucked but not drawn. The butcher will draw it for you, but after weighing and pricing. You will need to allow for this in estimating the size of bird you require.

Game birds are best eaten young. The plumage is a guide as all young birds have soft even feathers. With pheasants and partridge, the long wing feathers are V-shaped in a young bird, as distinct from the rounded ones of an older bird. Smooth, pliable legs, short spurs and a firm, plump breast are other points to look for. Most game birds need to be hung so check this with your butcher or poulterer. He will probably pluck and draw it for you if you ask. If game is not hung, the flesh will be tough and tasteless. Look out for game in supermarkets too, where the game is ready for the oven.

CHOOSING FISH AND SEAFOOD

Really fresh *whole fish* has clear, bulging eyes and bright red gills. Avoid any with sunken, cloudy eyes and faded pink or grey gills. The body of the fish should be firm and springy to the touch, with shining skin and bright, close-fitting scales. *Fish fillets* and *steaks* should look freshly cut, the flesh moist and firm-textured, showing no signs of dryness or discoloration. The bones should be firmly embedded in the flesh; if they are loose and coming away from the flesh this indicates that the fish has been cut for some time and is past its best.

When buying *frozen fish*, make sure that it is solidly frozen, clear in colour and free of ice crystals. Any smell should be mild and clean, exactly as for fresh fish. Breadcrumbs or batter coatings on frozen fish portions should be crisp and dry looking. Avoid frozen fish that has a brownish tinge or that is in any way damaged.

Shellfish should be very fresh as they are more perishable than other fish. They should have a clean sea smell and clear fresh colour; avoid any that are dull looking. Prawns and shrimps should have tails curled well under them. Look for tightly closed shells where applicable.

While it is unwise to freeze your own shellfish – since the temperature required for satisfactory preservation of shellfish is lower than that normally obtainable in any domestic freezer – commercially *frozen shellfish* are useful when the type you require is out of season. You can also freeze very fresh shellfish in made-up dishes such as soups, fish pies and quiches.

CHOOSING DAIRY PRODUCE

When buying fresh *milk*, *cream* and *yogurt*, look at their date stamps, then keep them cool, clean and covered to ensure they stay fresh.

Cheese can be bought from specialist cheese shops and supermarkets. Freshly cut cheese should look fresh, with no dried or greasy areas on the surface. It is important that the cut surface of cheese is always covered and that a mild-flavoured cheese is not kept alongside a strong cheese. If buying pre-packed cheese, check that it does not look sweaty or excessively runny and that it is within the life of its date stamp. If buying a ripened soft cheese, such as Lymeswold, well before the expiry of the date stamp, you may prefer to keep it to allow it to ripen to your liking.

When buying prepacked *eggs* in shops you can get some idea of how old they are by checking the week number given on the box. Week 1 falls at the end of December or beginning of January.

CHOOSING FRESH FRUIT AND VEGETABLES

When buying fruit and vegetables always choose them carefully and make sure that they are fresh. Fruits should be bought with unblemished skins. Root vegetables, such as potatoes, carrots and swedes, should be bought firm and unwrinkled. Buy little and often to ensure freshness.

STORING FOOD

Storage of perishable foods such as meat, fish, dairy products, soft fruit and vegetables is of vital importance to keep them as fresh as possible. The best place to keep them is in the refrigerator or, failing this, a cool larder. Perishable foods intended for long-term storage can be kept in a freezer.

All foods that are stored in the refrigerator should be covered or well wrapped to prevent the flavours drifting from one to another and to prevent the food from drying out. Store *cheese* in the bottom of the refrigerator, so it does not get too cold, but it's best to remove it from the refrigerator half an hour before serving to allow it to come up to room temperature and regain its flavour. *Milk*, *cream* and *yogurt* will keep for several days, but check date stamps when buying them. The same applies to cartons of fresh fruit juice. UHT milk will keep well even without a refrigerator but is best stored in a cool place.

Put *meat* in the refrigerator as soon as possible after buying. Remove any paper wrappings, rewrap the meat loosely in polythene or foil, leaving an end open for ventilation, and place the package on a plate in case it drips. If the meat is prepackaged in polythene or cling film, just loosen the wrapping to allow air to circulate. When buying meat in vacuum packs or controlled atmospheric packaging, follow the manufacturer's instructions.

Most fresh meat can be stored in the refrigerator for up to 3 or 4 days; minced meat and offal are more perishable and should be used within 24 hours. Cooked meat should be cooled quickly, wrapped in foil or polythene and, if possible, put into the refrigerator within 1½–2 hours of cooking. Store for up to 4 days. Frozen meat should be left in its wrappings and stored in the freezer or frozen food compartment of the refrigerator.

To store fresh *poultry*, remove the giblets from inside the bird as soon as you get it home. Remove any tight packaging, cover the bird loosely with a polythene bag that will allow the air to circulate and store in the refrigerator for 1–2 days. The giblets should preferably be cooked straight away, as they deteriorate more quickly than the rest of the bird, but in any case they should be stored separately. Stuffings can be prepared in advance, but store them separately too and stuff the bird just before cooking.

Fresh *fish*, from the fishmonger, should be loosely wrapped and stored in the refrigerator. Cook it within 24 hours of purchase. Store frozen fish in the freezer or frozen food compartment in its original wrapping.

Eggs are best kept in a rack in a cool place. If you have to store them in a refrigerator, keep them well away from the ice compartment (there is often a special egg storage rack) and away from foods like cheese, fish or onions whose smells may transfer to the eggs.

Store eggs pointed end down and use them at room temperature; eggs that are too cold will crack when boiled and are also difficult to whisk. Fresh eggs can be stored for 2–3 weeks in the refrigerator or 1–2 weeks in a cool place.

Salad ingredients should be kept at the bottom of the refrigerator, loosely wrapped in polythene bags. Unwashed, most will keep for a week. Mushrooms are best kept in a paper bag and then wrapped in a polythene bag. Once washed, dry salad ingredients well before returning to the refrigerator in a polythene bag.

Green leafy vegetables are also best stored at the bottom of the refrigerator. Trim away any damaged parts and wrap the vegetables in paper before refrigerating. *Root vegetables* like onions, potatoes and carrots should be stored in a cool, airy place such as a vegetable rack so that air can circulate around them. If you buy potatoes ready washed in polythene bags it is best to transfer them to a paper bag so that they do not become soft and spongy. *Fruits* such as apples and pears are best kept in a fruit bowl.

COMMERCIAL FREEZING OF BRITISH FRUIT AND VEGETABLES

All fruit and vegetables, from the moment they are picked, begin to lose their nutritional value and flavour.

Freezing is a convenient way of preserving fresh fruit and vegetables and if blanched and frozen with minimal delay, they remain as close to their natural state as possible.

Commercial quick-freezing produces small ice crystals, which means there is little deterioration of the flavour, colour and nutritive value of fruit and vegetables. Frozen produce can thus often be fresher than the fresh fruit and vegetables in the shops.

PICK YOUR OWN

Fruit and vegetable picking can be an enjoyable day out and it's satisfying to come home laden with fresh produce. There is a wide variety of produce available, including soft fruits, green and root vegetables. Don't, however, get so carried away that you have to spend hours freezing, or making jam which you didn't plan to do because you have picked too much to consume. Check with the supplier concerning the suitability of their produce for freezing.

Try to choose a part of the field that hasn't already been well picked – usually the further away from the entrance the better. The best fruit and vegetables tend to grow at the edge of the plant so tread carefully as you walk along the rows.

Select fresh, firm produce and when picking soft fruits don't pile them up so much in your basket that you squash the fruit below. The best way to pick fruits such as strawberries is to pinch the stem and snap it off above the fruit; don't pull the fruit from the plant.

When you get the fruit or vegetables home, use them quickly to avoid them going to waste. If you intend to freeze them, lay them singly on trays and put in the coldest part of the freezer. When solid, pack in polythene bags or rigid containers.

FROM FREEZER TO MICROWAVE

Home freezing is an ideal way of preserving food since you can have a store of produce readily available and you can buy food to preserve at the height of the season when they are cheap. A ✱ symbol beside the recipe in the book indicates which dishes can successfully be frozen.

A freezer and microwave cooker can be ideal companions. The microwave will thaw food in a fraction of the time normally required for complete thawing, which allows you the convenience of being able to select food from the freezer at short notice.

Most foods can be frozen and microwaved without impairing the quality. The thawing process is very fast and because there is a risk that some parts of the food will start to cook while others are still frozen always use the DEFROST or LOW settings.

Pack food in containers suitable for using in both freezer and microwave, never microwave in foil containers and remove metal tags. Open all cartons and remove lids and slit or pierce polythene bags.

To help foods thaw evenly, stir when possible, moving frozen parts to the outside of the dish, separate chunks of food and turn large items over.

Some foods, such as joints of meat, also need to be given a standing time after thawing to ensure that they are completely thawed.

MICROWAVE COOKERS

A microwave cooker can save much time and if used to its best advantage, can be a very useful appliance to have in conjunction with a conventional cooker. Many of the recipes in this book can be prepared and/or cooked in a microwave and instructions are given where appropriate. A ▨ symbol beside the recipe indicates that it is suitable for cooking in a microwave. Microwave instructions are then given at the end of the recipe.

HOW TO USE THE RECIPES IN THIS BOOK WITH YOUR MICROWAVE COOKER SETTINGS

Unlike conventional ovens, the power output and heat controls on microwave cookers do not follow a standard formula. When manufacturers refer to a 700-watt cooker, they are referring to the cooker's POWER OUTPUT; its INPUT, which is indicated on the back of the cooker, is double that figure. The higher the wattage of a cooker, the faster the rate of cooking. Thus food cooked at 700 watts on full power cooks in half the time of food cooked at 350 watts. That said, the actual cooking performance of one 700-watt cooker may vary slightly from another with the same wattage because factors such as cooker cavity size affect cooking performance. The vast majority of microwave cookers sold today are either 600, 650 or 700 watts, but there are many cookers still in use which may be 400 and 500 watts.

IN THIS BOOK
* HIGH refers to 100% full power output of 600–700 watts
* MEDIUM refers to 60% of full power
* LOW is 35% of full power

Whatever the wattage of your cooker, the HIGH/FULL setting will always be 100% of the cooker's output. Thus your highest setting will correspond to HIGH.

However, the MEDIUM and LOW settings used in this book may not be equivalent to the MEDIUM and LOW settings marked on your cooker. As these settings vary according to power input, use the following calculation to estimate the correct setting for a 600–700-watt cooker. This simple calculation should be done before you use the recipes for the first time, to ensure successful results.

Multiply the percentage power required by the total number of settings on your cooker and divide by 100. For example:

MEDIUM (60%) = % Power required
× Total Number of Cooker Settings
÷ 100 = Correct Setting

$$= \frac{60 \times 9}{100} = 5$$

LOW (35%) = % Power required
× Total Number of Cooker Settings
÷ 100 = Correct Setting

$$= \frac{35 \times 9}{100} = 3$$

If your cookery power output is lower than 600 watts, then you must allow a longer cooking time for all recipes in this book.

Add approximately 10–15 seconds per minute for a 500-watt cooker and 15–20 seconds per minute for a 400-watt cooker.

No matter what the wattage of your cooker is, you should always check food before the end of cooking time, to ensure that it does not get overcooked.

Don't forget to allow for standing time.

COMBINATION COOKER OWNERS
Combination cookers combine conventional and microwave methods of cooking so that food browns as well as cooking quickly. If you own a combination cooker you should follow your manufacturer's instructions regarding cooking times.

MICROWAVE COOKERY NOTES
Bowl Sizes
* Small bowl = 900 ml (1½ pints)
* Medium bowl = about 2.3 litres (4 pints)
* Large bowl = about 3.4 litres (6 pints)

Covering
* Cook uncovered unless otherwise stated.
* At the time of going to press, it has been recommended by the Ministry of Agriculture, Fisheries and Food that the use of cling film should be avoided in microwave cooking. When a recipe requires you to cover the container, cover with either a lid or a plate, leaving a gap to let the steam escape.

RECIPE NOTES
* Follow either metric or imperial measures for the recipes in this book. They are not interchangeable.
* All spoon measures are level.
* Sets of measuring spoons are available in both metric and imperial sizes to give accurate measurement of small quantities.
* Size 2 (large) eggs should be used except when otherwise stated.
* Plain or self-raising flour can be used unless otherwise stated.
* Brown or white breadcrumbs can be used unless otherwise stated.

WHEN VEGETABLES ARE IN SEASON
This is to show when British-grown vegetables are available.

	January	February	March	April	May	June	July	August	September	October	November	December
Artichokes – Globe						•	•	•	•			
Jerusalem	•	•	•	•						•	•	•
Asparagus					•	•						
Beans – Broad						•	•					
Runner							•	•	•	•		
Kidney						•	•	•	•			
Beetroot	•	•	•	•	•	•	•	•	•	•	•	•
Broccoli – Calabrese						•	•	•	•	•		
Sprouting			•	•	•							
Brussels – Top	•									•	•	•
Sprouts	•	•	•	•						•	•	•
Cabbage – January King	•	•	•	•						•	•	•
Drum Head								•	•	•	•	
Spring Green	•	•	•								•	•
Red	•	•										•
Carrot	•	•	•	•	•	•	•	•	•	•	•	•
Cauliflower	•	•	•	•	•	•	•	•	•	•	•	•
Celeriac	•	•	•						•	•	•	•
Celery					•	•	•	•	•	•	•	•
Chicory	•	•								•	•	•
Chinese Leaves				•	•	•	•	•	•	•	•	
Courgettes						•	•	•	•	•		
Cucumbers				•	•	•	•	•	•	•		
Endive					•	•	•	•				
Kale	•	•	•	•	•						•	•
Leeks	•	•	•	•				•	•	•	•	•
Lettuce	•	•	•	•	•	•	•	•	•	•	•	•
Marrows						•	•	•	•	•		
Mint					•	•	•	•	•	•		
Mushrooms	•	•	•	•	•	•	•	•	•	•	•	•
Mustard and Cress	•	•	•	•	•	•	•	•	•	•	•	•
Onions	•								•	•	•	•
Parsley					•	•	•	•	•	•		
Parsnips	•	•	•	•					•	•	•	•
Peppers					•	•	•	•	•	•		
Peas					•	•	•	•	•	•		
Potatoes – New						•	•	•				
Maincrop	•	•	•	•	•				•	•	•	•
Pumpkin									•	•	•	
Radishes					•	•	•	•	•	•		

WHEN VEGETABLES ARE IN SEASON
This is to show when British-grown vegetables are available.

	January	February	March	April	May	June	July	August	September	October	November	December
Seakale	●	●	●									●
Shallots	●								●	●	●	●
Spinach (best Mar/Apr)			●	●	●	●	●	●	●	●		
Spring Onions				●	●	●	●	●				
Swedes	●	●	●	●	●				●	●	●	●
Sweetcorn								●	●	●		
Tomatoes				●	●	●	●	●	●	●		
Turnips	●	●	●			●	●	●	●	●	●	●
Watercress	●	●	●	●	●	●	●	●	●	●	●	●

WHEN FRUITS ARE IN SEASON
This is to show when British-grown fruit is available.

	January	February	March	April	May	June	July	August	September	October	November	December
Apples – cooking	●	●	●	●	●	●			●	●	●	●
dessert	●	●	●							●	●	●
Blackberries									●	●		
Black/redcurrants						●	●	●				
Crab Apples									●	●		
Cherries						●	●	●				
Chestnuts										●	●	●
Damsons								●	●	●		
Elderberries									●	●		
Gooseberries						●	●	●				
Greengages							●	●				
Loganberries							●	●				
Medlars										●	●	
Mulberries							●	●				
Pears	●	●	●					●	●	●	●	●
Plums						●	●	●	●	●		
Quinces										●	●	
Raspberries						●	●	●	●			
Rhubarb			●	●	●	●						
Strawberries					●	●	●	●	●	●		

INDEX

ACKNOWLEDGEMENTS

The Publishers would like to thank the following for their advice and assistance:

Aberdeen Angus Cattle Society; Adgestone Vineyards; The Apple and Pear Development Council; Aspall Cyder House Products; Bacon and Meat Manufacturers' Association; Beenleigh Manor Farm Foods; Belvoir Fruit Farms; Berwick Glebe Vineyard; Brecon Brewery Ltd; Biddenden Vineyards Ltd; Breaky Bottom Vineyard; Brewers' Society; British Chicken Association; British Egg Information Service; British Food Information Service of Food from Britain; British Frozen Food Association; British Fruit and Vegetable Canners' Association; British Herb Trade Association; British Iceberg Growers' Association; British Poultry Federation; British Quality Vegetables and Salad Association; British Sheep Dairy Association; British Sugar plc; British Tourist Authority; British Trout Association; British Turkey Federation; British United Turkeys; British Watercress Growers' Association; Broadoak Cider Company; Bronte Liqueur Company Ltd; Bruisyard St Peter Vineyard; Butter Information Council; The Campaign for Real Ale; Carmathen Water; Cheddar Farmhouse Cheese Federation; Colman's of Norwich; Colston Bassett and District Dairy Company Ltd; Company of Scottish Cheese Makers Ltd; Copella Fruit Juices; Cornish Scrumpy Company Ltd; Cumbria Tourist Board; Dairy Crest; Delicatessen and Fine Foods Association; Ditchling Vineyards; Dittisham Fruit Farm; Dumfries and Galloway Tourist Board; East Anglia Tourist Board; East Midlands Tourist Board; Elham Park Vineyard; The English Farm Cider Centre; English Hops Ltd; English Vineyards Association; English Wine Centre; F. H. Mann (Bushy Park) Products; Farmhouse English Cheese Bureau; The Farm Shop and Pick Your Own Association; Felstead Vineyards; Flour Advisory Bureau; Food and Drink Federation; Fresh Fruit and Vegetable Information Bureau; Freshly Pressed Juice Association; Frozen Quality Food Ltd; The Game Conservancy Trust; The Goat Producers' Association of Great Britain; Hallgarten Wines Ltd; Hammond & Deacon Ltd; Health Food Manufacturers' Association; Heart of England Tourist Board; Highlands and Islands Development Board; Highlands Spring Ltd; Inch's Cider Company; Industrial Development Board; Infopress; John Murray & Co (Mull) Ltd; Knowle Orchard Produce; Lamberhurst Vineyards; Loch Lomond, Stirling & Trossachs Tourist Board; Meat and Livestock Commission; Meat Promotions Executive; Merrydown Wine and Cider Makers; Milk Marketing Board for England and Wales; Milk Marketing Board for Northern Ireland; Mushroom Growers' Association; National Association of Cider Makers; National Association of Soft Drink Manufacturers; National Dairy Council; The National Farmers' Union; National Farmers' Union – Scotland; National Farmers' Union – Ulster; National Farmers' Union – Wales; National Federation of Fruit and Potato Traders Ltd; National Veal Producers' Association; Norbury's Cider Company; Northern Ireland Tourist Board; Northumbria Tourist Board; North West Tourist Board; Sue Cloke of Paxton & Whitfield; Penshurst Vineyards; Potato Marketing Board; The Processed Vegetable Growers' Association Ltd; Quality British Celery Association; Quality Milk Producers; Royal Agricultural Society of England; Scotch Quality Beef and Lamb Association; Scotch Whisky Association; Scottish Development Agency; Scottish Milk Marketing Board; Scottish Salmon Information Service; Scottish Tourist Board; Seafish Industry Authority; The Shellfish Association of Great Britain; Southern Tourist Board; South East England Tourist Board; Spice Information Bureau; Stilton Cheesemakers' Association; Swiftsden Vineyard; A Taste of Somerset; A Taste of Sussex; Tea Council; Tenterden Vineyards; Thames and Chiltern Tourist Board; Thatcher's Farmhouse Cider; Three Choirs Vineyards Ltd; Torpeek Farm Products; Trofarth Industries; Wales Tourist Board; Welsh Development Agency; Welsh Lamb Enterprise; Westbury Vineyard; West Country Tourist Board; Whitbread Hop Farm; Wye Valley Fruit Farms Ltd; Yorkshire and Humberside Tourist Board.

Cheeses on pages 96–7 supplied by Duff & Trotter, 13 Leadenhall Market, London EC3

With special thanks to Ivan Fagent, Sheelagh Donovan, John Vanner, Geoff Grant, Clare Thomson, Christina Ball and Helen Mott of the Milk Marketing Board; Judith Hodge of British Food & Farming 1989; to David Hellard and Eve Thomson of the National Farmers' Union; and to Emma-lee Gow.

PHOTOGRAPHIC CREDITS

Page 10 Fotobank/England Scene/Andy Gordon; 11 Anthony Blake; 12 (top) *Farmers Weekly*/P. Allen; 12 (bottom) Stockphotos/Trevor Wood; 13 S & O Mathews; 14 Anthony Blake; 15 (top) Susan Griggs Agency/Simon McBride; 15 (bottom) Colin Molyneux; 16 Colin Molyneux; 17, 20 S & O Mathews; 21 Susan Griggs Agency/Robin Laurence; 22 (top) Andrew Lawson; 22 (bottom) South East England Tourist Board; 23 *Daily Telegraph* Picture Library/P. Titmuss; 24 (top) Stockphotos/Trevor Wood; 24 (bottom) S & O Mathews; 25 Holt Studios; 28, 29, 30 Colin Molyneux; 31 (top) Neil Holmes; 31 (bottom (2)) Jacqui Hurst; 32 (top) Roger Phillips; 32 (bottom) Colin Molyneux; 33 Susan Griggs Agency/David Beatty; 36 Susan Griggs Agency/Rob Cousins; 37 *Daily Telegraph* Picture Library/Charles de Jaeger; 38 John Vigurs ; 39 Susan Griggs Agency/Simon McBride; 40 Andrew Lawson; 41, 42, 43 Sefton Photo Library; 46 Stockphotos/Trevor Wood; 47 (top) Susan Griggs Agency/Adam Woolfitt; 47 (bottom) Stockphotos/ Trevor Wood; 48 (top & bottom) Jacqui Hurst; 49 Bruce Coleman Ltd/Eric Crichton; 50 Anthony Blake; 51 Neil Holmes; 52 Frank Lane Picture Agency/Silvestris-Meyers; 53 Susan Griggs Agency/Anthony Howarth; 56 Susan Griggs Agency/Adam Woolfitt; 57 Fotobank/England Scene; 58 (top) Susan Griggs Agency/Simon McBride; 58 (bottom) Fotobank/England Scene; 59 (top) Britain On View (BTA/ETB)/John Melville; 59 John Vigurs; 60 Bruce Coleman Ltd/B & C Alexander; 61 (top) Susan Griggs Agency/Rob Cousins; 61 (bottom) Patrick Thurston; 62 (top) *Farmers Weekly*; 62 (bottom) Simon Warner; 66 (top) Charles Tait; 66 (bottom) Bruce Coleman Ltd/Gordon Langsbury; 67 Susan Griggs Agency/John Marmara; 68 (top) Susan Griggs Agency/Adam Woolfitt; 68 (bottom) Anthony Blake; 69 (top) The Image Bank/David W. Hamilton; 69 (bottom) Susan Griggs Agency/ Adam Woolfitt; 71 (right) Susan Griggs Agency/Ted Spiegel; 71 (left) Stockphotos/Trevor Wood; 73, 74, 75, 76, 77 John Vigurs.

FURTHER INFORMATION

For further information on dairy products contact:
The Milk Marketing Board
Thames Ditton
Surrey KT7 0EL
01 398 4101

For initial enquiries about any other food produce contact:
British Food Information Service of Food from Britain
5th Floor, 542–544 Market Towers
New Covent Garden Market
London SW8 5NQ
01 720 7551

For a copy of the leaflet 'Vineyards open to the public' send a stamped addressed envelope to:
The English Vineyards Association
Information Service
English Wine Centre
Drusilla's Corner
Alfriston
East Sussex BN26 5QS

For a list of PYO farms in your area contact:
Mrs Tessa Crago
The Farm Shop and PYO Association
The National Farmers' Union
Agriculture House
Knightsbridge
London SW1X 7NJ
01 235 5077

Tours of a hop farm can be made at:
Whitbread Hop Farm
Beltring
Paddock Wood
Tonbridge
Kent
TN12 6PY
0622 872 068